EX • LIBRIS
GENERAL MAP
OF
THE WORLD
Dawn 2016

D1116484

Great Teams' Great Years

Kansas City Chiefs

by Dick Connor

A National Football League Book

Macmillan Publishing Co., Inc.
New York
Collier Macmillan Publishers
London

Other Books in This Series
Cleveland Browns
Dallas Cowboys
Detroit Lions
Los Angeles Rams
New York Giants
Pittsburgh Steelers
San Francisco 49ers
Washington Redskins

A National Football League Book
Prepared by Creative Services Division, National Football League Properties, Inc.
Publisher: *David Boss*
Editor: *John Wiebusch*
Managing Editor: *Tom Bennett*
Associate Editors: *Patricia Cross, Doug Kelly*
Project Coordinator: *Bill Von Torne*
Production Manager: *Patrick McKee*
Production Staff: *Amy Yutani, Rob Meneilly, Jere Wright*
Executive Director: *Jack Wrobbel*

Produced by The Ridge Press, Inc./Rutledge Books Division.
Copyright © 1974 by National Football League Properties, Inc. All rights reserved. No part of this book may be reproduced or transmitted in any form or by any means, electronic or mechanical, including photocopying, recording or by any information storage and retrieval system, without permission in writing from the Publisher.

Macmillan Publishing Co., Inc., 866 Third Avenue, New York, N.Y. 10022. Collier-Macmillan Canada Ltd.

Library of Congress Catalog Card Number: 73-21300
First Printing 1974
Printed in the United States of America

Contents

Introduction

Millionaires are not supposed to endure frustration. Anger, perhaps; envy on occasion; but frustration, never. Particularly if the millionaire is 26 years old, the son of one of the world's wealthiest men, and has set out with the ambition to buy a professional football team. Yet Lamar Hunt found himself frustrated in late 1958 as he flew back to his Dallas home from Chicago. He had met there with Mrs. Walter Wolfner, widow of Charles Bidwill, who had built the Chicago Cardinals football club. Hunt had failed in his attempt to buy the team and move it to Dallas.

Hunt was one of several men who had tried to buy the team. He then had spoken to National Football League commissioner Bert Bell about getting an expansion team. Again he was turned down. So he had gone back to Mrs. Wolfner one last time. Now he had failed again.

Professional football would never be the same after Hunt deplaned that day. Instead of buying a team, he would found a league. "It was sort of like a light bulb coming on," he said later. He reasoned that if men in Minneapolis, Houston, and Denver also had tried to buy the Cardinals and, like himself, had been rebuffed, they or men like them might be interested in a new league.

Hunt contacted several men, among them K. S. (Bud) Adams in Houston and Bob Howsam in Denver, and found them enthusiastic about the idea. In the summer of 1959, he offically launched the American Football League with charter members in Dallas, Denver, Houston, Minneapolis, Los Angeles, and New York. Late in the fall Buffalo and Boston joined the new league.

By that time the AFL and NFL were locked in open warfare. Hunt had tried to keep the peace, going so far as to ask Bert Bell to become commissioner of the new league in addition to the NFL. Bell had made the first public statement regarding the AFL, announcing the six original cities during a Senate hearing in late July and claiming that the NFL would "foster" and "nourish" the new kid on the block. His attitude had encouraged Hunt, who felt that both leagues could live and prosper. Then came August 29, 1959, and a press conference in Houston. George Halas of the Chicago Bears and Art Rooney of the Pittsburgh Steelers were in the Texas city to watch their teams play a preseason game. They announced the NFL was about to expand into Dallas and Houston.

Hunt struck back quickly. "The American Football League from its inception has tried to keep its relationship with the NFL on the highest plane and with an amicable attitude on all matters," he said. "Now it is apparent that Mr. Halas and the NFL are not interested in this type of relationship but have kept professional football out of Denver, Seattle, Minneapolis, Louisville, Buffalo, Dallas, Houston, and Miami despite efforts of these cities to expand into the National Football League."

Clint Murchison and Bedford Wynne headed one of the groups seeking the Dallas franchise in the NFL. In early fall Hunt was told that he could have the franchise provided that he abandon plans for the AFL. He and Murchison met in ensuing weeks to talk over the problem, but neither would compromise. Hunt felt responsible for having talked others into starting the AFL. Murchison was determined to get an NFL team. Gradually Hunt's position hardened. He was committed. He would fight the NFL.

The war was underway. Hunt fought it with talent, money, brains, and foresight. And he waged his battle with three men who remained with him for years – until long after the AFL finally was absorbed into the NFL. One of these men was Hank Stram, who joined Hunt almost at the start. Stocky, vain, inventive, and a brilliant football tactician, Stram had spent a long apprenticeship as an assistant coach in college. The second man was Jack Steadman, an SMU man like Hunt, who had shown a preference for business affairs and a talent for management. The third man was Len Dawson, a quarterback whom the NFL had discarded as a failure.

Together, this unlikely quartet – a millionaire, a tailor's son, a businessman, and a backup quarterback who had been waived by every team in the NFL – created one of football's most imposing records. They survived the lean years and the humiliation of having to leave Dallas in 1963 for a new start in Kansas City. They survived more hardships in Kansas City before moving into national prominence in 1966 as the first AFL team to challenge the reign of the NFL's Green Bay Packers. That they lost the game mattered little in perspective.

"Now you know how the rest of us in this league have felt for years," Cleveland's Art Modell told Hunt after the Packers' 35–10 victory in Super Bowl I.

The loss smarted, but Hunt's team moved on, changing, strengthening, and, finally, winning it all over the Minnesota Vikings in Super Bowl IV. It was a fitting victory. For ten years the Chiefs had carried the AFL battle, and for three years they had endured the taunts stemming from their failure against the Packers. Super Bowl IV was the final game pitting teams from the rival leagues; the next season the leagues were merged.

The Chiefs emerged from the sixties as the most successful team in the AFL's history. They had won the AFL championship three times. They had gone to the Super Bowl twice. They had set standards against which other teams measured themselves, and they had drawn that ultimate accolade: imitation.

But most memories of the early Chiefs are of the men:

Of Hunt, drenched with champagne, grinning broadly in the dressing room after the Texans' first championship in 1962; and asleep on Pete Rozelle's office floor during the marathon realignment meeting.

Of Abner Haynes, kneeling over Stone Johnson on the field in Wichita, Kansas, in August, 1963, while his friend gazed back, terrified, and paralyzed.

Of the haunted look in Len Dawson's eyes as he met newsmen in New Orleans before Super Bowl IV to refute charges he had consorted with a gambler.

Of E. J. Holub, a true Texan and one of the league's most boisterous players. Some swore he wore his Stetson and his cowboy boots to bed. Everyone was "a good ol' boy."

Of the fingers of Otis Taylor, stretching for one more pass to catch.

Of Mike Garrett's uncontrollable joy at scoring against the Vikings and then leaping into Taylor's arms.

Of the sweeping arc of Jan Stenerud's leg.

Of Willie Lanier and Bobby Bell belting a runner.

Of the poignant moments when men like Jerry Mays and Johnny Robinson called it a career.

Within a decade Kansas City (née Dallas) soared from a new team in a new league to a power in pro football. It established some high standards. "People expect us to go fourteen and oh every year," Hunt once said when his club finished second. That the Chiefs did not always excel was testimony to the fact that the league Hunt had created grew steadily stronger.

The Great Years

An unprecedented era of sports expansion began when Lamar Hunt founded the American Football League and the Dallas Texans, the team that would become the Kansas City Chiefs, in August, 1959.

A gymnasium full of crew-cut athletes and booster club members have just finished dinner, and the master of ceremonies is introducing Hank Stram, assistant coach at Miami University in Florida, as the featured speaker. It is early December, 1959. Stram is returning in triumph to address the annual football banquet at Lew Wallace High School in Gary, Indiana.

Stram had no trouble finding the place. This was his hometown and his old high school. As a 12-year-old, he had thrown a no-hitter in Gary. As a somewhat undersized prep, he had led Lew Wallace High to football victories. From there he had gone to Purdue, where he won seven letters and the Big Ten Award as scholar and athlete. He then remained at Purdue as an assistant coach, where he served, at times brilliantly, under Stu Holcomb. He moved on to other assistant coaching jobs. He went to Southern Methodist where the Mustangs had been losers. They won. He went to Notre Dame, where the Fighting Irish had been in a slump. They won. He went to Miami, where the Hurricanes had been losing. They won.

He had served each team well. But he had never had a team of his own. Now at 35 years of age, Stram was a frustrated, restless man. He even seriously considered leaving coaching to work for a sporting goods company.

The master of ceremonies touches on Stram's frustration. "The amazing thing to me," he says, "is that tonight's speaker has never been a head coach." The statement draws a round of sympathetic applause. Stram toys with a fork.

Finally Stram goes to the microphone and completes a rather routine address, saying all the right words of encouragement to the young people in front of him. He is seated again and listening to the concluding remarks when a man taps him on the shoulder. "Coach, there's a long distance call for you in the office." Stram excuses himself and follows the man to the office.

"Hank?" The voice is familiar but escapes Stram at first. "This is Lamar. Hawarr yew?" The twang is unmistakable. "Do you remember our visit in Miami?"

Stram and Lamar Hunt had had dinner and a long chat in Miami earlier in the 1959 season. It was a meeting that had left the young coach puzzled. Hunt had explained that he was forming a new professional league. He had spoken of the cities involved, his goals, and his plan to put a team in Dallas. But never in their several hours of discussion had he mentioned the head coaching job.

"What do you think?" Stram had asked Miami head coach Andy Gustafson after Hunt left.

"Well, what did he say?" Gustafson had asked.

"We talked a long time, but he never said what job he was talking about," Stram had said.

"He wouldn't have come all this way from Texas if he wasn't talking about the head job," Gustafson reasoned. "Just wait. He'll get back to you."

Still, as the season wore on and plans for Hunt's proposed league developed, Stram wondered. He had almost forgotten the talk when the phone call reached him in Gary that December evening. Yes, Stram replied, he recalled their visit. "We've got everything almost set up now," said Hunt. "I still need a head coach. Would you be interested?"

Stram flew to Dallas the next day, met with Hunt, and just before Christmas, 1959, became the first head coach of the Dallas Texans in the new American Football League. He would be the team's only head coach throughout its life in the AFL, and he would continue with it in the NFL in the 1970s. His flair and style would be stamped on the team indelibly, while he and Hunt would form a long, almost unique working relationship in a business not noted for longevity in such relationships.

By the time Hunt had contacted Stram in

Gary, the 26-year-old son of oil millionaire H. L. Hunt was already deeply involved in the formation of his new league. He felt that Stram would be ideal in a league that would have to stress scoring and excitement in its formative battles with the established NFL, especially in Dallas, where the older league was planning a direct confrontation.

Hunt had first met Stram in the dressing room at SMU when Stram was an assistant coach. "He said we talked after a Notre Dame game or something," Stram said years later, "but I honestly don't remember it." Something about Stram's almost cocky assurance and the results he had repeatedly obtained with his offense had remained in the back of Hunt's mind.

Stram was the fourth man Hunt added to the Texans' payroll that fall. In October he had retained Will Walls, a respected scout and former coach, to begin assessing talent for drafting purposes. In early November he hired Don Rossi as administrative director. Rossi, a former boxer, football player, and assistant coach at Michigan State, also had served as head of the extensive sports program in the U. S. Air Force. When Hunt hired him he was western promotion manager for Spalding Sporting Goods and an NFL game official.

Not long before the call to Stram, Hunt had signed Chris Burford for $12,000. The Stanford end and All-America became the first player ever signed by the Texans. Since Burford was regarded by some scouts as the top receiver in the country that year, his signing set a pattern that the Texans and later the Chiefs would continue to follow as they rose in the AFL: draft well, then sign 'em.

Events had moved quickly. In little more than five months, Hunt had put together an eight-team league, found owners for each franchise, helped arrange playing sites, organized and conducted a player draft, and issued the first challenge the NFL had faced since the ill-fated All-America Football Conference just after World War II.

It had been a frantic period for the young man who had set out merely to buy the Chicago Cardinals and move them to Dallas. The boom following World War II had sounded in the Southwest as elsewhere, and Hunt and others were growing tired of having to fly to Kansas City to watch major league baseball, or elsewhere for professional football. But because the NFL complacently clung to its no-expansion policy, Hunt had gathered support for a new league. Now he would have to fight the NFL, which had decided to install an expansion team in Dallas after all.

After setting up teams in Denver, Dallas, Minneapolis, Los Angeles, New York, Houston, and finally in Buffalo and Boston, Hunt next moved to draft players with which to stock the teams. The owners assembled in Minneapolis on November 22, 1959, even though the Minnesota franchise situation was already shaky. The NFL eventually would capture the territory as one of its first prizes. The AFL draft was one never seen in the NFL, opening with a so-called territorial claim of one man per club from the team's own area. The Texans chose SMU quarterback Don Meredith.

Then the owners proceeded. To insure that their teams would not be oversupplied at one position and bankrupt at another, each franchise selected a "team" of two ends, two tackles, two guards, a center, and four backs. Remaining names were drawn by lot from the pool established by a committee headed by former Notre Dame coach Frank Leahy, then associated with the Los Angeles Chargers.

Burford's name topped the alphabetical list of Dallas players, released the next day. Abner Haynes, the North Texas State halfback from Dallas, was drawn by Minneapolis, but Don

Rossi immediately announced that the Texans would try to trade for Haynes, the first black athlete ever to play for a major school in Texas. Other names on the Texans' list were Mississippi All-America guard Marvin Terrell and Louisiana State halfback Johnny Robinson.

Now the AFL needed a commissioner. One name mentioned was that of Lynn (Pappy) Waldorf, the former California coach who was the chief talent scout for the San Francisco 49ers. Waldorf chose a unique method of withdrawing his name from speculation: "It wasn't a very intelligent draft," he snorted. "How could it be? They had a few guys looking around and they pooled their information. It looks like they followed the All-America lists right down the line. It will be years before their scouting system can compete with ours. They got a little jump on us by drafting first, but all the top kids will wait to see who drafts them in our league before doing any business."

Hunt replied, "We feel that we accomplished exactly what we wanted. We were striving primarily for equalization, and we feel we did a good job in that respect. We had no intentions of going out and finding the Harlon Hills at Florence State Teachers Colleges. I doubt if anyone was lured to the stadium to see Harlon Hill play his first year in professional football. It takes time for a player to reach the greatness of a Harlon Hill. It also takes time for the public to realize that he's great."

Hunt already had admitted that the AFL had no delusions about testing the NFL's supremacy on the field for a while, but he also knew that time was against him. In Dallas, the Clint Murchison-Bedford Wynne group, although not yet officially awarded the NFL expansion spot, had settled on a name: Rangers. The name was changed to Cowboys in the spring of 1960. More important, they had Don Meredith's signature on a personal services contract. The SMU quarterback, one of the most sought-after collegiate passers in years, would be a direct competitor for Dallas fan interest. One late fall Saturday in 1959 a Dallas paper listed the day's scores as Navy 43, Army 12; Notre Dame 16, USC 6; and Dallas NFL 1, Dallas AFL 0. The score mounted. Johnny Robinson was signed by Detroit. Another draftee, Vanderbilt halfback Tom Moore, elected to go with Green Bay.

Finally the skid was stopped. As promised, Rossi had arranged a trade with Minneapolis for rights to Abner Haynes, and Haynes agreed to sign a Texans' contract as soon as North Texas State completed a Sun Bowl date.

What's more, Will Walls was proving to be as good a detective as he was a scout. He reported that Robinson almost certainly had signed an illegal NFL contract with Detroit and that he had changed his mind.

Even in that early stage, the fight for talent was underway. It was a furtive kind of war, waged with checkbooks, telephones, airline schedules, many promises, and ever relentless pressures.

"Will Walls is about the best recruiter there is," said an admiring Sammy Baugh. "He knows every kid in the country and they all like him."

With Haynes committed, the Texans also traded for Jack Spikes, a TCU fullback who had been drafted by Denver. Thus the Texans assembled the nucleus of a strong backfield. Spikes could use his power inside, and Haynes could turn his floating, graceful speed loose to the outside.

Meanwhile, Hunt found that his selection of Stram was a popular one in Dallas, where Stram once had been a strong candidate to succeed Woody Woodard as SMU coach. In fact, Stram still owned the home he lived in during his days as an SMU assistant coach.

A Dallas paper had observed that "his [Stram's] Miami team bore the Stram trademark

Open warfare erupted between two professional football leagues and the principal battleground was the Cotton Bowl in Dallas (left). There the established NFL placed an expansion team, the Cowboys, to challenge the Texans of the new AFL. The four men who operated the rival Cowboys are shown at right. They are., (left to right) head coach Tom Landry, part owner Bedford Wynne, general manager Tex Schramm, and principal owner Clint Murchison.

of widely flanked ends, slot halfbacks, and varying line splits, and won six of ten games. The material was virtually the same as that on the Miami squad of the previous year, but they had won only two of eight games." This had been the pattern through much of Stram's long assistantship.

An all-state halfback at Gary in 1940, he went to Purdue. There he lettered in baseball and football after a three-year stint in the army. Then he joined Stu Holcomb's staff in 1946. Even then ideas were churning in Stram's mind. It would be years before he refined them into the elaborate, confusing alignments he threw at early AFL opponents and at Minnesota in Super Bowl IV. But the genesis was there in Lafayette.

"I was the youngest assistant on the staff at that time, and the only one not married," Stram remembers. "When Stu had to speak somewhere in Illinois or Indiana and didn't fly or take a train, I was usually free to drive with him." As the headlights searched down Midwest highways and the windshield wipers brushed away the snow, the two men talked football.

Holcomb was the patient target for the thousands of ideas that spewed from Stram's imagination. Thousands of formations and plays still may be gathering dust in some forgotten file in the Boilermakers' athletic offices, filed there by the former coach who accepted all of them. "He would always listen, always take them," Stram said.

Even then Stram was locked on the coaching philosophy that eventually projected him into national prominence. He was a disciplinarian. Although his attitude is sometimes obscured by the flair of his attire or the flamboyance of his offenses, Stram insists, "There has to be one man. It has to be his way." Football he felt was not a democracy. It was a dictatorship, although a benevolent one if possible. Jerry Mays, the almost perennial all-league defensive lineman for Stram, describes him as "Little Caesar." It is a description of affection.

Stram also believed "in variety — variety on offense, variety on defense." Later other words would enter his public vocabulary, words such as "personality," which he uses frequently to describe the style of a team, and "movement by design," which he uses to describe the multiple patterns he hurls at opponents.

The winter and spring of 1960 were as busy as the preceding months. Charges and countercharges, suits and countersuits were exchanged as the struggle between the leagues escalated. The signing of players continued as Hunt and his baby league tried to grow teeth and prepare for their first playing season. There were some notable court triumphs, including one that awarded Billy Cannon to Houston instead of the Los Angeles Rams. Another released Robinson to the Texans instead of binding him to Detroit.

Murchison and Wynne had been awarded a Dallas franchise at the same NFL meetings in late January in which Pete Rozelle was elected commissioner. But the Texans seemed to be making inroads in Dallas against their NFL rivals. Hunt had tied up the preferred dates in the Cotton Bowl, and a booster group, called the Spur Club, had sold over 1,000 tickets by early January.

On the football front, a parade of strange-looking athletes was besieging the Texans' front office. The new league was a magnet attracting both disgruntled NFL players and faded stars who had scrapbooks and little else. "For every player we've signed," sighed Walls, "we've got maybe six more applications. We probably got three-hundred-fifty applications."

The Texans' first training camp was in Roswell, New Mexico. "We had three stacks of equipment," recalls equipment manager Bobby Yarborough, who like many others in the Chiefs'

28

The most exciting player in the AFL in 1960, the league's first season, was running back Abner Haynes of the Texans, carrying the ball against the New York Titans in a photo (left) that shows the sparse attendance for a Texans' game at the Cotton Bowl. Joe Foss, commissioner of the AFL, presented a trophy to Haynes (right) after the Dallas star was named player of the year in the AFL.

organization has remained with the club from the beginning. "One was for those we didn't think would make it; one was for those that might; and another, good stuff, was for the guys we knew were going to be around." The talented draft choices such as Haynes, Burford, and Spikes all drew their equipment from "the good stuff." And before long old NFL retreads, such as Paul Miller and Ray Collins, and free agents such as Sherrill Headrick, also were drawing from that stack.

"Put in both 'r's' and both 'l's'," Headrick used to tell interviewers. "My Mom likes that." He was the most unlikely linebacker candidate in either league. His shoulders slumped from a long neck and his belly protruded. Yet he was blessed with a rare gift. He seemed instinctively to know where a play would develop, and he was totally fearless and impervious to pain. His nickname was "Psycho," and eventually the Texans even named a defense for him.

Headrick had been a fullback and guard at TCU but not a scholar. He had flunked out prior to his senior season and then had gone to Canada. At 24, weighing possibly as much as 210, he came out of Canadian ball, where he was a defensive back. "If I hadn't gotten this job," he said of the Texans, "I don't know what I'd have done. Nothing, probably. I'd have been a bum."

The Texans began to build their defense around this improbable hero, who remained with them until Cincinnati picked him in the expansion draft. Through it all there was one habit he never lost. He never went onto the playing field without first throwing up in the locker room.

Other players slowly emerged from the sunburned mass Stram drilled relentlessly in the New Mexico heat. Guard Bill Krisher was one. A former Oklahoma star under Bud Wilkinson, he would provide much of the blocking on Haynes's sweeps. He was named the Texans' first captain.

Cotton Davidson, unsuccessful in a short NFL try after starring at Baylor, had gone back to coaching his alma mater before the new league enticed him into one more try. He came out of the summer as Dallas's quarterback.

Haynes more than lived up to expectations during the first season, winning the rushing title with a 5.6 average that also earned him player of the year honors. However, it still took a strong three-game winning streak at the finish to wind up 8–6, second to Los Angeles's 10–4. Krisher, Haynes, Headrick, and defensive end Mel Branch were voted to the all-league team.

Then despite one of the finest drafts in their history, the Texans were second again in 1961, this time with a 6–8 record. Spikes had been hurt early in the season, robbing the team of part of their running game and helping to launch a six-game losing streak. Davidson had continued an erratic career as a passer, due partly to the fact that the Texans were forced to rely heavily on their passing game.

But by 1962 the Texans had begun assembling the major parts of the machine that would serve them for the next decade. The 1961 draft brought in E. J. Holub, Jim Tyrer, Jerry Mays, Fred Arbanas, Curtis McClinton (a future choice who came in 1962), and Frank Jackson. Most of the parts were there, but Stram still was searching for the final part that would make the machine run. He finally found it in a slender six-footer with frosty blue eyes and an even icier demeanor. Len Dawson had arrived to join Stram for the first time since their careers had crossed in Ohio 10 years earlier. Dawson then had been a heavily recruited youngster from Alliance, Ohio, where he had earned a reputation as a fine passer. Stram had been recruiting for Purdue. "I remember one of the first things I ever noticed about him," Dawson said afterward, "was the trousers he was wearing. They had no hip pockets. I couldn't figure out

Chris Burford (left) was the first player signed to a contract by the Texans, and he became the team's star pass receiver. Defensive safetyman Johnny Robinson (right) was one of the biggest names signed by the Texans in the AFL's war with the NFL to enlist college football players.

where he kept his handkerchief and comb."

Stram, who has been a dapper figure all through his career, had kept after Dawson. Perhaps it was Dawson's curiosity that eventually lured him to the Boilermakers; he may have wanted to find out where Stram really did keep his comb. More likely it was Stram's promise that the Boilermakers would be a passing team and that Dawson would be their passer.

Stram had kept his promise and Dawson had lived up to expectations. In 1954, 1955, and 1956, he led the Big Ten in total offense and passing. And in 1957 he was the Pittsburgh Steelers' number one draft choice. He was offered a $12,000 salary and a $2,000 bonus. His only other choice was to play with Toronto, so he took the Steelers' offer and spent the next three years watching Bobby Layne. In 1960, Dawson was traded to Cleveland; this time he waited behind Milt Plum.

All the while Dawson grew rustier. There were a few plays here, a series there, part of a quarter when a game was out of hand. Through five seasons, the frustrated young quarterback played perhaps the equivalent of five full quarters. Over those five seasons, he threw 45 times, completing 21 passes for 204 yards. There was one touchdown pass with Pittsburgh in 1959 and another in 1961 with the Browns.

Stram and Dawson had stayed in touch. Once, when Stram had attended an NCAA convention in Pittsburgh, they had gotten together. "Lenny was very dejected," Stram said later. "I tried to assure him that he could still play, that probably all he needed was a different atmosphere. I told him I'd like to have him with our team if he ever got free."

After the 1961 season, Dawson went to see Cleveland's Paul Brown. He was put on waivers in early summer. He was not claimed. Free, he called Stram.

"When I got word that Lenny was free, I was at the practice sessions for the Coaches' All-America game, which was then held each summer in Buffalo," Stram recalled. "There were a lot of pro people there, and word got around that several other teams would like to sign Dawson as a free agent." Cannily, Brown had placed Dawson on waivers at a time when most clubs were on vacation, and Dawson still feels that this explains why no NFL team filed a claim on him in the summer of 1962.

Afraid that he might be beaten to his old pupil, Stram flew from Buffalo to Pittsburgh, meeting Dawson in the air terminal. "When he met me," said Stram, "I was embarrassed at worrying about anyone else getting to him first. He said, 'I told you I wanted to sign with you. What were you so worried about?'"

Within weeks Stram's worries had shifted. His Texans were in camp for their third summer. Davidson remained the number one quarterback. Hunter Enis of TCU was number two. Eddie Wilson, a high draft prospect from Arizona, was number three. Dawson was a distant fourth. His name didn't even appear in newspaper reports from training camp until late in the summer.

Had it not been for Stram's long acquaintance with Dawson, and his knowledge of the man's fiber, Dawson would have been cut early. "No question about it," Stram admitted a decade later. "He was awful those first few weeks."

Mechanically, Dawson was a mess. His footwork was bad, his execution was sloppy, and his passing was even worse. But Stram was patient, and gradually some of the old Purdue polish returned. "The rotation of his ball got a little tighter; he got sharper; his reactions got better," Stram said. As he watched his former pupil slowly regain form under the Texas sun, Stram's worries eased. "Maybe," he thought. "Yeah, just maybe." Stram and the Texans needed a maybe at that point.

The 1962 calendar had opened on a promising note as the Texans, including Davidson, played a big part in helping the West win the first AFL All-Star game in San Diego. During league meetings that same week, Joe Foss's contract as commissioner was renewed, and the player limit was raised from 33 to 36 men. That would help Stram. The Texans also announced that they had retained ex-Chargers personnel man Don Klosterman and that he would have full charge of the scouting operation. "We have been lax in contacting and following up on players," Hunt said. "For instance we drafted a boy from Purdue (Larry Bowie) and it didn't occur to anyone in our organization that we had the ideal man to deal with him in Hank Stram. So we lost him to the NFL."

Arbanas, who had missed the 1961 season with a back injury, was the talk of the camp early the following summer. Completely healed, he was rapidly answering the tight end problem that had troubled the Chiefs in their first two seasons. At 6-feet 4-inches and 233 pounds, the powerful first-year man was both a good receiver and a devastating blocker.

There were other encouraging notes. Walt Corey, a linebacker who had spent 1961 in the service, returned 30 pounds heavier than he had been as a 195-pound rookie in 1960. "My gosh, did you see his arms?" Stram asked. "He could crack walnuts with those biceps."

The Texans' number one choice, Ronnie Bull, the big fullback from Baylor, had been signed by Chicago in the NFL, but the Texans had signed their number two choice, end Bill Miller from Miami. They also had signed Eddie Wilson from Arizona, traded for rights to quarterback Bobby Ply of Baylor, and drafted Auburn quarterback Bobby Hunt. On the seventeenth round, they chose Alabama end Tom Brooker.

Dawson's debut was the kind that makes a man keep his bags packed. Coming in during the second quarter of a preseason contest in Atlanta, Dawson steered Dallas to one first down and three fumbles. Davidson rescued the game in the second half, directing the Texans to a 13–3 win over Oakland.

Dallas had a 2–3 record in preseason games that summer. Only one of its games was even noteworthy. Denver beat Dallas 27–24 on a field goal in sudden death overtime.

Dawson improved gradually. He won the starting job for the regular-season opener with a splendid second half against Houston. Even though Dallas lost 34–31, Dawson threw three touchdown passes while completing 13 of 19 attempts for 239 yards.

Dallas was a new team as it took the field in the Cotton Bowl for its season opener against Boston. One-third of the squad had never played an AFL game. Dawson was at quarterback, Arbanas at tight end, and Miller and Burford at wide receiver. Defensively, the fleet Johnny Robinson was starting a new career as a safety instead of a running back.

Haynes launched his greatest year by scoring four touchdowns against the Patriots, and Dawson threw two touchdown passes. The two men established a scoring combination that would carry the Texans often in 1962. Dallas won 42–28.

Afterward, Haynes, the first black captain in the league, stood in the dressing room and called his teammates to order. "Normally," he said solemnly, "we give the game ball to coach Stram after we win the opener." There were scattered snickers in the room. Dallas had never won an opening game before. "But tonight we want Len Dawson to have it."

Within a week Davidson was traded to Oakland – without Stram's approval – by owner Hunt in exchange for the Raiders' number one draft choice and negotiation rights to Fred Miller, the LSU tackle. Earlier the Texans had

Five years as a bench warmer in the National Football League had eroded the quarterbacking skills of Len Dawson (left) before he joined the Texans in 1962. His performance was so poor during training camp that only an association of many years with Hank Stram, coach of the Texans, kept Dawson from being cut from the squad. Before the season was over, however, he emerged as the leading passer in the American Football League. The prototype Texan during the Dallas years was brilliant linebacker E. J. Holub, nicknamed "the Beast" (right).

turned down an offer to swap Davidson and center Jon Gilliam for center Jim Otto.

More than a decade afterward, Stram still seemed reluctant to recall the loss of Davidson. He felt Davidson should have remained a Texan. "I can still see the coach that day the trade was made," says equipment manager Yarborough. "He went out on the practice field and sat there, all alone on a blocking dummy, staring at the grass."

It turned out that Dallas used the Raiders' draft choice to acquire Junious (Buck) Buchanan. The trade had been an enormous gamble, regardless of Davidson's inconsistency. He was, after all, the Chiefs' only proven veteran at quarterback. Wilson was the rawest of rookies, and Dawson, despite an excellent opening night, was relatively untested as a starter. And what if Dawson were injured?

Davidson's departure posed another problem: He was the Texans' punter. His departure created a chronic weakness in this department and ultimately some bizarre strategy in the title game against Houston.

In the meantime the Texans were faced with the immediate problem of their next game, which was against Oakland – and Cotton Davidson. "Cotton was like a coach on the field with us," said Stram. "He knew our offense, our defense, and our personnel. Fortunately, we hadn't put in any special plays for the Oakland game when he left."

During the Oakland-Dallas game, Dawson offered encouragement by throwing three touchdowns to Burford. The Texans won 26–16, but another event occurred that weekend that was even more vital to Dallas's future. Jack Kemp had guided the Los Angeles, and then San Diego, Chargers to two straight Western Division championships, and he had won three of four games against Dallas in the first two seasons. Kemp was a nemesis. But suddenly Kemp was no longer a Charger. In a rare misjudgment triggered by anger, San Diego coach Sid Gillman had placed his broken-fingered passing ace on waivers. A player put on this list within 24 hours of a league game was not recallable. Buffalo took Kemp, thus acquiring a man who would take them to two league titles in the mid-1960s. Gillman had to spend 1962 breaking in rookie John Hadl.

The effect on Dallas was the removal of a pesky enemy in the third week of the season, just as Dawson was starting to show Stram's judgment and patience were well placed. It was a happy coincidence for Stram's rambunctious youngsters, who were beginning to feel a little cocky. Averaging slightly over 23 years of age, the majority with little or no previous experience, they were beginning to believe their press clippings. They were good. They would get better.

Stram, the addicted doodler, kept turning would-be adversity into pluses. On a Friday night in the fifth week of the season, he devised a different blocking tactic to counter the notorious blitz used by the Boston Patriots. He went with two tight ends, putting Arbanas on one side and the rookie Brooker on the other. They nullified the Patriots' linebackers, while Burford roamed through the Boston secondary, catching 10 passes. Dallas won 27–7.

"Chris Burford has the equipment, speed, fine size [6-feet 3-inches, 210 pounds], and intelligence," said Stram. "But more than anything else, he wants to catch the ball. You can see it even in practice. Even in a routine passing drill, he catches the ball as if it were the winning touchdown in a championship game."

Unfortunately the Boston-Dallas game also saw Spikes carried off the field. His thigh was hemorrhaging as it had in 1961. He had missed the last half of the year, sending Dallas into a six-game slump. But this time Stram and the

Texans had depth, and McClinton was eager for the chance.

The previous fall the New York Giants' Jim Lee Howell had called McClinton the best college runner in the nation. And two years earlier the Los Angeles Rams had used a tenth round choice on him while he was just a sophomore. This unprecedented action was only legal because he had interrupted his college career to spend two years in the army. A former Big Eight hurdles champion, he could move his 6-foot 2-inch, 218-pound frame over a 100-yard field in 9.8 seconds. The Texans had lost Spikes, but McClinton was an awesome replacement.

Week by week the Texans found a new hero or a new way to win. Their next hero was Brooker. In the sixth game of the season, he kicked a late field goal to down New York 20–17. It was only the seventh in his entire career, pro or college, but three had won games and another had tied Texas in the 1960 Bluebonnet Bowl.

Stram surprised Houston with a new zone defense, and the Texans beat the Oilers 31–7 in Houston for the first time. The Texans intercepted six passes and recovered three fumbles. Haynes scored one touchdown and Dawson threw for three touchdowns, two of them to Burford. With Denver's loss to Buffalo, the Texans, who had been playing leapfrog with the Broncos since early in the year, were boosted back to the top of the Western Division.

Of the team Stram sent out against the Oilers in the light rain that day, only Dawson ever had appeared in an NFL game, while roughly half of the Oilers had previous pro experience. Haynes, James Saxton, Robinson, Jackson, Spikes, McClinton, Branch, Bill Hull, Mays, Tyrer, Miller, Burford, and Holub all had joined the Texans as rookies and were growing with the team, as Stram wanted.

In a quirk of scheduling common in the AFL in those years, the Texans were to meet the Oilers again the next week in the Cotton Bowl. The results of the rematch were unfavorable to the Texans. It took a late Dawson pass to Burford to avert a shutout; the Oilers gained revenge 14–6. George Blanda accounted for all the Oilers' points with two passes to Billy Cannon and two conversions. Worse, Denver beat San Diego 23–20 and reclaimed first place.

The Texans were scheduled to play the Titans in the Polo Grounds next, although early in the week nobody, especially the Titans, was certain whether or not the game would be played. For the second or third time, payroll checks had bounced for the troubled New York team, and its uniforms were being held for ransom in a laundry. It wasn't until midweek that assistant commissioner Milt Woodard announced that the checks had been covered and would be honored. Meanwhile owner Harry Wismer was still looking for a buyer. His asking price of $2.5 million was considered outrageous.

In the beginning of November, Dallas was 6–2 and Denver was 7–2, and two key showdowns were due between them in the next month. The Texans prepared by demolishing the demoralized Titans 52–31. Dawson again threw three touchdown passes; Haynes ran for 107 yards and scored three times; and Holub, playing linebacker on defense and center on offense, logged 58 minutes of playing time.

Holub could scarcely undress himself in the locker room. The 6-foot 4-inch, 230-pound Czech, nicknamed "the Beast," had majored in business finance at Texas Tech. If there was such a thing as a prototype Texan on the 1962 Dallas team, the Beast was it. He wore a wide grin, Stetson hat, size 50 coat, and 13-E boots. He was outgoing, loud, likeable, and immensely talented.

"When I was a little kid, three straight flash floods wiped out our farm in Schulenberg," Holub said. "My dad never got over it. He still

The 1962 AFL champions. Front row, left to right: equipment manager Bobby Yarborough, James Saxton, Eddie Wilson, Bobby Ply, Len Dawson, Bobby Hunt, Frank Jackson, and Abner Haynes. Second row: head coach Hank Stram, Jack Spikes, Curtis McClinton, Smokey Stover, Johnny Robinson, Dave Grayson, Duane Wood, E. J. Holub, Walt Corey, and trainer Wayne Rudy. Third row: owner Lamar Hunt, Al Reynolds, Marvin Terrell, Curt Merz, Jon Gilliam, Sonny Bishop, Carl Larpenter, Sherrill Headrick, and assistant coach Ed Hughes. Fourth row: assistant coach Tom Catlin, assistant coach Bob Ghilotti, Paul Rochester, Jerry Cornelison, Jerry Mays, Jim Tyrer, Charlie Diamond, scout Don Klosterman, and assistant coach Bill Walsh. Fifth row: general manager Jack Steadman, Tommy Brooker, Bill Miller, Fred Arbanas, Bill Hull, Dick Davis, Mel Branch, and Chris Burford.

drives to the country every weekend and sits all day just looking at the horses and cows. All my life I've wanted that farm back."

He was nearing that dream. Holub had become a must-sign player the previous year when the crosstown Cowboys had snatched away Bob Lilly in the signing wars. Now as the Texans neared the key part of their 1962 season, Holub owned 476 acres near Paris, Texas, and spent every possible moment listening to nearby foremen for advice.

"This is everything I want," he said that previous spring. "I live in an apartment in Paris and get to my ranch at four-thirty every morning. I stay until dark. When hay baling starts I'll run some lights and work later. At night I read books and pamphlets on soil and conservation. I don't want anything else – except a dog. I'm going to get a dog. I had one, but I had to get rid of him. I hate the city. There's nothing to do but pound the concrete and talk to people. I've got to be outdoors where you can accomplish something." In the year before he joined the Texans he had captained three different college all-star teams.

On the field, Holub, Headrick, Smokey Stover, and Corey helped form one of the young league's most formidable linebacking groups, one so versatile that Stram even experimented with using all four at once, leaving just three linemen. Holub was typical of the talent beginning to ripen on Hunt's new family tree. Ply and Hunt had abandoned any thoughts of being pro quarterbacks and were developing into fine safeties, as was Robinson.

Mays was being used at tackle. Tyrer had taken charge at left tackle on offense and never was displaced during the rest of his long, all-league career. Haynes was approaching some major records on this team, and was receiving national acclaim. "He runs like a fox," said sportscaster Elmer Angsman.

"I can get to top speed in two steps," the young halfback said. "But you know it's nothing you can work on. It's just instinct." Haynes had played both defense and offense at Lincoln High, a segregated school in Dallas. "In the part of town where I was raised, growing up was hard. It was a fight to get into school, to get back to school, and to stay in school."

Haynes had a gifted if untrained singing voice; a record he cut at a Dallas station came close to professional quality. He was a floating, graceful runner with a knack for setting up and using his blockers at precisely the right moment.

Stram continued to use the double tight end formation throughout the season. "Everyone sees the basic split end and flanker offense every week," he reasoned. "It's getting fairly easy to defend. They don't see the double tight end offense until they play us. As a result we're getting just one or two defenses thrown at us every week instead of eight or nine like we used to."

Finally it was time for Dallas to meet Denver in the showdown both teams had been pointing for. Dallas had a 7–2 record; Denver, leading the league in offensive statistics, was 7–3. Snow was packed about the playing field in Denver that Sunday and it was 25 degrees as the teams left the dressing rooms. Portions of the turf were frozen, and the temperature was falling.

The Texans held a 10–3 lead in the fourth quarter. Then Denver's Jim Fraser lofted a punt that went out of bounds on Dallas's 3-yard line.

Dawson twice sent runners into the line and got only five yards. Stram watched the two futile stabs and was worried. He considered having Dawson take a deliberate safety. "At least we'd be able to free kick from the twenty instead of possibly having to get one away under pressure off the icy footing from deep in the endzone."

But Dawson, using McClinton for a play-action fake, passed to Brooker at the 25-yard line. The rookie was all alone, and he headed downfield like a truck trying to negotiate a

snowy mountain pass. He just made it, crashing into the endzone with Denver defender Jim McMillin on his back. The 92-yard touchdown pass play gave the Texans breathing room. A little later Dawson extended the lead with a 48-yard pass to Arbanas. Dallas won 24–3.

Brooker, who saved his field goals for important occasions, apparently favored the same policy for receptions. The touchdown catch was his second catch of the year. Both passes went for scores.

On Thanksgiving Day, Denver fell further off the pace with a 46-45 loss to the Titans. Dallas had to win just one of its last four games to clinch a title tie. Oakland, trailing the league in almost every department, was the Texans' next opponent in Dallas.

Davidson, suffering from a shoulder problem, had completed only 36.2 percent of his passes that season. Dawson, on the other hand, was the hottest man in the AFL, with a 61.8 percent completion rate. He had 24 touchdown passes.

But Dawson scarcely had to pass during the game against Oakland. He threw only 13 times, completing 9 passes, netting 129 yards, and scoring 2 touchdowns. With the turf heavy and slippery, he elected to send Haynes and McClinton thundering off tackle on a relentless attack the Raiders never stopped.

The Raiders' seventeenth consecutive defeat – and Dallas's clinching of at least a title tie – were in hand. Dallas's second backfield (of Wilson, Spikes, and Jackson) was at work, so it was a mystery to all when Haynes, who already had scored one touchdown, came trotting out of the murk near the end of the game. He ran onto the misty field from the bench and told Wilson to run him on a sweep. Dutifully Wilson did. Haynes found the corner, waited for blockers, and then spurted. One Raider tried to stop him at the 3-yard line, but Haynes bowled him over and scored his eighteenth touchdown of the season, tying Steve Van Buren of the Eagles, Jim Brown of Cleveland, and Bill Groman of Houston for the record of most touchdowns in one season.

"Abner called that play himself," a lineman said afterward. "We laughed and told him he better score or cough up a hundred dollars."

Haynes netted 112 yards, McClinton 109. Years later Haynes said he didn't think he'd run out on his own. "I don't know," he said. "It doesn't sound like something I'd do. Coach Stram might have sent me out – or my teammates."

Whatever the reasons for Haynes's magnificent year, he had become one of the game's brightest running stars.

The game produced one major casualty: Burford twisted a knee and was out for the remainder of the season.

Assured of at least a tie for the title, Dallas headed to Buffalo. Denver was to face Houston. A Dallas win or a Denver loss would give the Texans the championship.

On the Saturday before the game, Dallas participated in one of its most important drafts, selecting Buck Buchanan of Grambling with the choice it had gained from the trade with Oakland. It also drafted Bobby Bell, Ed Budde, Jerrel Wilson, and Dave Hill. All of these men would remain as key elements of the Dallas-Kansas City organization for over 10 years.

Then on Sunday, the Texans were taken apart by Jack Kemp, whom Buffalo had acquired from San Diego. Kemp showed his hand had definitely healed as he completed 21 of 35 passes for 248 yards and two touchdowns in his second start after coming off the injury list. Buffalo won 23–14, but, since Houston beat Denver, Dallas won the championship.

Back in Dallas the next day, Gilliam, musing over the title, explained why the team did not seem particularly elated. "We knew we were going to win it," he said, "regardless of what

Denver or anybody else did. We knew we had it when we beat Denver up there in the snow two weeks ago. It was just a matter of time until we clinched it. The best team wins. We simply have the best team."

Buffalo coach Lou Saban put it another way. "Dallas has always had the talent," he said. "In Len Dawson they have the man who brings out that talent. Dallas is the class of the American Football League."

Two meaningless games were left. The Texans prepared for their second game against Denver by signing Buchanan, Stone Johnson, and Budde. They then moved Frank Jackson from his position as Haynes's backup to replace Burford at flanker. The Texans won the game 17–10.

The final game of the regular season was against the San Diego Chargers, who had been decimated by the loss of Kemp, plus 23 other injuries. They were hardly the Chargers of the past two years. Dallas won 26–17.

The victory over the Chargers was secondary to one Klosterman announced earlier. The Texans had pulled off a coup by signing Bell away from the Vikings. Minnesota officials said that the Texans had "made one of the most fabulous offers ever proposed to a collegiate player." They claimed Bell was given a long term, no-cut contract calling for about $150,000. The Texans denied it, although Bell's contract reportedly did cover a five-year period.

"The Texans very likely have signed the best all-around athlete in America," Klosterman declared. "Bobby Bell is a professional prospect at almost any position you can name – and a good one." Bell was UPI lineman of the year at the University of Minnesota, and the Football Writers Association of America had voted him the Outland trophy, which is awarded annually to the nation's number one lineman.

Bell had begun his career on a Shelby, North Carolina, team that played 6-man football. The school went to 11-man football when Bell was a senior and with a team of only 18 players it won the state championship. Bell was the team's quarterback. During one game he threw an 80-yard pass but shunned all praise, giving it instead to the receiver who was fast enough to get under the ball. Flooded with college offers but shunned by southern schools because he was black, Bell had narrowed his choices to Notre Dame, Illinois, and Michigan when Minnesota entered the bidding at the last minute. "They wanted to know more about me," said Bobby, "but we didn't have any game movies to send. I had to get a letter of recommendation from Jim Tatum, the North Carolina coach."

The Texans' 11–3 season in 1962 matched that of the Oilers in the Eastern Division. It was an impressive finish to a highly satisfying season, but the most important part was still a week away, when the game to determine the AFL championship would be played in Houston's misty Jeppesen Stadium.

The AFL championship was finally decided in a marathon battle lasting 77 minutes and 54 seconds. The Texans mastered Houston 20–17, finally winning what had eluded them through their first two frustrating years: the championship of the AFL.

The Texans won the title with a team averaging only 23.3 years, and they were hailed as a "dynasty" after the dramatic win over Houston. They had some excellent talent and had added to it with such draft choices as Budde, Buchanan, and Bell, the heart of the 1963 selections.

Dallas's overtime win had created an unexpectedly strong and favorable impact for the league as a whole. "The AFL was born at the age of three, so magnificent was the game . . . viewers were even given to wonder if Joe Schmidt or Sam Huff could excel E. J. Holub," wrote Shirley Povich in the *Washington Post*.

In addition to Dawson, who was player of

One year the Texans were AFL champions. The next year, they weren't even "Texans" anymore; they were now "Chiefs." The designer of the team's emblem accommodated the 1963 move to Kansas City easily enough. What had been a cowpoke racing across Texas (left) became an Indian racing across Missouri (right). Walking the streets of Kansas City to check out their new surroundings in the photo below are Chiefs players (left to right) Jerry Mays, E. J. Holub, and Frank Jackson.

Running back Mike Garrett (left), winner of the Heisman trophy at USC, joined the Chiefs in 1966. Kansas City obtained cornerback Fred Williamson (right) in a trade with Oakland in 1965.

the year, and McClinton, who was rookie of the year, Haynes and Headrick made all-league for the third straight season; Branch for the second season; and Burford, Tyrer, Mays, and Holub for the first time. Arbanas, Duane Wood, Dave Grayson, and Bobby Hunt were named to the second team.

On January 11, Foss said all league teams would remain where they were for 1963. "We have not really tested Dallas," Hunt said during the league meetings that week. "We have never reached a point where we were playing a 'must' game in Dallas. We had three 'must' games last season, but they were all on the road." He said that the Texans outdrew the Cowboys, "but the difference was very insignificant – only about three thousand. Two teams cannot succeed in Dallas . . . Dallas is not used to Sunday afternoon games. Basically Dallas is a church town and we're trying to change people's habits."

Presumably Kansas City was not as religious. On February 8, Hunt announced that he would move his team to Kansas City, provided that civic leaders there would sell 25,000 season tickets. The Missouri city offered other alluring concessions too, and Hunt's decision stood. The battle on the plains of Texas was over, decided ultimately by the ledger sheets of Lamar Hunt and reinforced by his realistic assessment that even a championship drive had not helped attendance.

The decision stunned his players. They had won; the Cowboys had not. They were champions of their league, and they were a young, vibrant, confident team. Yet they were being driven off to Missouri, while the Cowboys stayed to harvest all the work of the past three seasons.

Only Oakland and New York had less paid attendance than the Texans in their title year. In his prepared statement Hunt said, "I have always tried to run this team as a business, and, in fact, in the long run, it must operate on a businesslike basis. Put in laymen's terms, this means that there must be enough income to meet expenses."

It was a surprisingly amicable divorce; sad, but with no real recriminations on either side. Even the president of the Spur Club conceded it was probably necessary.

"People say Dallas is a poor sports town," Hunt said. "But I think the situation of having two teams has been the fault here. When I first went into it, I anticipated a one-team city." Hunt also said he hadn't anticipated how much television would hurt. "While one team is trying to sell tickets to a home game in the Cotton Bowl for five dollars," said Hunt, "the other team is beaming its game into town free.

"I can't be bitter at the city. And I can't be bitter at the situation that has existed," Hunt said. "I don't think they [the NFL] did the right thing. What they did was wrong for the game of pro football."

What Hunt did in moving, quite possibly, was release the first dove of peace between the AFL and NFL. The dove would not land for three more years, but it was en route. Hunt referred to this in his Saturday, February 9, press conference announcing the franchise shift. He said it could be the first step in interleague cooperation. "Obviously the leagues could never get together until the Dallas situation was resolved," he said.

In Dallas, civic groups had been afraid to take sides. "Don't do for one what you don't do for the other," had been the motto. If you buy two Texans tickets, buy two Cowboys tickets. Even the newspapers fell into the pattern. A two-column Cowboys headline drew a two-column Texans headline to balance it.

Public reaction followed that of players and media: sad but resigned. One lady called the Texans' switchboard and asked, "Is it true the Texans are leaving Dallas?"

"Yes, ma'am, that's right."

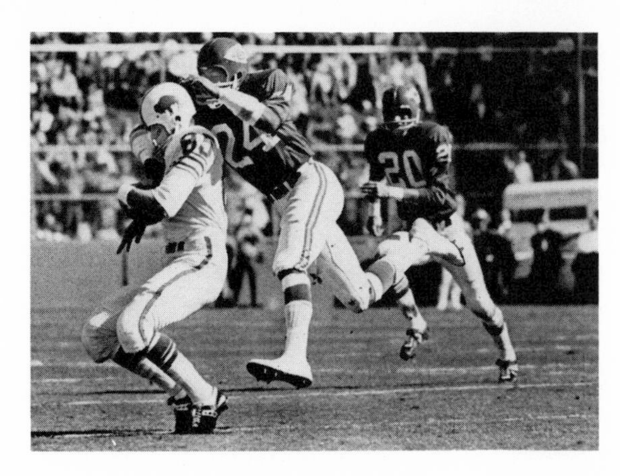

"Well, I'm sorry to hear that. We're sure gonna miss coach Schramm and his boys." (Tex Schramm was the Cowboys' general manager.)

Such confusion was not unusual during the three-year overlap. A national magazine once placed ads in the Dallas dailies, telling about an upcoming story on Tom Landry, "the brilliant young coach of the Dallas Texans." And when the Kansas City-based Rockne Club of America honored Stram as coach of the year after the 1962 season, they sent the letter in care of the Cowboys.

All did not go smoothly in Missouri. There was opposition in the City Council to the generous lease terms, but Mayor H. Roe Bartle stood firm. He said that he had sought the Texans; they had not come hat in hand to him. Ticket sales were not exactly booming either. The 25,000-ticket goal was an enormous one. Houston, even with the momentum of two straight league titles, had sold only 11,000 for the 1962 season. The average AFL advance sale was 7,500. The NFL average was 28,000. The Associated Press estimated Hunt had lost $200,000 in the previous season, as the Texans averaged 22,201 to the Cowboys' 21,794.

By May 22 (the deadline Hunt had set), only 13,025 season tickets had been sold in Kansas City, but Hunt said that the team would still move. He said that in five weeks Kansas City had produced more sales in dollars than the all-time record of 13 of the 22 teams then comprising the two leagues, and that sales totaled roughly $600,000.

The Texans were now Missourians, and four days later their name was officially changed to the Chiefs.

In the next three years there were moments when both Hunt and the players must have wondered if the shift was worth it. They went 5–7–2 and finished third in 1963, drew even at 7–7 in 1964, and were 7–5–2 in 1965. Attendance slid steadily downward,even though Stram drafted players like Otis Taylor, Frank Pitts, Gloster Richardson, Pete Beathard, and Ed Lothamer. Cornerback Fred Williamson and halfback Bert Coan had been added through trades. However, Haynes was gone. He was traded to Denver in 1965 after a good comeback season in 1964. Like most of the team, he had come down with some sort of malaise in 1963 just after the shift north.

Somehow the 1966 season was different from the start. The opening of training camp in July seemed almost anticlimactic after all that had happened in the first half of the year.

At halftime of the East-West Shrine Game the previous winter, the Chiefs had signed Mike Garrett, the Heisman trophy winner from USC. Most AFL teams had assumed Garrett was all but suited up with the Los Angeles Rams of the NFL. The Chiefs had waited until the twentieth round to name him in the draft. In Garrett, for what columnist Mel Durslag said was a $450,000 package, the Chiefs got the slashing, outside running threat they were missing previously.

In early January Klosterman quit. He had been incorrectly quoted regarding a possible franchise shift of the Kansas City team to Anaheim, but the misquotes stirred a storm in Missouri, where the Chiefs had just launched a high-powered season ticket campaign. This seemed to be the last leg of a collision course that Stram and Klosterman had been traveling for a long time. Two strong personalities were producing the wrong chemistry. Klosterman's wasn't the only face missing. Others included veterans Frank Jackson, Mel Branch, Alphonse Dotson, and Ron Caveness (who was claimed by Miami in the expansion draft).

Meanwhile, Hunt was under such pressure that he had to call a press conference to deny that he was planning to move the Chiefs. At the same time he said that the 12-day-old ticket

Coach Hank Stram compared Bert Coan (left, about to benefit from the block of guard Curt Merz) to legendary runner Tom Harmon. Defensive leader E. J. Holub, towering over Stram in the photo at right, typified the gung-ho spirit of the Chiefs.

campaign had sold 6,715 season tickets, of which 3,000 were new.

By early summer the war between the two leagues had ceased. Peace had come in the form of a merger agreement signed on June 8. The terms of the agreement were these: Rozelle would be the commissioner of both leagues; there would be an interleague world championship game; all existing franchises would remain at their present sites; there would be a combined draft; a new franchise would be added to each league in 1968; AFL teams would pay an indemnity of $18 million over a 20-year period; interleague preseason games would be played in 1967; and a single league would commence with interlocking schedules in 1970, the year current television contracts expired. "The two big things we wanted we got," said Hunt, "the championship game and the preseason games."

Within a month Hunt already was referring to the championship game as the Super Bowl, a name that quickly caught the public's fancy. It intrigued the players as well. From the start a theme ran through the Chiefs' training camp interviews – the postseason playoff against the NFL champion. At one point Williamson even speculated on what it would be like to cover Boyd Dowler and "drop the hammer" on the Green Bay receiver.

Stram pushed his team harder than before, as they trained through the muggy summer days at William Jewell College. In their first four games, the Chiefs would have to face defending league champion Buffalo twice, plus Oakland and Boston.

One thing was quickly obvious: Otis Taylor was about to live up to all the promise he had shown since being drafted in the fourth round a year earlier. "Wait and see," Stram had enthused, "just wait, boys. He'll be the most respected flanker in the league next to Lance Alworth. With Taylor in the lineup, we'll be able to do so much more with our offense this year." Stram was savoring the thought of Taylor's deep threat and Garrett's ability to open up the running game.

Pete Beathard was pushing hard for Dawson's job. As one veteran observed, "The decision's getting tougher for the man [Stram], isn't it? I think it depends on the situation. If the other team's line is bigger and slower, like Houston's, Beathard goes better because he's quicker and can roll out. If we're up against a quick, smaller line, Lenny is better."

The Chiefs won four games in a row in the preseason and then had a rest the opening week of the season. This was followed by three consecutive road games at Buffalo, Oakland, and Boston.

The league was changing in 1966. San Diego had been the major early rival, but the Chargers had been wounded in the signing wars. Houston had faded as another rival, but Oakland was rising.

The Chiefs got a sparkling job from Bert Coan and won their first game, beating Buffalo 42–20. "Tommy Harmon was the greatest I ever saw," Stram said one afternoon as he studied Coan in practice. "He was a picture runner, with great speed and great knee action. Bert Coan looks more like Tommy than anybody I've seen."

A week later the Chiefs marred the dedication of the Raiders' new stadium by blocking two field goal attempts and a punt, winning 32–10. In Boston the next week, the Chiefs' explosive start continued with a 43–24 rout. In three games Dawson had completed 60 percent of his passes for 10 touchdowns. Then the Chiefs went home to meet Buffalo again.

A crowd of 43,885, including 3,700 standing room patrons, was the first sellout in Kansas City. The Bills completely dominated the game, winning 29–14. The loss dropped the Chiefs into second place in the division, behind the hot

The development of Kansas City's offense progressed faster than that of the defense. There, Stram relied on the leadership of safety Johnny Robinson (below). Exciting wide receiver Otis Taylor (right) was a sensation as a Kansas City rookie in 1965.

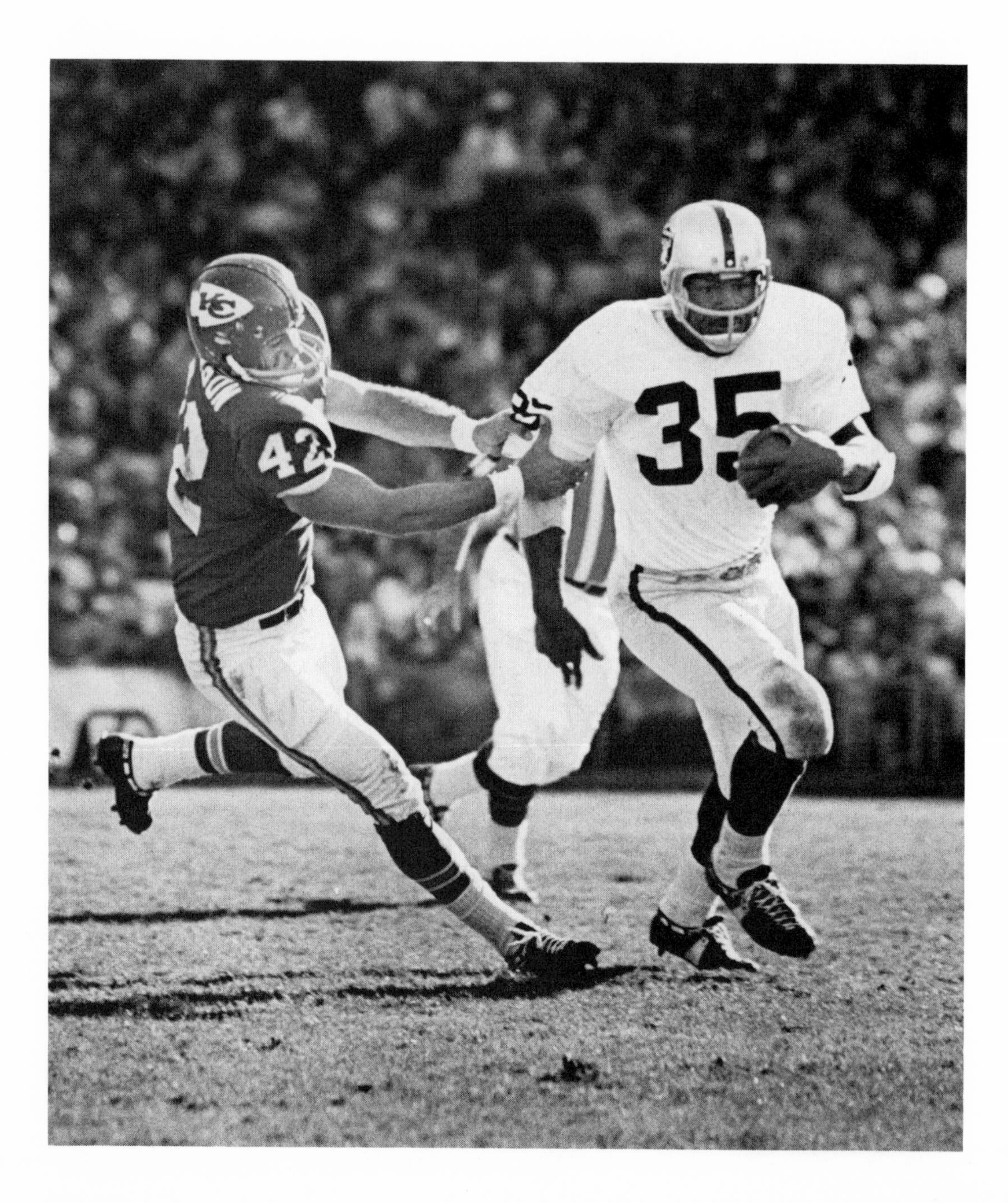

San Diego Chargers, who were still undefeated.

Another good crowd, more than 33,929 people, came out the next Saturday night as the Chiefs beat Denver 37–10. This crowd boosted attendance for two games to 77,814, more than half of the 1965 total. The Chiefs played a three-man line with four linebackers to assist rookie Emmitt Thomas, who filled in for the injured Williamson. Williamson had dislocated a shoulder dropping his forearm "hammer" on Glenn Bass the previous week.

The Chiefs' next game was again against the Raiders. The Raiders moved up in the king-of-the-hill battle in the West, beating Kansas City 34–13 as Tom Flores threw three touchdown passes in the second quarter. It was Kansas City's last loss until Vince Lombardi and his NFL Packers inflicted a final, humiliating defeat in the first Super Bowl.

Mauling Denver 56–10 the following week, the Chiefs regained first place with an awesome display of power. They netted 614 yards, plus a barrage of cans and bottles from Broncos fans, who felt that the Chiefs were trying to pour it on unnecessarily.

The next game was against Houston. "Kansas City is smelling the championship, and they played like it," said Houston coach Wally Lemm after the Chiefs won 48–23. It was a big-play day. A 79-yard interception and lateral involving Robinson and Willie Mitchell accounted for one touchdown; a 77-yard run by Garrett and a 77-yard pass from Beathard to Taylor accounted for another. Reg Carolan took 45- and 22-yard passes from Dawson for two more.

The next week commissioner Rozelle watched his first AFL game in person. Kansas City was playing the Chargers and beat them 24–14 for a 7–2 record. It was the first game all season in which Beathard did not play. Dawson went all the way before a crowd of 40,986 that increased the total for five games to 183,553, breaking the old Dallas record of 171,500, established in 1960.

Williamson came off the injury list for the game and drew boos, but he accepted them with the comment, "I love every one of those confused individuals."

Robinson, now five years into his job at safety, was named back of the week for his work against the Chargers. He had run with Billy Cannon in the LSU backfield on their national championship team in 1959, and he played his first two years as a pro on offense. Then Stram made him the first major AFL star to be moved to defense.

"At the time," said Stram in 1966, "the offense was ahead of the defense in the AFL. I was concerned with getting more quality athletes on the defense. We needed ability and leadership in the defensive secondary, and I was confident Johnny could provide that."

Robinson loved the change. "I think my career will be longer as a defensive player," he said after the San Diego game in 1966. "If I knew then what I know now, I would have wanted to be a defensive back from the start. If you make a mistake on offense, it may not make a difference, but everything you do on defense is important."

The next game was against Miami and it was an easy victory. Dawson passed for three touchdowns, raising his league-leading total to 22 and opening more room between himself and Beathard, who failed to move the team in the second half.

In the last quarter, Williamson's hammer incapacitated Miami receiver Howard Twilley, fracturing his cheekbone. "It was a cheap shot," said Miami coach George Wilson, but no penalty was called. Mays, playing at end instead of tackle, said, "I withheld my opinion until I saw the movies. I'm really sorry it happened, but I am convinced it was not a cheap shot. Fred came in for the tackle with both arms outstretched. It

Pete Beathard (left) was the reliable backup quarterback behind Len Dawson during the team's 1966 championship drive. The best trade made by the Chiefs in 1966 brought kicker Mike Mercer (right) to Kansas City from the roster of the Buffalo Bills.

was legal. If we can't play this way, we ought to go back to playing touch football."

Afterward, Jackson, the longtime Texans-Chiefs utility man who had gone to the Dolphins in the expansion draft earlier, was asked the difference between the 1966 Chiefs and earlier teams. "Age," he said. "This team is mature. And the development of Otis Taylor. I don't think there's any doubt about it, he's one of the best in the game."

By the first week in November, the Chiefs were moving steadily toward a title, and Garrett was being touted for rookie of the year. In his first eight games, he had 405 yards rushing, a 7.0 average (best in the league), and six touchdowns. And he didn't start until the eleventh game of the season.

"His power is amazing," said Stram, "but his best attribute may be his great sense of balance with that tricky lateral movement. He's always under control. Garrett is the greatest trouble runner I've ever seen. The more trouble he's in, the more impressive he is. And he thrives on work. The more he carries in a game, the better he gets. He has the torso of a two-hundred-forty pound man. He has broad shoulders and a thick neck. It's hard to get hold of him."

Garrett had gained 3,221 yards in three years at USC, but he did not learn to run there. "When I was playing in grade school and junior high sandlot ball, every boy in that area seemed to use that lateral movement. I just grew up with it. When I moved to a new neighborhood in high school, I was the only one who had it."

Garrett was not the only reason for the rising number of Kansas City wins. Dawson was enjoying his finest season, even better than the championship year of 1962. He was more confident and smoother, and he was leading a stronger team. In Garrett, the Chiefs had the outside threat. In Taylor, who led the league with an average of over 23 yards a catch, they had the super threat that forced other teams into special preparations. Their defense, although it had some flaws that would be exposed by the Packers, was beginning to move toward the levels it would maintain over the latter years of the decade.

As November wore on, the two leagues began to eye each other cautiously, wondering. In the NFL, Dallas led the East at 7–2–1, and Green Bay led the West at 8–2–0. Kansas City was carrying an 8–2–1 record into three final road games, just ahead of Oakland's 7–4–0.

After all their years of war, after the struggle in Dallas, would Super Bowl I pit the Chiefs (nee Texans) against the Cowboys (nee Rangers) at high noon in Los Angeles?

The Chiefs opened their road tour knowing that they could have the title in hand by the time their game against the New York Jets ended in Shea Stadium on Sunday. Oakland was home against Buffalo on Thanksgiving Day. A loss would eliminate the Raiders. The Chargers were to play in Denver on Sunday. A loss would take the Chargers out of it. The Chiefs would have the title, provided, of course, that they did their part by subduing Joe Namath and the New York Jets.

As the Chiefs took the field in Shea Stadium, Oakland was finished, defeated 31–10 by Buffalo. The largest crowd ever to see the Chiefs, 60,318, was watching. Kansas City entered the final minutes of the game with what appeared to be an insurmountable 29–10 lead. Dawson was on the sideline, his left wrist injured, while Beathard mopped up. The young USC quarterback had come on in the third quarter and taken the Chiefs 80 yards in 15 plays. Then he used up another six and one-half minutes to get Mike Mercer in place for a 33-yard field goal, his fourth of the day. Mercer hit from 32, 15, 47, and 33 yards.

The game's tempo was set early. On their

opening possession, the Chiefs were forced by penalties to cover 167 actual yards on an official 90-yard march to a touchdown. Mercer's 47-yard kick just before halftime staked Kansas City to a 16–10 lead.

Burford, meanwhile, was engaged in a running battle with Jets cornerback Johnny Sample. Burford caught 8 passes for 109 yards as he moved his career yardage figure over 5,000 yards.

"One," he would say to Sample when he caught a pass. "Two," he said the next catch. Goaded and growing madder, Sample committed two personal fouls on the drive that gave the Chiefs a 19-point lead.

Then Namath began one of his devastating hot streaks. Within four minutes he threw two touchdown passes. An apparently easy win had become a 29–24 cliffhanger. It was here that Beathard steered the Chiefs to Mercer's final field goal, making it 32–24. Since the AFL had the two-point conversion rule, the Chiefs' lead was vulnerable and they threw up a desperate defense as Namath came out throwing. Finally, Willie Mitchell intercepted at the Kansas City 32-yard line. The Jets never got the ball again.

The Kansas City charter plane was at 18,000 feet, heading west in the fading light, roughly over Elwood City, Pennsylvania. The time was 5:50 p.m. The pilot's voice broke in. "We have a score you might be interested in," he said. "Denver 20 . . . San Diego 17."

The Denver win, the Raiders' and Chargers' losses, and the Chiefs' triumph had combined to give the team its first title in four years. The Chiefs' first three years in Kansas City had been frustrating, sometimes sorrowful. Uprooted and unfamiliar with their new locale, they had fallen below .500 before struggling back.

As the plane droned on, somebody threw a wad of mashed potatoes. Another wad. A can of beer was shaken and sprayed. Beer flowed freely – down Stram's neck, over general manager Jack Steadman's horn-rimmed glasses. Nobody cared.

Garrett crouched in a corner, unseen for a while. "I can't even stand the smell of that stuff [beer]," he said. Beathard heard. Garrett was drenched. "I think we just bought ourselves a DC-6," sighed Steadman, surveying the incredible disarray.

Somebody asked Mays his feelings about the possibility that Kansas City might play Dallas in the Super Bowl. "Whoever plays for the NFL, it will be an emotionally charged game," he said. "But if we play the Cowboys, it would be over and above that. I can think of no team in the world that I'd rather beat than the Dallas Cowboys. For three or four of us it would really involve a lot of pride. For instance, Sherrill Headrick played with Bob Lilly at TCU. I played with Don Meredith; Smokey Stover was a real close friend of Mike Connally's. Jon Gilliam and I, being natives of Dallas, probably would be more emotially involved in a game than anybody else."

A crowd of over 1,500 greeted the Chiefs in Kansas City.

In the next game, the Chiefs used two of their white collar gang, McClinton (a banker) and Burford (a lawyer) to beat Miami 19–18. Then they wrapped up the regular season by defeating San Diego 27–17.

McClinton had spent the season as a blocker for Coan and Garrett. "Balance," Stram said. "Curtis has been one of the most unselfish players all year because we're utilizing his great blocking ability more than ever before."

"In the past couple of years, I've accumulated a lot of big statistics, but the team wasn't a big winner," McClinton shrugged. "Now we have a better attack, and we're the Western champs. How can I complain?"

Nine Chiefs – Robinson, Bell, Buchanan, and Mays on defense; Dawson, Taylor, Arbanas, Budde, and Tyrer on offense – were named to

56

Coach Hank Stram was carried from the field (left) on the shoulders of linebacker Walt Corey (56) and wide receiver Otis Taylor (89) after Kansas City defeated Buffalo 31-7 for the 1966 AFL championship. Later, the Chiefs carried the banner of the new league into the first Super Bowl game against the Green Bay Packers (right, the game program).

the Associated Press's AFL all-league team.

While the Chiefs completed an 11–2–1 year by beating the Chargers in the last AFL game in old Balboa Stadium, the Bills clinched the East by beating Denver. It would be Buffalo-Kansas City in Buffalo on New Year's Day.

Kansas City took a couple of days off for Christmas, then went back to practice. A blizzard hit the city, but it didn't bother Dawson. He completed 13 of 18 in practice. Temperatures remained in the teens through most of that week. In the East, Buffalo fled to Winston-Salem, North Carolina, to practice. They also ran into snow there.

When the Chiefs had won their last AFL title in 1962, it was worth $2,206 per man. The Houston Oilers had earned $1,471. The winner of the 1966 game would get $5,300.

Jack Spikes had been the most valuable player in the 1962 game. Now, in a twist of football fate, Spikes was in the Bills' backfield.

Although the game was in Buffalo, Kansas City felt no special trepidation at playing away from home. Including preseason games, the Chiefs were 10–0 on the road that year.

Ironically, the weather seemed to prepare the Chiefs for what they would encounter in Buffalo. The storm hit Kansas City on Tuesday, and it dumped up to eight inches of snow on some parts of the area. The sun was out by Wednesday, but snow was stinging along on a 24-mile-an-hour wind, and, according to equipment manager Bobby Yarborough, the temperature was 16 degrees when practice began.

Burford stood by the door trying to decide whether to wear sneakers or football cleats for the midweek practice. "The field's clear of snow now," Yarborough reported. This would be Burford's first title game. He was injured the last part of 1962 and didn't play in Kansas City's 20–17 win over Houston.

"Buffalo has the worst playing surface in the league," Burford said as he watched the weather outside. "Half of the field is in the shade and frozen; half is in the sun and mushy. Then, you have that baseball infield, too."

Just in case their rushing attack, which with a 162-yard average was the best in the league, stalled against the Bills' powerful defense, Kansas City worked hard all week on passing. There was good news on the injury front: Williamson came back after missing nearly a week with an ankle injury, and Dawson's left wrist was sound again.

Dawson had led the league with a 56 percent completion mark and 26 touchdown passes. Taylor and Burford each had caught 58 passes in a remarkable show of strength (Taylor for 1,297 yards and Burford for 758). Each had eight touchdowns. The figures graphically showed the extra dimension Taylor had brought to the Chiefs' attack.

The Bills had permitted only 75.1 yards a game rushing in winning the East. "I'd say Buffalo's front seven – the four defensive linemen and three linebackers – is as good as any in pro football," said Stram. Buffalo's linebackers – Harry Jacobs, John Tracey, and Mike Stratton – had played 74 consecutive games together.

On Thursday, while winds of up to 45 miles per hour whipped Buffalo, Hunt surprised Stram in Kansas City by giving him a new five-year contract. "This has been such a great year I really hate to see it end," said Hunt. "This year our team became successful. We were successful at the gate, and we finally worked out the merger between the two leagues. It's not often so many good things happen in one year."

The Bills were bothered by one disturbing statistic: Kansas City liked to score big and early. Of the Chiefs' 448 points, 158 had come in the first quarter. The Bills, on the other hand, had been blanked nine times in the first quarter.

However, few teams in football had been

Within two years after a Super Bowl in which the Chiefs could not stop the Packers, they had built a linebacking corps that was one of pro football's finest. Bobby Bell (left) had been a Chiefs' star for years. Jim Lynch (right) and Willie Lanier both were drafted by Kansas City on the second round in 1967.

dominated by one man as much as Kansas City had been by Jack Kemp. Kemp had moved to Buffalo in 1962. Since then in nine games against the Chiefs, he had lost only once.

Finally, the game began. The Chiefs' opening kickoff was taken by tackle Dudley Meredith, who fumbled on his own 31. Jerrel Wilson recovered for Kansas City. Two plays later, Dawson hit Arbanas for a touchdown and Kansas City led 7–0. Buffalo retaliated four minutes later when Kemp fired over a Kansas City blitz, hitting Elbert Dubenion at midfield. The play carried for 69 yards. The score was tied 7–7.

In the second quarter, Dawson threw to Taylor to restore a seven-point lead. But near the end of the half, the Bills again moved near the goal. Then the game turned. Buffalo's Bobby Crockett came down the left side and angled toward the goal post. Willie Mitchell, attempting to cover, slipped in the endzone. Crockett crossed a yard in front of the goal and seemed to be wide open. Kemp saw the inviting target and rifled the ball, but Robinson came from nowhere to make an interception. He ran all the way to Buffalo's 28-yard line before he was caught. Kansas City attempted one play before Mercer was brought on to kick a field goal. Instead of what had looked like a 14–14 deadlock at halftime, Kansas City led 17–7.

"I knew Robinson was there," Kemp said. "But I thought I could get the ball through." All day long, Kansas City plays succeeded and Buffalo plays failed. Not long before Robinson's theft, Dawson had attempted to hit Garrett on a swing pattern, only to have the Bills shift into a zone. Tom Janik came charging out of the murky drizzle wide open at the Chiefs' 20-yard line. Janik dropped the ball.

As the fourth quarter began, the Chiefs still weren't safe. Then Garrett scored the first of his two touchdowns. He wriggled out of Ron McDole's grasp to score by inches on fourth down. The Bills were seeing vintage Mike Garrett.

Much of what Dawson did that cold, wet afternoon was done on third down. The Chiefs converted 8 of 15, gained 154 yards, and scored three touchdowns.

Finally, it ended: Kansas City 31, Buffalo 7. "We thought we could run better," Kemp said quietly. "We thought we could pass better.... We even thought we were going to win."

As they walked off, Dawson and Buffalo's Al Bemiller shook hands. "Now show those other guys how tough our league is," Bemiller said to the Chiefs' quarterback. The "other guys," Green Bay, had used four touchdown passes by Bart Starr to outlast Dallas 34–27. It would be the Chiefs versus the Packers in Super Bowl I.

Arbanas, who had separated his shoulder against the Bills, dismissed his injury with a shrug. "I'll play even if Lamar Hunt has to go out and buy me a new shoulder," he said.

The Chiefs flew home to an airport reception of 12,000 people. They took two days off before heading for Los Angeles.

"I'm glad we're playing Green Bay," said Mays. "Now there won't be any doubt that the winner is the best team in pro football."

There weren't any doubts, either. The Chiefs lost to the Packers 35–10 and left Los Angeles a subdued team. But Stram refused to look back except to find out what the team needed to change. On the morning after, one thing was clear: The Chiefs' defense needed major repairs. (Stram made repairing the defense a priority, and by the time Kansas City played in its second Super Bowl, in January, 1970, half of the defensive line, two-thirds of the linebackers, and three-fourths of the secondary had been changed.)

"We've got to piece some things together and fortify certain areas as we go along to be ready for next year," Stram said. "I'm very disappointed we didn't win, but it doesn't mean Green

Bay or the NFL is 25 points better than this squad."

When official league statistics came out in February, they confirmed the potency of the Chiefs' attack in 1966. Dawson was the leading passer with 159 pass completions in 284 attempts for 2,525 yards and 26 touchdowns, plus a league high 8.9 yards average gain. Garrett was second in rushing, despite not having started until the eleventh game. Kansas City's ground game, led by Garrett's league-high 5.5 per try, netted 5.2 yards a carry and 19 touchdowns. McClinton and Coan also finished in the top 10.

In mid-March, the Chiefs' thinking was obvious. In the first common draft they turned heavily to defense. Gene Trosch, a 6-foot 7-inch, 260-pound defensive end from Miami of Florida, was the number one choice.

The second round distinguished the 1967 draft for Kansas City. Using a choice acquired by trading former quarterback Eddie Wilson to Boston in 1964, the Chiefs chose Jim Lynch, the All-America and Maxwell trophy winner as outstanding senior in the nation. Lynch was from Notre Dame. In their own spot on the second round, the Chiefs took little All-America Willie Lanier from Morgan State. Lanier and Lynch would reshape the Chiefs' aging linebacking corps. Within two years Lanier and Lynch, along with Bell, would become one of the most formidable threesomes in football.

There was more good news in June. Voters approved a bond issue of $102,385,000 for civic improvements that included funds for a two-stadium complex. One stadium would be for football, the other for baseball. Hunt immediately offered to purchase $5 million worth of bonds.

When the preseason games began in August, Kansas City seemed to have recaptured all the confidence of the previous championship season. They moved easily past Houston and the Jets, and destroyed Oakland 48–0. They unveiled one variation. Stram had them bringing the tight end into the I and shifting out of it regularly (instead of occasionally, as they had in 1966).

"Do you know what I like about it?" Stram said. "It even bothers our own defense, and they have been looking at it since we opened camp. And our defense is experienced and adjusts well." Stram, hoping to create a "crisis in recognition" and a moment's indecision, was succeeding even against his own defense.

The draftees that year were even better than Stram anticipated. In spring camp he had seen the dimension Jan Stenerud would bring to the kicking game. The Fetsund, Norway, native had stood near the 50-yard line repeatedly kicking balls over the crossbar.

"He's great," said Stram. "He's six to fifteen yards better than any kicker we've seen." Stenerud, a ski jumper whose father had him jumping off the kitchen table at an early age to strengthen his legs, had drifted into placekicking by accident at Montana State. His teammates had to show him how to put on shoulder pads. He had missed his first collegiate try; then he kicked nine in a row.

Stenerud had gone to Montana on a skiing scholarship and had been good at it, finishing fourth in the NCAA and winning the conference. He had not seen his first football game until September 22, 1963, when relatives whom he was visiting in Buffalo took him to a game. Ironically, the game pitted the Bills against the Chiefs. In the first period, Brooker had lined up to kick a field goal.

"What's he going to do?" Stenerud asked.

"Try a field goal."

"Oh, it really doesn't seem very difficult – for a soccer player, I mean," said Stenerud. A few years later the slender 6-foot 2-inch skier and soccer player would make it look easy.

Lynch and Lanier were also delighting the Chiefs' staff that summer. "These are probably

Of all the factors that contributed to Kansas City's success during the Great Years, none was more important than the presence on the Chiefs' roster of two superb kickers, Jerrel Wilson (left) for punts and Norwegian Jan Stenerud (right) for placements.

the best middle linebacker prospects we've ever had," Headrick said as he studied Lynch and Lanier. Noland Smith was also delighting the staff. Super Gnat, as Hunt called him, was a 5-foot 6-inch bundle of speed on kickoff returns.

The next game coming after just four days' rest following the victory over Oakland, was one of the most memorable games ever played in Municipal Stadium. The Chicago Bears were the opponent. They were the first NFL team that the Chiefs had faced since their Super Bowl defeat, and the Chiefs had endured many taunts. "We've had to live with that Super Bowl stuff for months," snapped Dawson.

On a muggy Wednesday night, Chicago took the ball after the opening kickoff and seemed to have little difficulty moving into range for a field goal and a 3–0 lead. There was some squirming among the patrons.

The score stayed 3–0 until late in the quarter, when Dawson delivered a pass from his 30-yard line. Taylor caught it at midfield, eluded a defender, and ran for the score. The Chiefs scored 32 more points in the second quarter to take a 39–10 lead at halftime.

Kansas City added another touchdown in the third quarter and three more in the fourth, annihilating the Bears 66–24.

Stram tried to say afterward that this was "just another game," but this charade was shattered when the team awarded four game balls: one to Hunt, one to Stram, one to Dawson, and one to Willie Mitchell. Dawson and Mitchell, of course, had been labeled goats in the team's loss to Green Bay.

The Chiefs had never scored more than they did that night. Chicago had never been scored on more in its 48-year history. Stram had unloaded the Chiefs' vast arsenal: the I, which shifted sometimes and not others; the moving pocket; the double tight end from Dallas days; and even a two-point conversion.

"Do the Chiefs compare favorably with other NFL teams?" George Halas was asked in the shocked losers' locker room. It was a pointed question. Seven months earlier Vince Lombardi had twisted the knife before dozens of newsmen in the Packers' rooms, saying there were several NFL clubs better than Kansas City.

"Yes, you've got to say that they do compare with other NFL teams in every way," said Halas. "They certainly played a spirited game. They've been pointing toward this since January."

It had been a crusade. Stram had shown his team the NFL highlight film in camp, letting the snide remarks carry the message. "We didn't talk much about revenge for the Super Bowl," Stram admitted, "but I wouldn't be truthful if I said we didn't have revenge in mind."

Dawson had mesmerized Chicago with play-action passing, completing 10 of 15 for four touchdowns. "He's a great one," Halas said. "Len Dawson is as fine a quarterback as any in the game. Buck Buchanan is an outstanding football player. I can only be most complimentary about Hank Stram. He has a well-coached ball club."

Kansas City's cup ran over that night, but the blissful string of summer victories ended in Los Angeles the following week when the Rams rolled over the Chiefs 44-24. Kansas City had a 24–13 lead at halftime, but in the second half the Rams scored the first three times they got the ball.

So the Chiefs came to their season opener in Houston with a 4–1 record. With seven rookies on the roster, they had high hopes of a return to the Super Bowl. They began the season with a 25–20 win over Houston. Then they shut out Miami 24–0. With a 2–0 record, it seemed as if they might be headed for a return to the Super Bowl. The offense, featuring a 54-yard field goal by Stenerud, had done the job against the Oilers, who were playing without Blanda for the first time. The defense had choked the young

3
71
16

Dolphins, keeping them from the endzone.

But the Raiders were next, and they also were 2–0.

Final cutdown time produced two surprises. Center Wayne Frazier was dropped and was quickly taken by Buffalo. And the Chiefs cut linebacker Smokey Stover. He had played in 141 consecutive games, every game the Texans/Chiefs had ever played. He was the only player who had done this. His release left four original Texans – Robinson, Burford, Headrick, and Al Reynolds.

The Raiders beat the Chiefs 23–21. The big plays that had contributed so much to 1966 success were missing. Taylor, for instance, missed a wide-open touchdown pass that would have changed the outcome. "We're victims of our own mistakes," groaned Stram. "Defensively, we're playing superb football, but we're making mistakes that give the other team points."

Then the Chiefs went home for the first time since the Bears game to face Miami. Kansas City beat Miami handily (41–0), but the big news came some 45 minutes later. It was announced that the Chiefs had traded Beathard to Houston for Ernie Ladd, quarterback Jacky Lee, and the Oilers' number one draft choice for 1968. Stram called it "the largest and most significant trade in the history of the team."

The next game was against the Chargers. It was then that the injuries started, and they would plague the Chiefs throughout all of 1967. Holub pulled a hamstring and Gilliam developed an aggravated knee as the Chargers laced the Chiefs 45–31. The following week Houston beat the Chiefs 24–19.

Now third in the division and 3–3 for the year, the Chiefs faced Denver, whom they demolished 52–9. However, Lanier, who had sustained a head injury against San Diego and then had missed two days of practice with the flu, collapsed in the defensive huddle. He was taken from the field unconscious. "He was having a hard time calling defensive signals a couple of plays before," Mays explained. "Somebody said he was in on three tackles in a row, head on."

For the next game, which was against the Jets, Headrick returned to the middle. He wasn't the only new starter, either. Frazier was back, claimed off the Buffalo waiver list when the Chiefs lost Gilliam, Tony DiMidio, and Mike Hudock, all centers, through injuries. The Chiefs finally regained their 1966 form. Garrett ran for 192 yards (a Chiefs' record), and Dawson threw two touchdown passes as the Chiefs beat the Jets 42–18. The following week they rolled up 30 points by halftime, beating Boston 33–10. It seemed that the big plays that had been missing in September and October had returned in November, but Stram was premature when he said, "I think we can go the rest of the way."

A storm of controversy swirled about the Chiefs a week later after a 17–16 loss to the Chargers. Preparing for a Thursday date with the Raiders, they couldn't get away from the questions: Why had Garrett carried 26 times and McClinton only twice? How could they have had five first downs inside the 15-yard line and come away from them with only six points? The Chiefs now had lost four games, three of them by a total of eight points.

At a Chiefs' Club gathering, Stram was subjected to heckling by one member who was incensed over the use of Garrett on four goal-line plays. Garrett had not scored. Stram explained that McClinton had not succeeded on an earlier try, so the Chiefs had elected to run their best runner behind their best blocker.

"That's no answer," the voice snorted.

Stram's temper could be gauged by the rising red creeping up his neck and face. "Stand up," he demanded. The man did.

"What business are you in?"

"I'm a lawyer."

A bizarre preseason followed Kansas City's appearance in Super Bowl I. Angered by critics who scoffed at how decisively they had been defeated in the world's championship game, the Chiefs lashed out at the first NFL opponent they faced as interleague preseason games began. They smashed the Chicago Bears (left, running back Mike Garrett in action) by a score of 66-24. A week later, Kansas City faced another NFL team, the Los Angeles Rams (right), and lost the game 44-24.

"Have you ever lost a case?"

"Yes."

"Have you ever had fifty-thousand people second guessing your loss?"

"No."

"Well, sit down and behave yourself."

Injury reports added to the pre-Thanksgiving lack of good will. Burford had hurt his shoulder. Lanier again had left early, suffering from double vision. "I remember chasing John Hadl toward the sideline," he said later. "I saw two of him. I tackled the wrong one and said, 'Hey, no, man, that's it.' I took myself out." Lynch was moved to the middle to replace him.

Holub still was not at top form, and on the day before Thanksgiving, the Chiefs sent him home to Texas. He was out for the year and would undergo his eighth knee operation. Both Mays and Chuck Hurston were given work at middle linebacker.

Somehow, in the midst of all this, the Chiefs emerged as eight-point favorites for their game against the Raiders.

If Sunday had been controversial, Thursday left no room for anything but condolences. The Raiders sacked Dawson six times, intercepted four passes and ran an effective series of power sweeps in a 44–22 romp over the Chiefs.

Although three games remained, the season might as well have been over. Kansas City won its final three games, finishing 9–5, a good year in most cases, but Oakland went 13–1 that season en route to an appearance in Super Bowl II.

Jim Kearney was used more at defensive back in those final games. Meanwhile Lanier had been dispatched to the Mayo Clinic, which reported that he had a skull contusion, resulting in swelling with the pressure on the optic nerve. He was finished for the season.

Hunt admitted he was disappointed, but he said that the year had not panicked him. "I wish we had done better. Looking back on the season, I feel we were three plays away from having a ten-and-two season," he said.

More and more, it appeared that the Chiefs had peaked in August against the Bears, soaring to an emotional height they never again scaled. "I hate to mention the effect the Bears' game had on us," said Stram late in the season. "It could sound like an excuse if I was not careful, and I certainly don't want that. I've never seen a team at the emotional level we achieved then. All the resentment, all the bitterness had been building up since the Super Bowl. We tried to curb it, to tone it down. It was no use.

"There's no question it was our inability to make the big play at crucial times . . . and don't think that luck doesn't help. You can't be long in this business before you realize how important luck is when you have a big year – or miss a big year. It's important, too, that you be lucky enough to remain healthy. Last year we had only two injuries of any significance. Now we have eight players on injured waivers, plus people like Bobby Bell, Ed Budde, Johnny Robinson, and Mike Hudock, who have been playing injured."

Three charter members departed in 1968. Burford (the first Texan), Headrick, and Reynolds were chosen by Cincinnati in the expansion draft, along with Bobby Hunt and Fletcher Smith. Burford had caught 390 passes for 5,505 yards and 55 touchdowns.

There were other personnel changes, too. Gilliam's knee forced his retirement, and two weeks later, Williamson, the controversial cornerback, was released. "This has been a real swinging year for me," he mused. "I've been in an accident, divorced, unemployed, and now released . . . and just about everything else. As I said before, the release is just another event in the life of Fred Williamson." Movie stardom lay just ahead for the handsome athlete, who like the others had given the Chiefs' fans much to remember.

Of all the losses, Gilliam's was feared to be

the most damaging, since the center position had been a chronic problem in 1967. Holub was moved permanently from linebacker to center. Lanier, wearing a specially constructed helmet and tackling more with his arms and shoulder than his head, settled into the middle linebacker slot.

Then despite a wave of injuries that struck first the Chiefs' runners and then the receivers, Kansas City and Oakland launched one of their classic title chases in 1968.

Stenerud kicked eight field goals in the first two games, the first a 26–21 victory over Houston. The Chiefs' second game was against New York. In the final 5:56 of the game, the Chiefs had drawn within a point, but New York held the ball and beat Kansas City 20–19. Namath's fine ball control had sealed the win. "I thought nobody in the world could do that against us," Stram said afterward.

It was the first time the Chiefs' offensive unit had failed to produce a touchdown since 1966, which also was the last previous home opener loss. The passing game had fallen below 100 yards. Only Stenerud's field goals and an 80-yard return by Noland Smith for a touchdown had kept the Chiefs in contention.

The next game was at home against Denver, and the first half was almost a wipeout. Coan left the game with a pinched nerve in his neck almost as soon as play began; Garrett was hospitalized with rib injuries; McClinton refractured his cheekbone. All in the first half.

"I never went through anything like that in my coaching career," said Stram, surveying the wreckage of his running corps. "We went into the game with just two healthy backs, Coan and McClinton. [The latter was barely recovered from a factured cheekbone]. We didn't want to use Garrett [arm injury], but we had to. Robert Holmes developed an infection on his shin, and he had a high fever before the game. We had to keep his leg on ice in the first half so that he could play in the second."

The crowd, which had booed both Dawson and Stram during pregame introductions grew uglier during the game, booing the entire,offensive unit repeatedly during the first half. Insults were showered on the bench from the stands. The Wolfpack – the rabid fans who sat in the temporary north stands directly behind the Chiefs' bench area – was howling.

Two Stenerud field goals provided a shaky 6–2 halftime lead. Then Stram delighted the crowd by benching Dawson in favor of Jacky Lee. Lee, favored with excellent field position, moved the Chiefs 55, 41, 44, and 29 yards, much of it on the running of the tank-like rookie Holmes. Jerrel Wilson had joined Holmes in the backfield, but Holmes was a one-man gang in leading the Chiefs to a 34–2 win.

Lee received a roaring ovation when he was introduced to the booster club luncheon later that week, but Stram cautioned the group, "We can't get emotional and sell somebody down the river. I feel this is the time Dawson should start. If we're not moving the ball, I won't hesitate to bring in Lee."

The next game was played in the sweltering heat of a Miami night in late September. Dawson and the Chiefs recaptured the scoring touch with a 48–3 victory. In the next two games they beat Buffalo 18–7 and Cincinnati 13–3 with a pair of powerful defensive displays. Since Oakland had lost to San Diego, the Chiefs were now in first place.

But the injuries continued. Two receivers, Taylor and Gloster Richardson, were on the injured list as one of the most important games of the year drew near. The next game was against Oakland, which had the league's best pass defense.

Stram's ability to adjust to the situation showed again. Resurrecting the old full-house

Cornerback Jim Marsalis (far left) and defensive tackle Curley Culp were Chiefs newcomers in 1969. Mike Livingston (right) quarterbacked the team for six games during the 1969 season while Len Dawson was out of action with a knee injury. The tenth, and last, season in American Football League history was the grandest ever for the Chiefs. They marched into the playoffs at Shea Stadium in New York against Joe Namath and the Jets (pages 42-43).

T, Stram sent his now healthy backs on a game-long ground attack, slamming behind ferocious blocking. Short of receivers, the Chiefs threw only three times – an AFL record low. They completed two for 16 yards.

Unable to believe that the Chiefs meant it, Oakland stayed in its normal defensive alignment until only nine minutes remained. It was too late. Kansas City, in a throwback to football's stone age, won 24–10.

Budde, the immense guard stationed on Tyrer's left side, was voted the offensive player of the week. This was the only time a lineman was so honored in the AFL. It recalled a prophetic remark Mays had made in the summer of 1963. When he first saw the 6-foot 5-inch, 265-pound Budde and the 6-foot 6-inch, 280-pound Tyrer work together, he said, "It scares you to see what they do to people."

A couple of weeks later Oakland gained revenge with a 38–21 win, but by then the Chiefs were settling in behind the growing power of their defense. They ran off five victories in a row to finish the 1968 regular season with a 12–2 record, the same as Oakland's.

It was the best record the Chiefs had ever had, but it left one more hurdle before a hoped-for return to the Super Bowl. For the fourth time that year, the Chiefs would play the Raiders, this time in the Western Division playoff at Oakland. The clubs had split in the regular season, and Kansas City had won 31–21 in a preseason game. But the Chiefs had shown more strength in the stretch. They had limited Houston and Denver to a touchdown each and had held San Diego to a single field goal in a 40–3 victory, which may have to rank among the best overall efforts any Chiefs team ever produced. Oakland, on the other hand, had struggled in its last three games against Buffalo, Denver, and San Diego. As the season ended, it seemed that the Chiefs were growing stronger while at the same time the Raiders grew weaker.

The morning of the playoff game, the Chiefs seemed grimly determined. Yarborough remembers, "I was sitting by the door at the Mark Hopkins Hotel in San Francisco at the pregame meal when Duffy Daugherty came by to say hello to Hank. I remember him saying 'I've never seen a group more ready to play a football game and more up for a game in my life.'"

But the good spirits did not last for long. Kansas City, which had set an AFL record by limiting 14 regular season opponents to only 170 points, was buried quickly by Oakland. Oakland scored three first quarter touchdowns to take a 21–0 lead. Then, in the second quarter, Kansas City ran 10 plays inside the Raiders' 10. The Chiefs could not score a touchdown, however, settling for two field goals. The final score was 41–6. Oakland had administered the worst loss in the Chiefs' history.

"After the game," Yarborough said, "it was silent. It was the quietest packing and moving out job that there ever was. And the thing was that everybody knew we were going to beat the hell out of them."

"I just can't believe it," Stram said on the somber ride home. "I just can't believe it. We're twelve and two. We win sixteen out of nineteen. And now this."

Ernie Ladd, who had chronic knee problems, had surgery and finally retired as new faces moved into old positions and old faces moved into new positions in the summer of 1969. McClinton was moved to tight end and Arbanas was shifted to tackle. James Marsalis, a cornerback from Tennessee State, was the Chiefs' number one draft choice, adding another ingredient to the defense. Curley Culp, whom the Chiefs had obtained from Denver a year earlier for the outrageously low price of a fourth round draft choice, was installed at defensive tackle. Marsalis's addition completed the secondary,

75

Kansas City's victory over the Minnesota Vikings in Super Bowl IV culminated a decade of struggle by Lamar Hunt, the Chiefs, and the AFL. Hunt personally ordered the commemorative patches (left) worn on the jerseys of Chiefs players during the Super Bowl game. Hunt and commissioner Pete Rozelle must have reflected on the tempestuous 1960s when they met before the game (right).

while Culp proved the perfect complement to Buchanan, Mays, and Aaron Brown, who was back at defensive end where he belonged. Ed Podolak and Jack Rudnay, two other prized draft choices, joined Marsalis in the Chicago All-Star game.

The Chiefs then moved through the most productive summer in their history. They went undefeated through six preseason games, which included their first win over the Rams. The score was 42–14 and Rams safety Ed Meador was impressed. "We would be in a defense for their I formation, and before we could get our defense audibled after the shift, they would be running off a play. Dawson always seemed to be a play ahead of us. We would be in the right defense, but he would exploit the weakness in that particular defense," Meador said.

Since the regular season opened with four straight road games, the Chiefs would need all their summer momentum. The first game was not auspicious. Dawson was nursing a slight crack in the base of the ring finger of his right hand. An infection had set in, and his hand was stiff. Nevertheless Dawson guided Kansas City to a 27–9 victory over San Diego.

The next game was in Boston. Kansas City won easily, 31–0. Late in the third quarter Dawson attempted a rollout pass to Taylor and was injured. Extensive examinations showed that Dawson had suffered a slight tear of the medial collateral ligament in his left knee, but the doctors differed on possible courses of treatment. One doctor recommended surgery, as did some other specialists. However, another doctor felt an operation could be circumvented. He said if Dawson kept his leg completely rested for two weeks, he might be able to play before the end of the season. The decision was Dawson's. He chose rehabilitation, accepting it as a "calculated risk."

It was estimated that Dawson would miss six games. The year that had begun so well was now uncertain. For the next game, which was against Cincinnati, Lee replaced Dawson. Mike Livingston was in reserve.

Late that Sunday afternoon, with shadows drawing patches on Nippert Stadium's surface, Mays ran all the way across the field, through a gate, up a flight of stairs leading from a group of buildings housing the dressing rooms on a hill, and into the Chiefs' dressing room. "He took off his helmet when he hit the door," Yarborough remembers. "Then he threw it. That helmet went sailing through the air, making that funny noise – ka-woo, ka-woo, ka-woo. It hit a two-by-four and broke it. The helmet didn't break though; it richocheted into a wire mesh and knocked it down. Mays was mad. He was hollering and raising hell. I've never seen a greater display of emotion by one individual. I can still hear that helmet!"

Kansas City had just lost to Cincinnati 24–19. The big plays were two long touchdown bombs by Greg Cook and Sam Wyche. But the Chiefs had a worse problem: Lee had suffered a cracked ankle during the game.

Stram quickly brought in John Huarte and Tom Flores to back up Livingston, who was now the starting quarterback. Podolak, who had played quarterback at Iowa and was just coming off a pulled muscle, also was considered.

The next game was against Denver. Livingston, with the help of field goals from Stenerud and a rocklike defense, led the Chiefs to a 26–13 victory on a snow-wet field. "His composure was outstanding," said Dawson, who watched, leaning on crutches.

Livingston, the 6-foot 4-inch 212-pounder who had been drafted second in 1968, went on to direct successive wins over Houston, Miami, and Cincinnati. He then started against Buffalo, before Dawson returned to relieve him.

On a rainy afternoon in Buffalo, two months

into the season, Stram sent Dawson into action just 30 seconds before halftime "to handle the ball a couple of times and to get the feel of it again." Dawson stayed on for the final half to complete a 29–7 victory. He also completed 7 of 14 attempts for just under 100 yards. It wasn't a headline-grabbing performance, but since Oakland had lost to Cincinnati, it was important. The Chiefs were now back in first with a 7–1 record compared to the 6–1–1 record of the Raiders.

Defense continued to be the key. In their next game, the Chiefs routed the Chargers 27–3, maintaining their lead in the standings. Of nine opponents, only Cincinnati had scored more than 13 points. Two games had been shutouts.

In the season's tenth week, the Chiefs moved to Shea Stadium for a showdown between the division leaders. Both the Chiefs and Jets came to the game with six-game winning streaks. Dawson carried an extra burden into the game. His father had died in Alliance, Ohio, on Friday. On Sunday morning he asked a Chiefs' official to help arrange transportation home for the funeral after the game. He then completed 23 of 38 attempts for 285 yards and three touchdowns. All three touchdown passes were caught by Otis Taylor. For one catch Taylor moved undetected out of a camouflaged slot formation between guard and tackle. Warren McVea added another dimension to the game as he collected 109 rushing yards. Kansas City won 34–16.

The Chiefs' run of victories ended a week later with a 27–24 loss to Oakland. The Raiders intercepted five passes and recovered two Chiefs' fumbles, converting them into 17 points. The loss knocked Kansas City out of first place.

On Thanksgiving Day in Denver, Dawson was hit while he threw a 44-yard pass. He returned to duty later in the game, which the Chiefs won 31–17.

The final home game of the season was against Buffalo. Stenerud kicked 5 field goals, which extended his string to 16 in a row – an NFL record – as the Chiefs stayed close to Oakland with a 22–19 win.

The showdown with the Raiders was on the last weekend of the regular season. Basically it made no difference which team won. Both were assured of playoff berths. Kansas City, which passed only six times, lost 10–6.

The Chiefs then advanced to a first-round playoff against the Jets in New York. In one·of their best games the Chiefs won 13–6. Now the Chiefs returned to Oakland, this time to battle for the AFL title and the right to advance to the Super Bowl.

The dawn broke cloudy and cold. Bay area Januarys, save for the ever-present early morning fog, are usually crisp and invigorating, but this day was to be an exception. It was not a great day for a football game.

The Raiders were a four-point favorite, but that meant nothing. It never does in a Kansas City-Oakland game – especially with the AFL championship on the line. The Chiefs had won two championships already, in 1962 and 1966, and on the afternoon of January 4, 1970, they made it three, winning 17–7 over the Raiders. Super Bowl IV, with the Minnesota Vikings, terror of the northland and the NFL, was next.

Kansas City went into Super Bowl IV as a two-touchdown underdog, but the Chiefs outran, outpassed, and outplayed the Vikings. The final score was 23–7, but no score could have told the entire story. A goal had been achieved. The Vikings – along with the rest of pro football – had learned just how good the Kansas City Chiefs really were.

If there was any single summary of 1970, it came from a 10-year-old fan named Scott Ferguson. One evening in early October he was questioned by Bill Grigsby, the Chiefs' radio announcer, at a fan club meeting. As Gary

Warner of the *Kansas City Star* reported, the conversation went this way:

Grigsby: "What do you think of the Chiefs?"

Scott: "They're pretty good."

Grigsby: "Is that all you can say about the world champions?"

Scott: "Well, that was last year."

There is nothing more immediate than winning, as Kansas City rediscovered in 1970. Following the glories of 1969, the 1970 season bore some resemblance to a morning after.

There were shock waves in mid-October when Garrett was traded to San Diego for a number two draft choice. The popular back had drawn headlines earlier that season when he said he planned to go back to baseball at the end of the year. Garrett and Stram had seen their relationship grow increasingly strained, and Stram, who insists he'll trade anyone who won't adhere to his way of doing things, made good on the promise. "What could I get for him two months from now?" he asked.

On the other hand, Garrett felt some of the Chiefs' innovations were done only for the sake of saying they could be done, and that they cost effectiveness. He also felt he was not being used as Stram had promised he would be.

As the 1970 season began, Buchanan's knees were ailing, and Brown's performance was hampered by a bad ankle. The Chiefs were stunned by Minnesota 27–10 in a season-opening rematch of Super Bowl IV. Eight days later, on a Monday night in Baltimore, the Chiefs responded by producing one of their most devastating games, routing the Colts 42–24 on national television. The following Sunday Kansas City lost to Denver.

Victories over Boston and Cincinnati gave the Chiefs a 3–2 record and set up a rematch with Dallas. The Chiefs had beaten the Cowboys in preseason play in Dallas in a highly emotional homecoming for the six old Texans still on the roster. But, when it counted, the Cowboys responded. Dallas took advantage of Brown's ankle injury and ran at him in the course of a 27–16 win that dropped the Chiefs back to .500.

As always, there was volatile chemistry involved when the Chiefs and Raiders collided, and their first meeting of 1970 was no exception.

Late in the game, with Kansas City leading 17–14, Dawson startled everyone by bootlegging from the Oakland 48 to the 29. Tripped by his own man, he fell. Oakland's huge Ben Davidson pounced on the prostrate Dawson, and Taylor jumped Davidson. Both benches emptied.

Technically, since Dawson was not "downed" by an opponent's action, he was fair game. It was the relish with which Davidson delivered the hit that earned the Oakland defensive end a 15-yard penalty to match Taylor's. Officials stepped off the penalty to the Oakland 14. Middle linebacker Dan Conners argued the penalties should be offsetting, the play going back to midfield. Officials took the ball back while Kansas City fans howled in protest. The officials, who had lost the original scrimmage line at the 48, replaced the ball on the 49. Kansas City couldn't move. Oakland took a punt and moved up field. Blanda eventually kicked a 48-yard field goal for a 17–17 tie.

Confusion over the rulings and the timing with which they were made drew criticism from the league office, although the offsetting penalties were upheld. Films proved that the rulings were correct. The next year, however, changes were made in the interpretation of continuing action, and better communications between the pressbox and the field were installed.

But the tie stood, and as the disappointing season wore on for the world champions, it would loom immense. In the next game Dawson celebrated his first return to Pittsburgh in more than 10 years with three touchdown passes and

His work done, quarterback Len Dawson reached for the hand of coach Hank Stram as he left the field during the fourth quarter of Super Bowl IV (left). A triumphant Stram was outlined on the cover of the 1970 Kansas City yearbook (right) by the numeral that only the Chiefs could claim.

a 31–14 rout of the Steelers. The Chiefs then suffered another tie, 6–6 with St. Louis.

Still, by the time Kansas City prepared for the annual season clash with the Raiders, they were tied for first place with the Raiders at 7–3–2. Now, in the next-to-last game of the season, the two teams were to confront each other on the West Coast.

Stram took his team west to train in Palo Alto early in the week. "I think you could describe our camp with the word 'Spartan,'" he said. "We will eat our meals as a team; we'll have meetings in the morning; and we'll practice each afternoon. We'll also have a curfew. There's only one time to celebrate, and that's after you've won it all. That's what we're trying to do."

Meanwhile, playoff and championship ticket options were mailed to Kansas City season-ticket holders.

Ben Davidson's hate mail from Kansas City had tapered to "just a few a week" in the intervening six weeks. He taped the best ones to the locker-room wall. "You don't play football for revenge. You play to win," Lanier said, publicly disavowing a grudge match.

The Chiefs were concentrating on a full 60-minute effort. In contrast, Oakland had captured the imagination of the football public with a series of last-second victories or ties.

It was the third December in a row that the clubs had battled into a championship showdown. Kansas City came to the game with the conference's best defense; Oakland had the top offense. The Raiders had amassed 4,147 yards, while Kansas City had allowed only 2,977. Conversely, the Raiders were twelfth in defense and Kansas City was tenth in offense.

A record Oakland crowd of 54,596 turned Oakland-Alameda County Coliseum into a deafening chamber of air horns as their Raiders clinched the West with a 20–6 victory. Oakland gained 324 yards and allowed only 121. Kansas City scored two field goals, but no touchdowns. It was only the second time all season that Kansas City went without a touchdown. Even Stenerud fell victim, missing a 29-yard field goal, his first miss inside the 30-yard line all season.

During a 7-minute, 56-second drive by the Raiders, which ended in Kansas City territory at the gun, the Oakland public relations department distributed playoff game ticket data.

The happy Raiders were shouting and pummeling each other all the way to their dressing room, with ex-Chief Alphonse Dotson hollering to nearby writers; "We beat 'em at their own game. We rammed it down their throat."

The Chiefs' 17–17 tie with Oakland in their first meeting and the 6–6 frustration of missed chances against St. Louis had caused Kansas City to lose its chance to return to the Super Bowl. If the Chiefs had won both of these games, they would have been 9–4. Like 1967, it was another year of "ifs."

Oakland fullback Marv Hubbard probably summed up feelings on both sides when he said, "I don't like the Chiefs, and I hope they hear what I'm saying. I have an intense hatred for them." The Kansas City-Oakland feud would simmer for another winter.

The Chiefs could have squeezed into the playoffs the final week by beating San Diego while Buffalo beat Miami. However, Miami had wrapped up a 45–7 triumph by the time the Chiefs took the field against the Chargers on a dismal, rainy day in San Diego. The Chiefs lost 31–13, while Mike Garrett of the Chargers enjoyed his best day of the year with 95 yards against his former mates.

The ominous season ended in the rainy letdown in San Diego. But there were to be no wholesale changes in the team. In mid-January, Hunt offered a new 10-year contract to Stram. As the new stadium 11 miles east of the downtown district took shape, other news dominated

Shafts of Missouri sunshine streaked through the roof as Wendell Hayes scored a touchdown against the San Diego Chargers at Municipal Stadium in 1970. A year later, the Chiefs occupied Kansas City's palatial Arrowhead Stadium (pages 50-51).

the winter and spring. Mays, one of the last links with Dallas, retired to join his father in the construction business.

And the Chiefs lost another nine-year veteran when Fred Arbanas retired in late spring. "He has been our regular tight end for nine years. That has to be a first in professional football," said Stram of the one-time Michigan State player who had overcome a series of injuries. He had even lost an eye to an unknown assailant while walking along Troost Avenue in Kansas City in 1964. The next spring he had gradually adjusted to his handicap in daily, noonday workouts with Dawson. It began with just tossing the ball back and forth. "We met every day during the lunch break of our off-season jobs and threw the football around. I caught footballs for an hour each day. We had to start five yards apart," said Arbanas.

Morris Stroud, a 6-foot 10-inch third-year pro who had started late in 1970, replaced Arbanas, while Marvin Upshaw moved in at Mays's old left end position.

The "Grease House Gang," the offensive line that had eaten together on Saturday nights on the road, also was breaking up.

One night, shortly after camp opened, Holub slipped quietly out of camp and back to Lubbock, Texas, where he already had undergone one hamstring and eight knee operations. "I saw him at dinner," said Jim Tyrer, his teammate for a decade. "He said, 'See you later.' At ten o'clock I went to his room, and he was gone." "The Beast," the holler guy, the emotional catalyst of the offense, had left without a sound.

Jack Rudnay, who had replaced Holub at center the previous year, furnished the last word. "He's not the greatest football player in the world," said Rudnay. "He yelled at everybody. He got veterans mad at him, and he made the rookies nervous. But he got the job done. It's not going to be the same without him."

When Stram was asked if such departures touched him, he said, "Do I allow myself to get sentimental? Yes. It's tough not to. Last year with Curtis [McClinton], and this year Fred [Arbanas] and Jerry [Mays]. It's always tough when people who have played such a prominent role in your success leave you."

Back home, Holub submitted to the surgeon for his ninth knee operation.

The Chiefs' camp continued to be productive. In fact, Dawson was wearing a cap reading "Super Bowl 1971." "I wear it all the time," he said. "I wear it to remind me of where I intend to be in 1972 – and not as a spectator as I was in 1971." He had bought the cap in Miami in January.

Dawson threw more in preseason games, a forecast perhaps that the Chiefs would live up to Stram's promise to restore big plays to their arsenal in 1971. The previous season, the team had turned conservative. They had thrown just 289 times, the lowest total in professional football.

Stenerud's toe was as prominent as Dawson's arm through the summer. The Chiefs compiled a 4–1–1 preseason record. However, they opened their season by dropping a 21–14 decision in San Diego. Fortunately, Oakland also lost.

The next week the Chiefs mounted a late drive to nip the Oilers in the Astrodome, giving them a 1–1 record. In the next game, which was against Denver, Bobby Bell jarred the ball loose from Don Horn and Aaron Brown made a mid-air recovery and dashed to a score that pried open a 16–3 win over the Broncos. In the following games, the big plays came back: The Chiefs won 31–10 over San Diego and thrashed Pittsburgh 38–16 on a Monday night.

This set up a home game against undefeated Washington, which was gathering steam under its new head coach, George Allen.

Taylor, who had caught six passes for 190

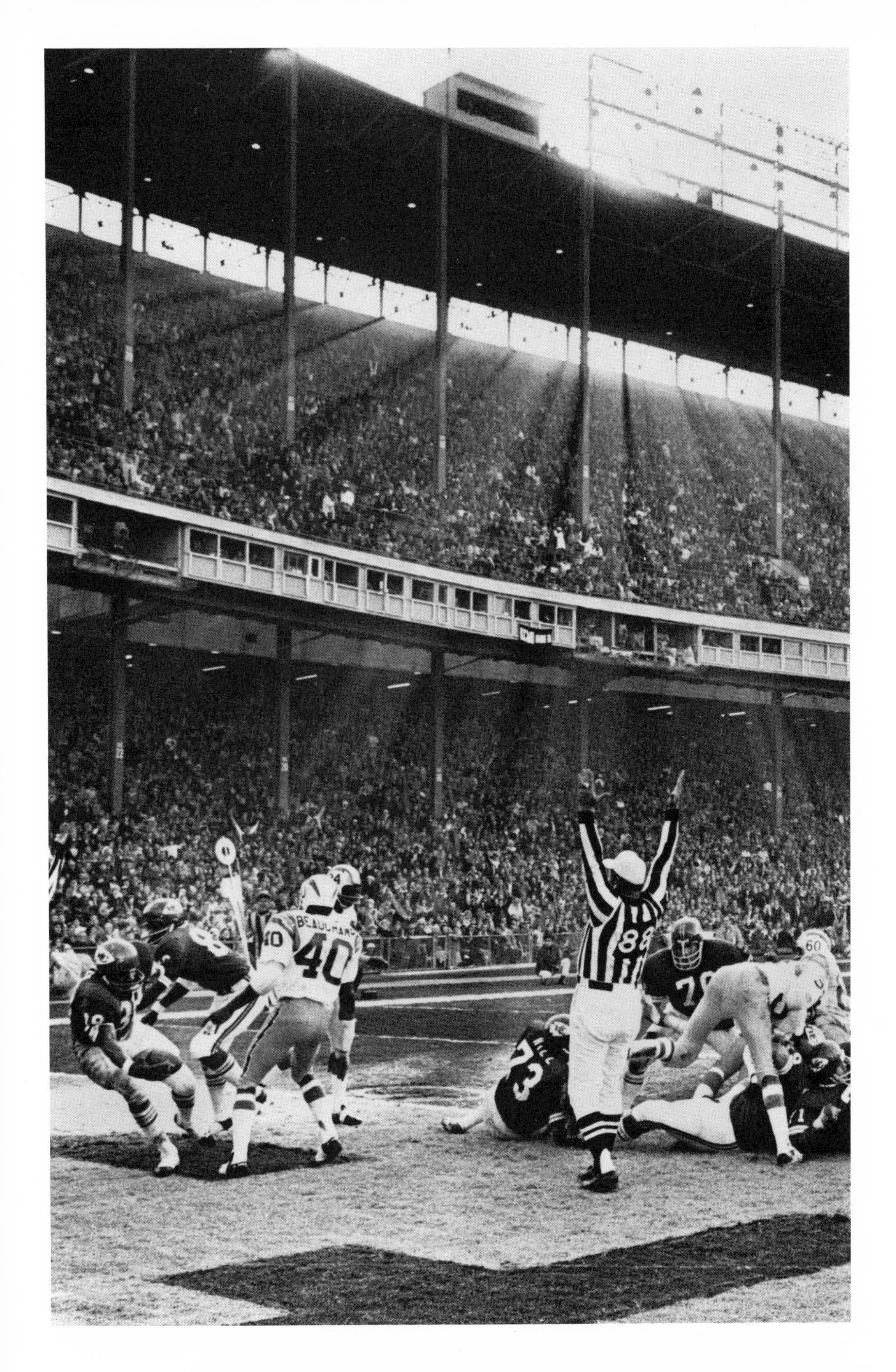
BEAUCHAMP
40
88
73

Ed Podolak accounted for over 5,000 yards rushing, catching passes, and returning punts and kickoffs for Kansas City from 1970 through 1973.

yards against the Steelers, was right back in form against the Redskins, catching five for 105 yards, including the game-winning touchdown in the last quarter of a 27–20 victory. Trailing 17–6 at halftime, the Chiefs staged one of their finest comebacks as Taylor snared the winning pass one-handed and ran across the goal line with Pat Fischer draped all over him. The Chiefs were 5–1, tied for first place with the Raiders.

The Chiefs then faced Oakland and Blanda. The 44-year-old tormentor of the Chiefs continued to work his magic as he brought the Raiders from a 20–10 deficit to a 20–20 tie.

The Chiefs' next game was with the Jets in Shea Stadium. With a biting wind robbing them of Dawson's deep throws to Taylor, and two Chiefs penalties helping the Jets, Kansas City lost 13-10.

The Chiefs rebounded the following week, presenting Stram with his hundredth coaching victory as they won 13–7 over Cleveland. Robinson, a member of Stram's first winning team, presented him with the game ball. A win over Denver and a Thanksgiving Day loss at Detroit gave the Chiefs a 7–3–1 record compared to the Raiders' 7–2–2.

The Chiefs took the weekend off after Thanksgiving. Early the following week they left for a few days practice at Santa Barbara before a Monday night game with San Francisco, which held a half-game edge in its division. From the Chiefs' point of view, the game took on new dimensions on Sunday: Atlanta beat Oakland 24–13. A Kansas City win would give the Chiefs a half-game lead. "We owed Atlanta the professional courtesy of a victory for beating Oakland," a straight-faced Brown said after the Chiefs beat the 49ers 26–17. The Chiefs' big-play year had continued. Against San Francisco the Chiefs had pulled off a 54-yard pass on third-and-one, a 25-yard scoring reverse by Taylor, and a fake field goal.

The Chiefs then faced their second meeting of the year with Oakland. "Here we go again," said Stram.

It was the seventh time in the past four years that the clubs had met with first place at stake. Going back to 1966, the Chiefs had won two, lost eight, and tied two. This time, the Chiefs had an 8–3–1 season record to Oakland's 7–3–2.

For a change it was the Chiefs who came from behind, marching nearly 90 yards in the final minutes to a game-winning field goal by Stenerud. The Chiefs' 16–14 win gave them the West, ending Oakland's four-year reign. Stram awarded 40 game balls. The next Tuesday he put his charges through a 45-minute practice in the rain to get ready for the regular season finale at home – a 22–9 win over Buffalo.

On Christmas Day, Miami played at Kansas City in the first round of the playoffs. In the longest pro game ever played, the Dolphins finally edged Kansas City 27–24. "It was a bitter loss, a bitter end to a really great season," said Stram.

Stram had signed a 10-year coaching contract that extended his tenure into the 1980s, while tightening his grip on Kansas City's football operation. Said Hunt at the press conference: "In my opinion, coaching is ninety-five percent of professional football. There is an old expression about football coaches, and I think it applies to Hank. He can take his boys and beat your boys, or take your boys and beat his boys."

In 1972, Hunt fittingly became the first AFL representative to be voted into the Pro Football Hall of Fame.

On April 4, Dawson ended speculation that he would quit by signing a two-year contract.

There was another question, though: Would Arrowhead Stadium be finished in time? Some 70,000 season ticket holders were ready, but the 1971 construction strike and legal hassles had delayed the stadium complex.

The last of the original Texans, Johnny Robinson, retired in July. The new breed had virtually replaced those who came north from Texas. Dawson and Tyrer had Dallas experience, but Podolak, Hayes, and McVea were now the running backs, along with the new number one choice, Jeff Kinney of Nebraska. Taylor remained to anchor the receivers, aided by Elmo Wright. The Cornelisons, Gilliams, and Holubs of other years also were gone, replaced by the Moormans, Daneys, and Rudnays.

Old names such as Haynes and Burford dotted the record books, but it was the new ones that suffered through a frustrating opening year in their magnificent new home. After beating St. Louis soundly in the August 12, 1972 inaugural, the Chiefs found Arrowhead strangely alien, winning only three of their seven home games.

The Chiefs finished the season with an 8–6 record.

In many NFL cities such a record would have been cause for rejoicing. It's a measure of the Chiefs' success that their 8–6 record was regarded with some concern.

The Chiefs' erratic play continued in 1973 as, more and more, the phrase "they're growing old" crept into conversation and stories. Dawson continued to be troubled with shoulder problems, and injuries hobbled offensive linemen.

Kansas City, that many-splendored point machine of the 1960s, had problems scoring. The Chiefs averaged only one touchdown per game for the early part of 1973. Only their defense kept them in contention.

In a Monday night loss in Buffalo in late October, Dawson's shoulder forced him to the sideline. Livingston came in and remained the starting quarterback for the last half of the season.

The Chiefs were not without problems, but they remained in contention. After 12 weeks of play, Oakland (7–4–1) led Kansas City and Denver (both 6–4–2) by one-half game. And the Chiefs' opponent in a thirteenth-week showdown was the Raiders.

For the first time since 1967, a Chiefs-Raiders game was not a duel between Len Dawson and Daryle Lamonica. In this match, Ken Stabler directed the Raiders, while Mike Livingston quarterbacked the Chiefs.

It wasn't even close. The Raiders used a powerful running game to overwhelm the Chiefs 37–7 and end their title chances.

In the end, Kansas City finished in a tie for second place with Denver, a rising power, at 7–5–2.

Twice before, in the years prior to each of their Super Bowl appearances, the Chiefs had seemed to be fading. That they should not surge back again seems unthinkable. Rarely has a team been so identified with success.

The Memories

Lamar Hunt (left) is president of the Kansas City Chiefs. In 1972, he became the first AFL representative to be elected to the Pro Football Hall of Fame.
Hank Stram (above) has been the Chiefs' only coach. He was the AFL coach of the year in 1962, when the Dallas Texans won the AFL championship (below) with an overtime victory over Houston.
One of the stars of the '62 game was Abner Haynes (right), who played with Kansas City through 1964 and remains its leading career rusher with 3,837 yards.

The Chiefs played the Green Bay Packers in Super Bowl I. The Packers held only a 14-10 halftime lead, but Willie Wood's interception of a Len Dawson pass led to a 35-10 Green Bay victory.

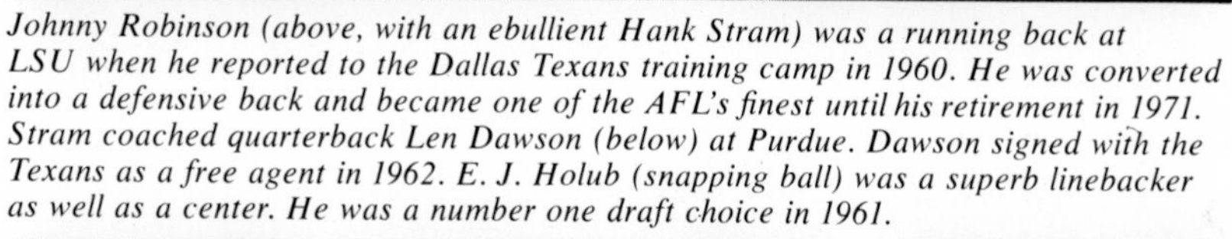

Johnny Robinson (above, with an ebullient Hank Stram) was a running back at LSU when he reported to the Dallas Texans training camp in 1960. He was converted into a defensive back and became one of the AFL's finest until his retirement in 1971. Stram coached quarterback Len Dawson (below) at Purdue. Dawson signed with the Texans as a free agent in 1962. E. J. Holub (snapping ball) was a superb linebacker as well as a center. He was a number one draft choice in 1961.

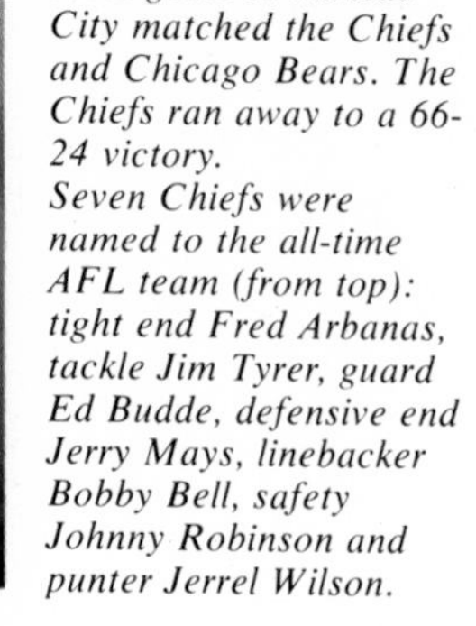

The first AFL versus NFL game in Kansas City matched the Chiefs and Chicago Bears. The Chiefs ran away to a 66-24 victory.
Seven Chiefs were named to the all-time AFL team (from top): tight end Fred Arbanas, tackle Jim Tyrer, guard Ed Budde, defensive end Jerry Mays, linebacker Bobby Bell, safety Johnny Robinson and punter Jerrel Wilson.

1:52
2
KC
0
OAK
7
45
45

Wendell Hayes barrels into the Oakland end zone for a touchdown in the AFL's final championship game, in 1969. Kansas City defeated the Raiders 17-7, the third AFL championship in 10 years for the team.

The Chiefs went into Super Bowl IV as 21-point underdogs to the Minnesota Vikings. But their defense, with Buck Buchanan and Curley Culp leading the charge, harassed Vikings quarterback Joe Kapp all day in a 23-7 Kansas City surprise.

(THE *Morning* KANSAS CITY STAR)

The Kansas Cit· Times

KANSAS CITY, MONDAY, JAN.

CHIEFS CHAMPS OF WORLD

Sing 'We're No. 1' In Celebrations

Len Dawson Steers the Kansas City Team to 23-7 Victory Over the Minnesota Vikings, Who Were Favored to Win the Game

FIRST 9 BY STENERUD

Kicker Makes Field Goals of 48, 32 and 25 Yards for an Early Edge in Last A. F. L.-N. F. L. Meeting

Parade Set For Victors

PRIDE IN THEIR TEAM

Boosters of Kansas City Chiefs Who Made Trip to New Orleans Are Warm ...

AFTER A WEEK WHICH HE HAD DESCRIBED AS AN ORDEAL, he was Lenny the Cool again last night. Len Dawson, the Kansas City quarterback, is shown (left, No. 16) taking his lumps in the game and (right) composed again in the Chiefs' dressing room following the 23-7 victory.—(Wirephotos.)

BIAFRAN LEADER FLEES

On the morning after the Super Bowl, Kansas Citians woke up to this headline in the Kansas City Times. *Mike Garrett (right) was an offensive star for the Chiefs in Super Bowl IV. He gained 39 yards rushing, caught two passes for 25 more, and scored the decisive second-quarter touchdown.*

Otis Taylor (above) has been Kansas City's leading receiver since he joined the Chiefs in 1965.
Jan Stenerud (right) attended Montana State on a skiing scholarship, but he soon found his way to a football field. The Chiefs drafted him as a future in 1966. He has become one of the NFL's finest percentage kickers.
Arrowhead Stadium, the Chiefs' 78,000-seat home, was opened in 1972.

The Chiefs and Miami Dolphins played pro football's longest game, 82 minutes and 40 seconds, in the first round of the 1971 AFC playoffs. Miami won 27-24 on Garo Yepremian's sudden death 37-yard field goal (above). Ed Podolak (left) was the Chiefs' big gun against the Dolphins, gaining 350 yards rushing, receiving, and returning kicks.

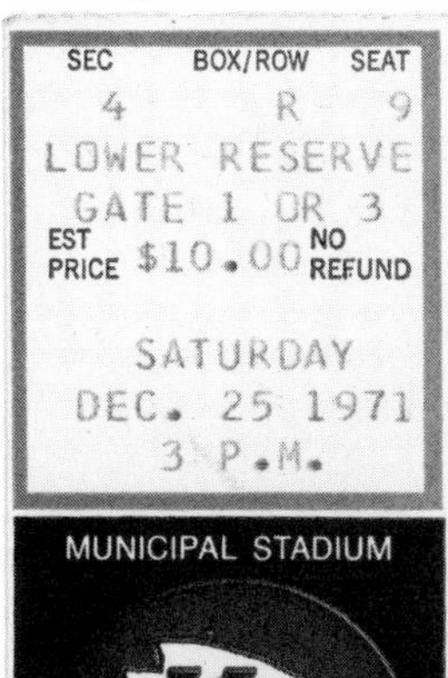

The Miami-Kansas City playoff of Christmas Day, 1971 (ticket stub, left), was not a happy Christmas for the Chiefs. The team's despair was etched on the faces (above) of Chiefs linebackers Willie Lanier (63) and Jim Lynch (51) as they trudged off the Municipal Stadium field, the team's home from 1963 through 1971, for the last time.

3

The Great Games

December 23, 1962

As evening approached, 37,981 fans were wedged into every corner of Houston's Jeppesen Stadium. The mist had slackened for the moment as Len Dawson looked around the circle of expectant faces in the Dallas Texans' huddle. The time out just ending had seemed to last forever as the tension built with each second. "Hold your positions," Dawson cautioned. "They'll try to draw you offside. Ignore them. Don't move."

Rookie kicker Tommy Brooker took a sodden towel and carefully wiped tiny patches of mud from the toe of his kicking foot. Across the murky field Houston coach Pop Ivy used the final second of the time out to call Tom Goode to the sideline. "Put all eleven men up on the line," Ivy ordered. The Oilers would not attempt to guard against trickery. There was no question of a fake field goal. Too much was at stake.

For both teams, exhausted by over five quarters of play on the merciless hard surface, everything had come down to this one climactic moment. Brooker, finishing his first year out of Alabama, marked off a spot and lined it up with the goal posts.

"I remember in the huddle," fullback Curtis McClinton said. "Some of the guys started to say something to Tommy about the kick, and somebody else hushed them up, afraid they would make Tommy nervous. But Tommy just looked at us and laughed. 'Don't worry about it,' he said. 'It's all over now.'"

E. J. Holub snapped. Dawson placed the ball at the 25-yard line on the precise spot Brooker had indicated, and Brooker delivered his fourteenth field goal of 1962, clearing the crossbar by about 10 feet to end what was then pro football's longest game. After 77 minutes and 54 seconds, the Texans had won the American Football League championship 20–17.

The game itself, televised nationally, did much to enhance the prestige of the young league and drew the attention of sports fans to its new stars.

An awful silence had hung over the Texans' dressing room prior to the game. They were a young team, engaging in their first championship test. Nearly half the Oilers had NFL experience, and they had won the AFL championship in 1960 and 1961. Big games were not new to them. Among the 33 Texans, only Dawson had ever played in a regular NFL game.

The tension was visible. One writer said that the Dallas team "looked as if it were heading out on a patrol from which no one expected to return."

Chris Burford, Dallas's top receiver, had missed the final three games after knee surgery. Leaning on his crutches, the most relaxed man in view, he grinned at middle linebacker Sherrill Headrick. Headrick, as usual, was throwing up. "He's been doing that before games for three years," Burford said. Headrick received sympathetic looks from his teammates, some of whom appeared about ready to adopt his habit.

It was misting, and the television crews had asked that the lights be turned on. Coach Hank Stram walked into the room. "The field is terrible," he said. "It's like concrete. Poorly laid concrete. When it rains, the field is nothing but mud. It gives pass receivers a big advantage." The Oilers had planted grass seed to help the sparse turf, and it had left a Mohawk effect down the crown from goal line to goal line.

Stram was worried. His team had blended 2,407 yards rushing with 2,456 yards of Dawson's passing to win the Western Division almost a month early, finishing with an 11–3 record. Houston, despite the presence of Charley Tolar and Billy Cannon in the backfield, had earned nearly two of every three yards by passing.

But if the Oilers had the experience, it was Stram's young Texans who responded to the pressure with the first big play of the day – after their punting got them in early trouble. A 22-

Texans	**3**	**14**	**0**	**0**	**0**	**3**	**20**
Oilers	**0**	**0**	**7**	**10**	**0**	**0**	**17**

yarder by the Texans' James Saxton gave the Oilers good field position in the opening quarter. Then Blanda confidently mixed Cannon, Tolar, and a 19-yard pass to Charley Hennigan. With third and goal at the Dallas 9-yard line, Blanda threw his second pass of the game. Holub leaped awkwardly at the goal line, grabbed it, and ran back to the 43-yard line. Inspired by the reprieve, the Texans produced a march of their own, climaxed by a 16-yard field goal by Brooker.

In the second quarter Dallas moved 80 yards in four plays, the last 28 on a pass from Dawson to Abner Haynes, the brilliant halfback who had been moved to flanker to take Burford's place in the game. The pass gave Dawson his thirtieth touchdown of the year, Haynes his twentieth. The score was 10–0.

To the growing consternation of Houston fans, the Texans scored again late in the half. Duane Wood stole another Blanda pass, setting up a two-yard touchdown for Haynes. Dallas led 17–0.

Halftime was a somber affair with the mist continuing. The homemade signs reading, "Go Big H, Crush Little D" looked bedraggled in the dismal setting. Incredibly the six-point underdog Texans were on the verge of humiliating the defending champions in their own stadium.

In the second half, however, Houston quickly changed the tempo. Following the second-half kickoff, Blanda began to find Willard Dewveall, and Houston went 67 yards in six plays to make it 17–7. Tight end Dewveall accounted for 51 yards on receptions. Only a third interception by Johnny Robinson in the endzone prevented another touchdown as the third quarter ended.

By now Dawson was being subjected to a merciless blitz on nearly every down. Ed Husmann and linebackers Doug Cline, Mike Dukes, and Gene Babb hurled themselves into the Texans, and the game was being played almost exclusively on the Dallas end of the field.

Twice more, short fourth-quarter punts put the Texans in jeopardy. The first, 35 yards by Eddie Wilson, gave Houston the ball at its 43-yard line. The Oilers drove to a 31-yard Blanda field goal just into the final quarter, but it could have been worse. Cornerback Wood produced one of the day's key plays when he hit Cannon just as a pass reached his fingers, jarring the ball loose and preventing a touchdown. Blanda's successful kick followed, narrowing the margin to 17–10.

Unable to move on their next possession, the embattled Texans again had to punt. When Wilson kicked it out of bounds at the Dallas 49, Blanda went to work. His first pass went 16 yards to Cannon at the Dallas 33, where Cannon was immediately tackled by Walt Corey.

Two plays later Blanda passed for 21 yards, also to Cannon, for a first down at the 10. A 9-yarder to Charley Hennigan put the Oilers on the 1. From there Tolar, the fireplug-sized fullback, went around the right side to score. With 5:58 left, the score was tied 17–17.

Blanda still wasn't through. After a 23-yard Wilson punt rolled dead at the Dallas 41, Blanda managed 7 yards on a pass, then wiped his toe to attempt a 42-yarder that would end the game.

But the next big play kept the Texans' hopes simmering. Headrick came bursting up the middle to block the kick. "Shoot, I wasn't even going to rush on that play," he said. "I never had before. But I took a step forward, and I saw a hole in the middle. So I decided to blast in there. I went right through two blockers, who probably knew I never rushed and were thinking about blocking someone else."

Two totally different halves had resulted in a stalemate and the second overtime in professional football championship history. Four years earlier, Baltimore defeated New York 23–17 for the NFL title after 8 minutes and 15 seconds

As Texas oil millionaires, the two men in the photo at left could have afforded finer tweeds. Yet Lamar Hunt (left) and Bud Adams wore the blazers of their respective teams, the Texans and the Oilers, for the 1962 championship game of the American Football League. Dallas blunted Houston thrusts five times with interceptions, the first of them by E. J. Holub at the Texans' 9-yard line (below). Soon, the Texans led 17-0. Quarterback George Blanda brought the Oilers from behind with his placekicking (right).

of overtime play. That game had done much to popularize the NFL brand of football, and now the AFL was presented with the same dramatic chance.

What happened next left everyone, including both teams, confused. At the center of the field referee Harold (Red) Bourne summoned the team captains for the coin toss to determine who would kick to get the overtime underway. Haynes trotted out for Dallas and won the toss. Bourne turned expectantly to Haynes.

"We'll kick to the clock," Abner said.

Bourne was dumfounded. In one sentence, Haynes had given away both possession and the benefit of a tricky and gusty wind, which was blowing at times 14 miles an hour out of the north and toward the clock behind the south endzone.

"I couldn't correct him, of course," recalled Bourne, since retired. "As I remember it, he had the choice, and when he made it, I told him, 'Captain Haynes, you made the choice and said you'll kick.'"

The ABC commentator on the field was equally astonished and said so to the millions watching. Never does a team facing sudden death give away possession. Never.

Yet Haynes's mistake that gray holiday afternoon was one of wording, a tension-induced misstatement of a tactical decision that Stram had made on the sideline during the three-minute intermission. Dallas did, indeed, want to give up possession. But it didn't want to yield the wind as well.

"I was afraid Blanda would kick off out of the endzone, and we'd take over on the twenty. We'd be unable to move and have to punt from deep in our endzone," Stram explained later. "We weren't punting well, and a short punt into the wind would give them the ball near midfield, almost in range for a quick field goal. Our offense had not been moving the ball the second

half, but our defense had been playing well.

"There was a lot of confusion all around, and Abner just said it wrong. He should have said, 'We'll take this end of the field – facing the clock.' Then the Oilers would have chosen to receive and we would have had what we wanted. Instead, Abner said first that we would kick. That gave away our option on the wind."

Dallas's strategy was not new. The Texans had won the pregame coin flip and elected to kick off rather than receive several times during the season. This had its roots in a trade between the first and second games, when owner Lamar Hunt, against Stram's wishes, shipped quarterback Cotton Davidson to Oakland for the Raiders' number one choice in the draft that fall. Davidson had been the team's punter. Wilson, a rookie quarterback, was pressed into replacing Davidson. At one point in October, he was averaging just a little more than a center snap. Consequently, Stram had adopted the strategy of taking the wind in the first quarter if he won the toss. "That way, we'll have it at our backs if Eddie has to punt," said the coach.

Now amid the expectant throng in the Jeppesen bleachers and the fans crowding the endzones, the strategy was resurrected again – except that Haynes, caught up in the moment, prefaced it with the words "We'll kick . . ."

"When we went into the overtime," he said a decade later, "coach Stram called me to the sideline and told me that we did not want to receive. He explained that the defense had done an excellent job. They had held Houston to either very short or minus yardage. The offense was not moving well. It had damn near stopped completely.

"With Burford hurt, they had moved me to flanker, although I also played at running back that day, too. We had an excellent specialty team. Our plan was to kick the ball to them, hold them, try to get a good runback on the punt return, and get on the board with a field goal."

Two words had ruined that.

"We thought they were crazy," said Blanda. "But it turned out all right for them, so what can you say?"

Neither club could move. A second interception by Robinson stalled one Houston thrust. The Oilers' blitz dulled anything that Dawson attempted.

Finally as the day darkened, Houston began to move from its 12 after a 39-yard punt from midfield by Wilson. Blanda had decided to throw out of the endzone if need be. He had already tried a pass to Cannon on third and 1 in the overtime. Cannon dropped it. This time, Blanda aimed at Dewveall and hit him with a 12-yarder. Three more passes got the Oilers to midfield. Blanda was nearing his field-goal range, and he had the wind behind him. Another pass got them to the 35, where a run lost a yard. It was second and 11.

Throughout the season, Dallas occasionally had dropped end Bill Hull, a 6-foot 7-inch rookie, back into pass coverage. It gave them, in effect, four linebackers and just three rushing linemen.

"I'm just second-guessing myself," Blanda said, "but if I had called a hook-in pass instead of a down and out, we'd have made it." But Blanda didn't call a hook-in. Trying for one more completion, extra insurance for a shorter kick, he suddenly saw Hull rise in the gloom between himself and intended receiver Hennigan.

Hull ran the ball back to midfield. On the final two plays of the fifth quarter, McClinton netted two yards.

Houston never touched the ball again. As the sixth quarter opened, Dawson flipped a short pass to Jack Spikes, and the ex-TCU All-America ran 10 yards to the Houston 38. Then, finally catching the Houston blitz coming on the right side, Spikes burst 19 yards off the left

55
28

30
81
31
74

Sudden death would end the struggle that was tied 17-17 at the end of four quarters. The Texans needed the football and a score, any kind of score. Yet captain Abner Haynes declared, "We'll kick to the clock," when Dallas won the coin toss to start overtime play (left). Houston could not take advantage of Haynes's blunder, however, and a second overtime period later, Tommy Brooker's field goal won the game for Dallas. It was the longest professional game up to that time—77 minutes, 54 seconds. In the locker room later, Jim Tyrer (77) seemed calm enough, while Fred Arbanas looked over the shoulders of celebrants Lamar Hunt, AFL commissioner Joe Foss, and a dampened Hank Stram.

to the Oilers' 19. The Oilers had been rushing Dawson from alternate sides all through the second half. "They had guessed right on just about every play," Dawson said. This time they guessed wrong.

With the ball at the 19, Dawson daringly tried for Spikes on a pass that went incomplete. There would be no more gambles. McClinton lost a yard, then Dawson kept it himself, positioning the ball in the middle of the field, 18 yards from the endzone. During the time out that followed, Brooker prepared himself while Dawson calmed his teammates.

"There wasn't anything to do but kick," said Brooker. "I kept my eyes on the ground. When I finally looked up, I saw the ball going through the goal posts. I asked Lenny, 'How far was it?'"

Dallas had won 20–17 and the bench erupted. Brooker was given a hero's ride into what quickly became a champagne-soaked dressing room. "Hey, you're wasting that stuff," Dawson cautioned Fred Arbanas, who was dousing everyone in sight.

Hunt, his team a champion for the first time, was so exuberant that he leaped to grab an overhead pipe and chinned himself 11 times. Later, trying to free a champagne-soaked tie knot, he solved the problem by cutting the tie, leaving the ends dangling from his collar.

It had been worth the wait. "We're the champs. We're the champs," a toothless Holub shouted repeatedly through the din.

Spikes, whose key runs had set up the winning field goal and a second quarter touchdown, netted 77 yards on 11 carries, and was voted the game's most valuable player. It was a heady honor for a man who had lost his job to the rookie McClinton at midseason. Spikes had gone out with a knee injury, and by the time he got back, McClinton was well on his way to rookie of the year. McClinton climaxed his brilliant opening year with 70 yards in the championship game while Haynes, running at times from his old halfback spot, added 26. Tolar's 58 yards led the Oilers.

Blanda threw 46 times and completed half for 261 yards. He might have enjoyed a better fate except for a half dozen dropped throws at critical times. Dawson threw only 14 times, completing 9 for a modest 88 yards.

"Dallas was a conservative team," Blanda snorted. "If we played it that conservative, we would never score."

"I've been sitting here thinking of the game," Stram said on the plane ride back to Dallas's Love Field. "I just can't say what was the big play of the game, or what was the deciding point. There were so darn many. You'd have to say that the pass Spikes caught and ran to set up the field goal was important. So was Headrick's blocking Blanda's field goal in the fourth quarter before the game went into sudden death, and Duane Wood's knocking Billy Cannon's catch loose in the endzone, and Johnny Robinson's interception on the goal line. There were just too many big plays. The game was full of them."

Dallas	3	14	0	0	0	3 – 20
Houston	0	0	7	10	0	0 – 17

Dal – FG Brooker 16
Dal – Haynes 28 pass from Dawson (Brooker kick)
Dal – Haynes 2 run (Brooker kick)
Hou – Dewveall 15 pass from Blanda (Blanda kick)
Hou – FG Blanda 31
Hou – Tolar 1 run (Blanda kick)
Dal – FG Brooker 25

January 15, 1967

That moment in January, 1967, is frozen on game film, forgotten in the panoply of events that have seized the national imagination in the years since Green Bay's Jim Taylor tried to run over Kansas City's Buck Buchanan. But of all the events on that sunwashed Sunday in Los Angeles, that one play dramatized the pent-up emotions let loose after seven years of what amounted to civil war in professional football.

Ever since 1960, when the American Football League first challenged the National Football League, taunts had flown back and forth. Which was better? The tradition, prestige, and glamour of the NFL's big names? Or the AFL, the upstart, the challenger, the brash new kid on the block?

"It's been a war of words," said Kansas City's Hank Stram. "Now we settle it where it should be decided, on the grass."

It was a publicity man's dream, played in Los Angeles, a city that epitomized, more than any other, the art of making something even bigger than lifesize.

Peace had been declared. A merger of the warring leagues was at hand. But first David must venture out to confront Vince Lombardi's Goliaths on a televised stage. The game would be watched by one of the largest audiences in sports history.

Baseball's World Series, the Kentucky Derby, and other major sports events had taken decades to grow into classics.

But the Super Bowl, pairing the two league champions in professional football, was launched full-bearded and with no previous tradition. All it had was an overwhelming curiosity generated by the end of the war and an immense press corps on hand in Los Angeles.

Was the NFL better? Was Kansas City as devastating as it had proven in 1966 in the AFL? Or were the Packers invincible?

More than 300 musicians marched on the floor of the Los Angeles Coliseum. With them were glee clubs, baton twirlers, and enormous floats, as well as 10 astronauts and 170 photographers. None of this disturbed the 61,946 fans in the 90,000-seat Coliseum.

In the tunnel at the end of the field, the Chiefs and the Packers waited for pregame introductions. The faces of the white-shirted Chiefs were grim, intense, and devoid of humor. Years later, Buchanan admitted he had come down the tunnel to the field so emotionally charged he wept.

Not even the volcanic performance of the 6-foot 7-inch, 280-pound Buchanan could slow the Packers that day, even though he remained totally unintimidated. "I cursed and screamed all day," Buchanan said later. "I cussed everybody I possibly could. I'll never forget one time that they ran a play with Elijah Pitts, and I laid a hit on him.

"'You can't run this hole here, man,' I told him.

"'I'll be comin' back,' he said.

"'Every time you come back, I'll be right here waitin' on you,' I shot back."

Finally, after Green Bay had built an insurmountable lead, Buchanan's growing frustration reached its height. When Taylor, Green Bay's powerful fullback, attempted to run through Buchanan's hole, Buchanan wrapped his arms about the former Louisiana State star. But Taylor kept his legs churning, driving for one extra yard on this day when league pride demanded the ultimate effort.

Buchanan, by now a raging torrent, picked up Taylor and hurled him to the ground. "I have never felt that way before," he admitted later. "I was going to hurt him. I had seen him kick tacklers before; I had watched it on film during the week. I wasn't going to stand for it."

Of such stuff was Super Bowl I built – although it took some time before the league offically adopted the name. For the first three

Chiefs	**0**	**10**	**0**	**0**	**10**
Packers	**7**	**7**	**14**	**7**	**35**

bowl games the official name was "World Championship Game." But everyone, coaches included, used the Super Bowl label applied by Lamar Hunt. He had adapted it from a bouncing ball his daughter played with.

Green Bay and the Chiefs were ideal opponents for the first Super Bowl. The Packers epitomized the NFL of the early 1960s. In the previous seven years, they had played in the championship game five times and had won four of them.

Kansas City, in its way, reflected the image of the younger league. An imaginative, struggling, gradually successful team, it had finally gained the AFL's first real moment in the sun. "There are two motivations in this game," said Kansas City captain Jerry Mays. "Number one is the Packers' pride to prove their reputation is justified. Number two is the underdog role we have. We're the poor kids from across the tracks coming over to play against the rich kids. They've had everything their way all the time. I don't think there are very many motivations as great as that."

The Chiefs were facing the Packers near the end of Green Bay's dynasty. Paul Hornung, the quarterback Lombardi turned into an all-pro halfback, pinched the nerves in his neck and could only watch the latter half of the 1966 season. Fuzzy Thurston and Jerry Kramer, who had raised the social status of guards with their execution on the power sweep, were also nearing the end of great careers. Forrest Gregg was a 10-year veteran with gray showing at the temples. Other signs of advancing age were evident on the squad.

"Off the field, they look like a reunion of the class of 1944," said one AFL writer who saw the Packers up close for the first time. It was one of the oddities of the Packers' reign that they seldom seemed impressive, either on film or in hotel lobbies waiting for the bus to the game. They simply did a job. They did it with flawless execution week after week.

As a youngster in Dallas, Mays had two idols. One was Doak Walker, who had led SMU to a 1948 championship. The other was Gregg, who had also been a Mustang. When Mays enrolled at SMU, he asked for Gregg's old number, 75; he still wore it as a pro. Now the two men would face each other: Gregg at right tackle on offense for the Packers; Mays at left defensive end for the Chiefs.

Green Bay had won its way into the game by beating the Dallas Cowboys, a team born in the same year and place as the Chiefs. The Chiefs had breezed by Buffalo in the AFL title game. Green Bay was 12–2 and Kansas City 11–2–1. The showdown was so promising that CBS and NBC charged as much as $85,000 for one-minute commercials.

The Packers had remained in the frozen north for an extra four days after the Chiefs had encamped at Long Beach on January 4. Lombardi hadn't wanted to come west at all until just before the game, but league pressure finally prevailed. The Packers wound up in Santa Barbara, 90 miles up the coast from the city.

Mountains looked down in the distance, and the Pacific washed the beach across the road. Birds sang in the eucalyptus trees. It was an idyllic setting, but Lombardi hated it.

"Phil, these mountains, what is this?" he asked assistant coach Phil Bengtson, when they arrived. "This place is like a resort. We wanted something barren." The Packers went to sleep at night lulled by the surf instead of the wind-driven snow they had left in Green Bay.

The Packers' late arrival gave the Chiefs the publicity stage to themselves. One of their defensive backs, Fred Williamson, made the most of it. Violating Stram's warning against saying anything inflammatory, Williamson ridiculed the Packers as a team and as individuals.

Ironically, Williamson had said many of the same things early in September, before the season ever began. "I'd love to play against that Boyd Dowler of Green Bay. I'd like to see how he reacts under the Hammer. NFL flankers don't worry me. We've got topnotch receivers in this league, speedwise. Look at Lance Alworth, Bo Roberson, and Elbert Dubenion. I don't believe all those press clippings about the fanTABulous National League." Four months later, he still felt the same, and he said so. He said he felt the Chiefs, before the game, had succumbed to a state of awe, even fear, regarding their upcoming opponent. He wanted to snap them out of it, focus any Packers anger on himself. Some of his teammates focused theirs on him.

The Packers, resting near the sea, didn't seem especially disturbed. Film studies of three Chiefs games had already convinced them that the Chiefs could be vulnerable to passes on the weakside, into the middle. The Chiefs were a fast team, said Lombardi, but he wasn't sure how fast since he could judge them only against teams he had not played.

"Our plan was to get inside [Willie] Mitchell," Lombardi said. "We were to send Dowler or McGee into Mitchell's area and let Starr throw to them. It worked out very nicely."

The Chiefs' stacked defense, he said, was good against the run, but it left them with little defensive help against the pass. "They were daring us to pass so we did. We're familiar with the stacked defense because Detroit once had it. We could get inside Mitchell. Because he didn't get any help from his linebackers, we went right at him."

Starr, 33, was in his finest year. He had 156 completions for a 62.2 completion percentage. He had thrown 14 touchdowns and only three interceptions. Rescued from obscurity by Lombardi when the latter took over a 1–10–1 team after 1958, Starr had been to Green Bay what Len Dawson was to Kansas City.

Dawson also had enjoyed his finest season, completing 159 passes for a 56.0 percentage and 26 touchdowns. He had been intercepted 10 times.

Each team had superb receivers: the Packers had Dowler, Carroll Dale, and the aging Max McGee; Kansas City had second-year man Otis Taylor and veteran Chris Burford. The 34-year-old McGee had been used sparingly and had caught only four passes in the regular season, plus another against Dallas. He did not expect to play.

"I'm kind of anxious to see what they are like," tackle Henry Jordan confessed when the Packers opened practice. "They came from the same colleges we came from."

The Chiefs' Curtis McClinton agreed. "Nobody around here is getting shook up because Green Bay is a thirteen-point favorite. Where do they get that? Just because we come from the American Football League? Look, maybe I could give Green Bay three points for the game. Maybe, I said. And those would be on intangibles that disappear when the whistle blows. The Packers get one for being at the peak of their maturity, another for having played in the big ones, and a third for tradition."

Many of the Chiefs, including McClinton, had been drafted high by NFL clubs. "Did I all of a sudden get worse because I went with the AFL?" McClinton said.

The preparations and publicity leading up to the game almost matched the event itself. Each fact, down to the smallest bit of trivia, was reported by the cadre of 338 newspaper, magazine, and wire service reporters. There were 262 radio and television people on hand. The media was everywhere. In Long Beach, for instance, a group overheard the Chiefs raucously singing the Mickey Mouse song in their dressing room.

The game program described it as "a day that can never happen again." So it was—the first AFL-NFL championship game, Super Bowl I. The Chiefs' opponents were the proud Green Bay Packers of Vince Lombardi (far left). Thirty-four-year-old Max McGee, who had not even expected to play in the game, caught seven passes and scored the first touchdown in Super Bowl history (left). Len Dawson massed the Chiefs' forces and kept the game close for a half (below, he's rushed by Willie Davis.)

BUCHANAN
86
BELL
78
25

The challenge and the growing might of a young league could be seen in this vignette from Super Bowl I. Towering Buck Buchanan met Green Bay's Jim Taylor at the line of scrimmage and threw him back, spinning him around in the process (right). Buchanan's chutzpah was answered a play later; the Packers sent Taylor over him for a first down.

Mickey Mouse song? It turned out the song had become Kansas City's battle cry after Tex Maule of *Sports Illustrated* had called the AFL a Mickey Mouse league during a conversation after the Green Bay-Dallas game. Somebody overheard and printed it, and the clipping found its way to the Chiefs' bulletin board.

Lombardi refused to accept the premise that the Super Bowl was the biggest game in football history. "Hell, no," he said. "We've been in other historic games. I wouldn't rate this over regular NFL games. Maybe next year this will be the most important thing in the world. Right now it isn't. It's just a big football game."

The Packers were not likely to succumb to overconfidence. "Look," said Thurston, "I'm going to be blocking a guy [Buchanan] who is eight inches taller than I am, seventy pounds heavier, and about seven years younger.

"I'm just a little old man. How am I going to be overconfident?"

Finally, after a buildup of two weeks, Super Sunday dawned. The game started, and for nine minutes the teams probed. Starr was thrown for a loss on his first third-down pass attempt. The Packers came patiently back to another third down, needing three yards at the Chiefs' 37-yard line. Starr threw to his left, where McGee, suddenly in the game because of an injury to Dowler, had maneuvered himself between Mitchell and Williamson. Somehow McGee cradled the ball one-armed in the crook of his right elbow and ran for the touchdown. McGee, who had spent the two weeks wondering if he'd even get to play, became the first man to score a Super Bowl touchdown. By the end of the game he would make seven catches, two of them for touchdowns.

But if NFL partisans had expected a quick rout, they grew silent as Kansas City retaliated. Dawson, moving the Chiefs with play action passes that seemed to trouble the Packers, finally threw 31 yards to Taylor, who got to the 7-yard line. From there Dawson again froze the Green Bay defenders with a run fake. Then he threw into the endzone to McClinton for the score. Bert Coan was equally open 5 yards deeper. It looked almost simple.

At halftime the Packers led 14–10, but Kansas City was optimistic. "I sincerely felt we could win," Stram said later. "And I think our people felt that way. I'll never forget it. One of our players walked into the locker room and blurted out, 'We've got them. They're a bunch of old men, getting tired. They're not in real good shape.'

"And they really felt this way," Stram continued. "Then all of a sudden it blew up in the second half with the quick interception."

One play, in the third minute of the second half, turned the game. "I would like to think that one play doesn't make that much difference, but in this case it did," said Stram. "Our personality changed. We diverted from our game plan, from the things we had set out to do and had accomplished the first half."

Under pressure from the first blitz the Packers ran all day, Dawson had thrown off balance. The ball was tipped and wobbled out to the right side in the direction of Fred Arbanas. Willie Wood intercepted at the Green Bay 45-yard line and ran to the Chiefs' 5 before he was caught by Mike Garrett. Pitts stabbed between Chuck Hurston and Andy Rice on the next play, and the once-close ball game had become Green Bay 21, Kansas City 10.

Dave Hill, the Chiefs' right tackle who had handled Davis nicely in the opening half, described what happened next. "After that interception he just came," said Hill. "He didn't worry about the run or anything. Of course, when you get an eleven-point lead you can expect that."

On the opposite side, Jim Tyrer experienced the same problem. "Their linemen grew more

The goal post temporarily shielded the photographer from the action as Max McGee scored his second touchdown of the game for the Packers (left and below). The sterling silver trophy for the winner of the first Super Bowl was presented to Lombardi by Pete Rozelle, commissioner of the NFL (right).

bold after that interception. They wound up and started rushing the passer every play. They even took wide splits. They didn't worry about the run. It changed the whole complexion of the game."

Kansas City's play action passes, a staple of its success all season, were useless. In the first half Dawson had been thrown for a loss only once. In the second half he and Pete Beathard were caught five times for 53 yards.

After Wood's interception, the Chiefs made one more concerted move. They got up to another third down at midfield, only to have somebody miss a block on Lee Roy Caffey. Coan was pulled down for a loss that forced a punt. The Packers' rush was so consistent by now that Dawson could do little to counter it.

Late in the third quarter, Starr passed, moving the Packers deep into the Chiefs' end of the field. Then he unleashed Jim Taylor, who punched it to the 13-yard line. From there Starr threw his second touchdown pass to McGee. Another long drive and a 1-yard run by Pitts midway through the last quarter made it 35–10 at the finish.

Starr had faced nine third-down situations the first half and had turned seven into first downs. But in the last 30 minutes, he made good on five of seven in another brilliant display of championship accuracy.

"The moving pocket? Did it move?" Lombardi asked sarcastically in the incredible crush of the Packers' dressing room afterward. His team had filed in like commuters heading for a rush-hour train.

Lombardi flashed his gap-toothed grin as he stood coatless under the glare of television lights, accepting the first Super Bowl trophy from commissioner Pete Rozelle.

After the interception and the undermining of the play action attack that had worked so well earlier, the Chiefs were through. "If you throw, throw, throw against Green Bay, you're just not going to win," Stram said.

"They had the kicking, the offense, and the defense. You can only get so far unless you have all three. If you've got two of those elements you have a chance of getting to the Super Bowl, but you cannot win it. We had the kicking and the offense. We didn't have the defense."

Someone asked Lombardi how the Chiefs compared to other NFL teams.

"Kansas City has a good team," he said. "But it doesn't compare with some of the top teams in the NFL. Dallas is a better team. That's what you want me to say, isn't it? There. I've said it."

Kansas City	0	10	0	0	– 10
Green Bay	7	7	14	7	– 35

GB – McGee 37 pass from Starr (Chandler kick)
KC – McClinton 7 pass from Dawson (Mercer kick)
GB – Taylor 14 run (Chandler kick)
KC – FG Mercer 31
GB – Pitts 5 run (Chandler kick)
GB – McGee 13 pass from Starr (Chandler kick)
GB – Pitts 1 run (Chandler kick)

January 4, 1970

Hank Stram surveyed his grass- and blood-stained team in the locker room. Halftime was nearly over.

Outside, the scoreboard lights showed Oakland 7, Kansas City 7. Huge chunks of soggy turf were being tamped back like enormous divots as Oakland-Alameda County Coliseum was repaired for the last 30 minutes in the history of the American Football League. When the final gun sounded, the AFL would disappear, swallowed up in the merger with the NFL.

But that was another matter. Stram had more immediate problems. Although his team was even with the Raiders, the statistics said they were in trouble. It had taken a long pass play in the closing minutes to set up that halftime tie. The Raiders had dominated and the Chiefs had committed mistake after mistake. Once, two Kansas City backs even crashed into each other.

Stram was also fighting a psychological problem. The noise of the air horns penetrated the deep concrete caverns all the way to the Chiefs' dressing room. This crowd was hostile, as Kansas City or Oakland crowds usually were when the two teams played each other. And the stakes on this January 4, 1970 – the AFL championship and a trip to the Super Bowl the next week – were among the highest ever.

"I dwelt on that championship thing," Stram said of his short halftime message. "I said I thought we were a little tight, but that we could work it out. And I said it had been going on for six months, and now we were within thirty minutes of a championship."

At that point, he paused and looked at his team. "We have it in the grasp of our hands. All we have to do is squeeze."

For three years, ever since Kansas City had gone to the first Super Bowl, the two AFL giants had been at grips. Oakland had squeezed harder.

In 1967, when the Chiefs attempted to repeat as champions, Oakland fashioned a 13–1 record and went instead to Super Bowl II. In 1968, when the Chiefs enjoyed their best regular season record ever at 12–2, Oakland matched it. The Raiders then humiliated the Chiefs 41–6 in a special playoff to determine who would play the New York Jets for the AFL title.

The Raiders, at that stage, had a virtual stranglehold on the Chiefs. Since 1966, the Raiders had won seven of eight games, including the last four in a row. The rivalry, always intense, grew more bitter with each game until players described their feeling with one word, "hatred."

"We're like tough old partners of an unhappy marriage, each knowing just where to kick, scratch, and scream to cause each other the most anguish," veteran Oakland center Jim Otto said of the twice-a-year grudge matches. A diabolic schedule-maker contributed to the feud. It seemed that each time the teams played against each other, first place or a division title was at stake.

"Each game has always been a monumental one," says Kansas City's middle linebacker, Willie Lanier. "If they beat us twice, they'd damn near gotten the league wrapped up. And if we beat them twice, we'd done the same thing."

"We could always tell when we were going to play Kansas City," said Rod Sherman, a receiver from USC. "Usually that would be the week Al Davis showed up to coach us."

Davis, Oakland managing general partner, was a former coach of the Raiders.

Kansas City's lone victory against the Raiders in three years had come in 1968. The Chiefs had lined up in an old-fashioned T formation and had run all but three plays on the ground for a 24–10 triumph. The Raiders avenged their defeat 38–21 two weeks later.

Just three weeks before their current showdown, the Raiders had won the AFL Western

Chiefs	0	7	7	3	17
Raiders	7	0	0	0	7

Division on the same field, beating the Chiefs 10–6. Len Dawson had thrown only six times. The win gave the Raiders their third straight division title, but it was a deceptive victory. For one thing, due to the special playoff rules in effect for this lame duck year of the AFL, both teams were already assured of spots in the playoffs. Only the home field advantage and the honor of winning a division were really at stake. For another, both teams knew that the Chiefs were like a fighter protecting a sore hand that day. Dawson's duty was to hand off to his runners. Kansas City wanted to take no chances on his being hit on a pass rush or slipping on the unpredictable Oakland surface. Earlier in the season Dawson had missed five games because of a knee that nearly required surgery. Then on Thanksgiving Day against Denver, he bumped that same knee, forcing him to miss yet another start the following week. The Chiefs had relied on Jan Stenerud, who kicked 5 field goals to set a pro record of 16 in a row, as Kansas City defeated Buffalo 22–19.

Oakland's win over Kansas City in the final regular season game left the Chiefs with an 11–3 record compared to the Raiders' 12–1–1. But both clubs suspected they would face each other one final time. The Chiefs, despite their loss, had had no sense of doom as they flew back to the Midwest. In one respect, in fact, there was elation. Lanier felt the Chiefs' defense had reached title form. "The first playoff game in New York's Shea Stadium was important because it had some big plays in it," Lanier said years afterward. "But I thought that our defense had come together and played one of its finest games ever in that ten-six loss in Oakland. Actually we had played well defensively all season."

As testimony to the rebuilding job Stram had accomplished since the 1967 defeat by Green Bay, the Chiefs dominated the AFL statistics in the league's final season. Lanier and Lynch had joined Bell as linebackers. Curley Culp and Aaron Brown had moved in with Buck Buchanan and Jerry Mays on the line. Jim Kearney had become the strong safety, next to the veteran Johnny Robinson, and Emmitt Thomas was at right cornerback. Rookie James Marsalis had come into the lineup in preseason, solving a chronic weakness on the left side. This unit, reinforced by seven new players in the past two seasons, had started every game since August. They had helped carry the club while Dawson was out. With Dawson back, they felt they could go all the way.

"I remember the wind," Dawson says of that showdown with the Jets on the Saturday before Christmas. "It was terrible. The field was hard. No grass. Cold. It wasn't wet, but the wind was blowing, gusting up over twenty-five miles an hour. And the temperature was one degree above freezing at kickoff. If I threw the ball easy, the wind would just take it. The wind was taking Namath's ball too. He was all over the place."

Under these conditions the game settled into a battle of defenses and infrequent field goals. The Chiefs nursed a 6–3 margin into the early stages of the fourth quarter, but it was increasingly shaky as Namath, finally gaining his touch in the wind, stirred New York's passing game to life. Slowly, he worked his team downfield. Then the crowd was brought to its feet as the Chiefs were penalized for interference in the endzone. It was first down on Kansas City's 1-yard line.

It was here, with the wind shrieking in off Flushing Bay, that Lanier led the Chiefs on what Mays later called the most inspiring single defensive series he experienced in his 10 years with the club.

Lanier was a man possessed. "I went crazy," he says.

"It was something that doesn't happen once in ten or twenty years," said Mays. "It was

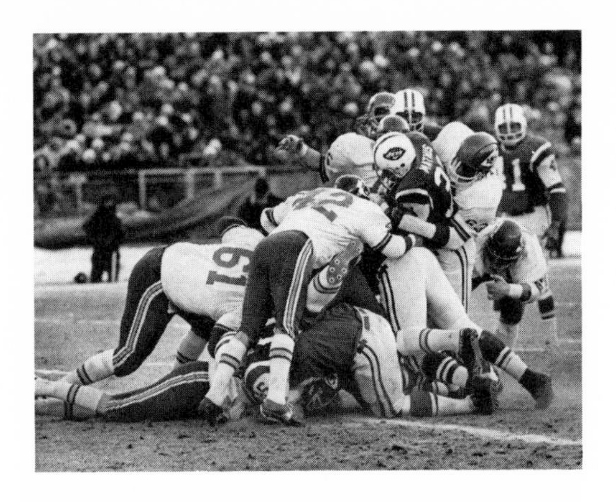

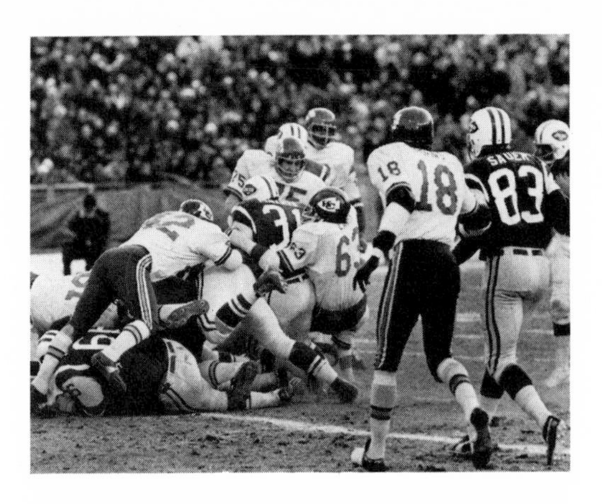

indescribable. We were high. The defensive unit had played well the entire game. Then Willie Lanier got us. He fired me up. It was the way he did it – tears in his eyes, teeth gnashing."

Shouting, screaming, crying, pleading, and pummeling, Lanier was like a 240-pound electrode as he recharged a unit that had been crushed by the disastrous interference call. The unit was ready.

Bill Mathis was stopped for no gain. Then Matt Snell lost a half yard. Both ran into a wall of Chiefs. It was third down. Namath surveyed the scene, and Lanier continued his curses and pleas. Namath faked a pitchout to Snell, who continued running to the right while Namath turned and faked a handoff to Mathis over guard. But the Chiefs didn't buy either fake, and Bell raced into the flat to cover Snell.

"He was out there with Snell, and he had no right being there," a dejected Namath said. Bell had stopped in the middle of a blitz and whirled to stay with the New York fullback just as Namath turned to throw to him. "If he hadn't been there, it would have been a touchdown," Namath said. But Bell was there, and Namath, who was rushed, had his pass land at Snell's feet.

The Jets settled for Jim Turner's second field goal of the day and a 6–6 tie.

Dawson then solved the Jets' defense and the winds, too, in two lightning thrusts. Starting from the 20-yard line after Turner's kickoff, and using a play that Otis Taylor had sketched on the sideline dirt, Dawson threw to Taylor for 61 yards. From the Jets' 19 he then passed to Gloster Richardson for the game's only touchdown. Kansas City 13, New York 6. It ended that way, although it took more fourth-quarter defensive heroics by Lanier and his friends to stop the Jets at the 16 and again at the 13. The defense that had cemented itself in Oakland had met the test in New York. Now it was ready for the Raiders and a championship test.

Stram practiced the team lightly before Christmas. He gave the team a couple of days off before they flew to the 68-degree sunshine in California, barely in time to escape a snowstorm. Stram headquartered his team in Santa Barbara for the week before the January 4 date with the Raiders. There was a certain irony in this. The Chiefs were staying at the same place the Packers did before Super Bowl I. Stram even occupied the same suite Vince Lombardi had.

The week was a good one. If the players had expected a semi-vacation amid the sand, palms, and sun, Stram dispelled it by calling a practice within four hours of landing. One of his major targets was to erase the memories of having lost so many recent games to the Raiders, including the two in the regular season just ended. "We are thinking positive. The next game is the only one that counts," he said.

Stram had thought of everything, even ordering special Oakland uniforms for use in practice. The black jerseys with silver numerals – each corresponding to a key Raider – were worn, if somewhat self-consciously, by Chiefs defenders during offensive drills.

Lanier wound up with Dan Conners's number fifty-five. "We don't get the vivid picture we're seeking without the actual numbers," Stram explained. "We want instant recognition." But Mays wasn't too sure. So deep was his dislike of the Raiders, he said he felt like a turncoat putting on the hated colors.

In Oakland the Raiders drilled in secret as usual. One Raider was quoted as saying, "We even had four guards on the gates today. That's the first time we ever had Pinkertons." Oakland obviously was not taking the game for granted.

John Madden, a rookie coach at 33, was the youngest head coach in the AFL. He had done an exceptional job in bringing the Raiders to this climactic date and was named coach of the

The resolve and the might that would make the 1969 Chiefs the champions of the world was apparent this day at the Shea Stadium goal line. There middle linebacker Willie Lanier denied Jets' running back Bill Mathis a touchdown (left). The Jets had been stopped and the ball given to the Kansas City offense. Lanier retired to the bench to receive Hank Stram's approval and a squirt of refresher (right).

year. Daryle Lamonica had thrown 34 touchdowns in the regular season and then 5 more in a 56–7 playoff rout over Houston. He had thrown six touchdown passes in the first half of a 50–21 win over Buffalo during the regular season. He was voted most valuable player in the AFL.

The Raiders were an explosive team. Lamonica could throw deep to Fred Biletnikoff or Warren Wells or hit Hewritt Dixon or Charlie Smith coming out of the backfield. Dixon, a converted tight end, was one of the finest fullbacks in the league. "He was a combination of halfback, fullback, and nastiness," said Lanier. "You don't see any like him running now. He was just a real nasty one. Nothing personal. Just a mean sonofabitch."

By late in the week, Stram stood on top of the Santa Barbara stands and watched his team and commented, "They're coming along just like I want them to. I don't see how Oakland can beat us." Madden, meanwhile, was concerned about Wells's shoulder, which had been injured in his team's 10–6 victory over the Chiefs.

Oakland fans were confident. On Friday, the team staged a luncheon with a New Orleans motif. "Just watch us Sunday," the supremely confident Lamonica proclaimed. "We are ready." So were the Chiefs. Brown, the 6-foot 5-inch, 265-pound defensive end from the University of Minnesota who had been a major reason for the improved defense all season, had fidgeted all week. As he waited for the elevator to the lobby the morning of the game, he said, "I don't think we could stand to wait another day for this game."

The Raiders made it look almost easy in the opening quarter. They outgained the Chiefs 101 to 20 yards and took a 7–0 lead on a three-yard run by Charlie Smith. Kansas City had stumbled through a series of broken plays, muffed assignments, and dropped passes. The Chiefs didn't get their second first down until late in the half. Then, with just over three minutes remaining, the team seemed to straighten out. Chip Oliver blitzed, and Dawson ducked under it and threw 13 yards to Taylor, getting the Chiefs out to their own 40-yard line. Two penalties and a short run by Robert Holmes advanced the ball to the Raiders' 42 as the two-minute warning was given. The Chiefs capitalized on their deepest penetration on their next two plays. Their passing plan was to take deep safety Dave Grayson out of the middle and occupy him. Dawson did this by sending Warren McVea in motion to the left while Frank Pitts raced down the right side, isolated on Nemiah Wilson. The strategy worked as Dawson hit Pitts in the clear. Wilson, badly beaten, recovered to make a saving tackle at the 1-yard line, but Wendell Hayes scored on the next play. The score was 7–7.

Stram was worried as he addressed his team during halftime. Still, he admitted later that "Pitts's catch had loosened us up a little. The noise of the crowd created confusion. Our players couldn't hear the automatics. At halftime, the line asked Lenny to call them out twice, once to each side."

The second half started badly for the Chiefs. George Atkinson fielded Stenerud's kickoff, picked up a wall of blockers, and ran it back 53 yards to the Chiefs' 45. Mixing a pass to Sherman with two runs by Smith, Lamonica took them to the Kansas City 26.

But the third and fourth quarters of this final AFL championship game were to produce some of the year's most dizzying shifts in momentum and luck. All week in Santa Barbara, the Chiefs had worked hard on an altered pass rush technique, sending Mays and Brown up the middle instead of along their normal outside lanes. This was the time to spring it, the Chiefs figured. They would give Lamonica the outside if he wanted it.

The gamble worked. Brown came crashing up the middle past a startled Bob Svihus and hurried Lamonica into an incompletion. That wasn't the worst of it for Oakland. On the pass, Lamonica drove his hand into Brown's helmet on the follow-through.

Lamonica kneaded the hand tenderly as he called the next play. He then missed Biletnikoff as the crowd groaned. Blanda attempted a 39-yard field goal on fourth down, but Lamonica bobbled a low snap and it was wide to the right.

Given this reprieve, the Chiefs should have taken charge. Instead Mike Garrett fumbled at the 33-yard line and the Raiders were again ready to put the game away. But again Brown stormed up the middle past Svihus. "Hell, I shut Brown off the last couple of games," the Raiders' tackle said in disgust. "Maybe I was a little lazy today. They were all coming hard and Daryle didn't have time."

Brown, who had spent his first years with the Chiefs being shuttled from position to position before settling at end in 1968, agreed. "Svihus had always been tough on me. He's talked to me in games before. He'd say stuff like, 'good rush,' or 'good play.' Today, he didn't say a word."

But Lamonica had spoken. Once he was seen shaking a fist at his offensive tackle on the sideline. The Raiders had total confidence in their passing game, but it had deserted them under the growing ferocity of the Chiefs' rush and blanket coverage in the secondary.

Lamonica gave way to Blanda but returned to finish the game. Later, Blanda would complain that he should have been left in. He also said the game plan had Biletnikoff stationed so wide that it was impossible to throw to him. Biletnikoff, the league's top receiver, never caught a pass, and he had only two directed his way all day.

After Garrett's fumble, Lamonica left the game with his injured hand. Afterward it was swollen and discolored. Blanda, replacing Lamonica with no warmup, missed an open Larry Todd. Then he was wide on a second field goal, this one from 40 yards out.

The Oakland defense, matching Kansas City's, held the Chiefs without a yard, and a 27-yard punt positioned the Raiders on the Kansas City side of the 50 for the third time in the quarter.

Lamonica was still in pain on the sideline as Blanda and the Raiders' offense came out. The crowd noise was deafening. A pass was incomplete. A screen gained nothing. On third down Blanda threw to Smith for a 23-yard gain to the Kansas City 24. The fans went wild.

On the next play Blanda went for the big one, trying to hit Wells in the endzone. Wells was open but he slipped on the 5-yard line and the ball was intercepted by Thomas in the endzone. Thomas ran it out to the 6.

"Hell, all Wells had to do was turn in on that play and it would have been a touchdown," Blanda said. "There was nobody there and he fell down."

So, for the third time in seven minutes, the Raiders had blown a chance to take the lead.

Now the Chiefs had the ball at their own 6. As the Oakland defense poured in, Robert Holmes barely escaped a safety, taking a four-yard loss to the 2-yard line.

On third down, Dawson retreated into his own endzone, ducking under another fierce blitz and buying an extra second. "I wanted to throw to Holmes over the middle, but they were knocking him all around. Then I saw Otis coming open upfield." Taylor had lined up in a camouflage slot on the right side between guard and tackle. Now he was angling toward the Chiefs' sideline with Wilson and Howie Williams in pursuit.

"That was one of my beauties," Dawson said facetiously of the arching floater, "but it looked real pretty when it was caught. I threw it so that it would go out of bounds if he couldn't get it."

In pro football, there are heated rivalries, and—on some even more torrid plane—there are games between the Kansas City Chiefs and the Oakland Raiders. A week after dispatching the New York Jets in a playoff game, the Chiefs met the Raiders for the AFL championship, the last ever to be played. Defensive end Aaron Brown (left, rushing Daryle Lamonica) played what may have been his finest game for the Chiefs. Robert Holmes scored the deciding touchdown (right). Kansas City won 17-7.

Taylor leaped and pulled the ball in at the Kansas City 37. Whether he caught it inbounds is still debated among the Raiders, but Dawson labeled it "a great call by the ref. I had to throw there. I didn't want us punting out of our endzone."

The pass ignited the Chiefs' offense. Holmes drove for 6 yards, then took a 23-yard pass to the Raiders' 34. From there a disputed interference call against Wilson on Taylor gave the Chiefs a first down at the 7. Three plays later Holmes scored, and the Chiefs had a 14–7 lead.

But the Chiefs had used up their offense. Three times in the fourth quarter – at their own 24, 31, and 13 – they fumbled the ball. The Raiders' offense sputtered, too. Trying to pass with the injured hand, Lamonica completed just 3 of 13 when he returned to the game. He also threw three interceptions. Thomas returned one interception 62 yards to set up a 22-yard Stenerud field goal with a little more than five minutes left, insuring a Chiefs' win.

The final score was Kansas City 17, Oakland 7.

The Chiefs were finally freed of the Oakland grip. "From my standpoint, I think this was our biggest victory ever," said Mays. "This was also the last AFL game that will ever be played. This will be the last Super Bowl in a strict sense. These two things make winning something special."

Stram called it the finest game he had ever seen Aaron Brown play. Brown, who couldn't wait for the game to begin, was credited with three sacks of Lamonica, plus seven unassisted tackles. The Raiders gained only 79 yards rushing and 154 yards passing as Lamonica and Blanda teamed to complete just 17 of 45, with four interceptions.

The Chiefs, with 20 fewer plays, had won it with their defensive stands and the two long drives. "I sure put our defense to the test today," Dawson sighed. "There were things about that game I wasn't too proud about." He was in a minority in the dressing room.

"We have a lot to be proud of," said owner Lamar Hunt. "Looking back over the years we've spent in the AFL, we've won three league championships. That is more than any other team. Buffalo and Houston each won two. Oakland won one, San Diego won one, and New York won one. That makes us the all-time AFL champions.

"Hank is the winningest AFL coach, and no team won a series from us. Oakland had a one-game lead over us going into today's game, but we tied it eleven-eleven. We also have the best preseason record and the best record against NFL teams. That's quite an accomplishment."

Kansas City	0	7	7	3	– 17
Oakland	7	0	0	0	– 7

Oak – Smith 3 run (Blanda kick)
KC – Hayes 1 run (Stenerud kick)
KC – Holmes 5 run (Stenerud kick)
KC – FG Stenerud 22

January 11, 1970

The first hint of potential crisis before Super Bowl IV had come while the Chiefs were on the West Coast to play Oakland for the 1969 AFL championship. The NFL learned that a major story was brewing. It involved a known gambler. And somehow it also involved Kansas City quarterback Len Dawson. A year earlier Dawson had voluntarily submitted to a lie detector test when the NFL learned a number of Kansas City games had been "taken off the board" by the nation's bookmakers. The test had exonerated Dawson.

This time, when questioned by Chiefs officials, Dawson said he could think of no reason why he was mentioned in the report. The incident was not released, and it was dismissed by the Chiefs. The Chiefs went on to beat the Raiders 17–7 to advance to Super Bowl IV, the last to match teams from rival leagues. After the game on January 11, 1970, the merger of the NFL and AFL would create one big happy family composed of two 13-team conferences.

The Chiefs flew into New Orleans on Monday night, January 5. A rain squall heralded a front that would keep temperatures unseasonably low all week. The next morning, the team turned out for a session of pictures and interviews.

Back in the team's hotel, the Fontainebleau on Tulane Avenue, Dawson was eating lunch when publicity man Jim Schaaf quietly took him aside. What Schaaf said left Dawson shaken. The National Broadcasting Company was about to use his name and those of some other athletes in connection with a story on the arrest of a Detroit gambler. The story would break later that day.

Dawson, shaken, went upstairs to Hank Stram's suite. Some of the other team officials also were there. They were on the phone, trying to obtain more details.

Then, late in the afternoon, the NBC Huntley-Brinkley report declared, "In Detroit a special Justice Department task force conducting what it described as the 'biggest gambling investigation of its kind ever,' is about to call seven professional football players and one college head coach to testify on their relationships with known gamblers, most notably Donald (Dice) Dawson of Detroit, who was arrested on New Year's Day with four hundred and fifty thousand dollars in checks and gambling records on him. Among the players scheduled to appear is Len Dawson, quarterback for the Kansas City Chiefs, who will play the Minnesota Vikings in the Super Bowl this Sunday."

Incredulous, Dawson sat to one side in the suite while Stram, owner Lamar Hunt, and security people from the league tried frantically to get more information.

Dawson, within days of what could be the most momentous game of his career, fought to retain his composure as he listened unbelievingly to the words coming from the television set in the suite.

The league's first reaction was to say nothing, but pressure grew as day turned to night. Reporters gathered at the special press suite that the Chiefs had established on one floor of their hotel. Schaaf sent out for some snacks. Upstairs, in Stram's suite, a statement was drafted, revised, and revised again.

Dawson came downstairs near midnight and, flanked by his coach, crossed the hall to the smoky room now crammed with writers and broadcasters.

The strain of the recent hours showed on Dawson's face as he read his statement: Yes, he knew Donald (Dice) Dawson but only casually. He had met him some 10 years earlier while playing in Pittsburgh. Dice Dawson had called him twice, each time to extend sympathy for events that had happened during the year. They were among many such calls. He had never had business dealings with Dice Dawson and had no

Vikings	0	0	7	0	7
Chiefs	3	13	7	0	23

idea why his name would be in the gambler's possession. Then, without submitting to questions, the quarterback went across the hall and back upstairs.

The next morning, Dawson reread the statement to his teammates. Stram asked if there were any questions. "Yeah," said center E. J. Holub. "Have our tickets come in yet?"

"When Lenny explained his side, we had no doubts whatever," one veteran said afterward. "We never had anyway. If you knew Lenny, you knew there was nothing to it."

His teammates were angry at what they considered the total injustice of the story.

Dawson endured a hard week. "Lenny said he's never been through anything like it," said his roommate, veteran safety Johnny Robinson. "I know it hit him real hard. It ate him up inside, and it looked to me as if he aged five years from Tuesday to Thursday."

The 1969 season had been rough on Dawson already. Early in the year, he had suffered a knee injury that kept him from starting five games. Almost on the eve of a critical game with New York, his father died; he had waited until after the game to fly back home for the funeral. Now he faced something he had no control over.

The initial practice was on Wednesday. The Chiefs began working on Stram's intriguing game plan. Dawson was subdued as he tried to pull himself together. At a noon press conference, reporters moved quickly into the gambling story, but their questions were squelched by Stram. Dawson avoided any further questions, but he was still getting calls at night.

"Let the guy alone," Robinson snapped at a caller who phoned the room he shared with Dawson. While Dawson stared at the ceiling sleeplessly that night, Robinson also tossed and turned. His problem was physical. He had torn some rib cartilage when he crashed into a wall during the Chiefs' 17–7 victory over Oakland the previous weekend. Even breathing pained him. Early in the week, he was still listed as doubtful for the Super Bowl.

Kansas City's problems almost seemed part of a pattern. The Chiefs had done everything the hard way that year. They had to call on an overworked defense to sustain them during the loss of Dawson. Then they had to fight their way up through the playoffs after finishing second, being forced to beat both the Jets and Oakland on the road. Now they were in New Orleans to face one of the most powerful teams the NFL had produced in its 50-year history.

Minnesota had won the NFL championship by beating 12 straight opponents, the longest single-season winning streak in 35 years. In three of the wins, the offense produced over 50 points. The Purple Gang's defense allowed only 133 points, a league record low.

Joe Kapp, the Minnesota quarterback, typified the bone-cracking image of the Vikings. "Other quarterbacks run out of bounds," said coach Bud Grant. "Kapp turned upfield and looked for a tackler to run into." Kapp was characterized as a man who played quarterback with faith and fury instead of finesse; he was a hungry gut fighter. Sometimes his passes wobbled or went end over end, but they seemed to get there. Against Cleveland, he ran over linebacker Jim Houston and knocked him out.

"Kapp was a great leader," said Kansas City captain Jerry Mays later. "I respect him as much as any guy I ever played against. He was a sorry passer and he really wasn't a smart quarterback. But he was a great leader, a real fireball. I hated to play against him. You could hear him on the sidelines and on the field, and you could see him on the field. You felt his presence no matter where he was. He'd look at you and challenge you with his eyes. He was always firing his players up. When I think of him, I think of his eyes."

Super Bowl IV...The Chiefs, battered 35-10 four years earlier by Green Bay, had made it back to ***the*** *game in professional football, this time to face the Minnesota Vikings. Len Dawson (left), calm and efficient, led the Chiefs. Joe Kapp (right), vocal and rowdy, directed Minnesota's Purple Gang. Defense was Minnesota's game, but the Chiefs knew of a weakness, and exploited it from the start, throwing quick, short passes such as the one below to Frank Pitts, in front of the Minnesota cornerbacks.*

Minnesota kept Kansas City away from the goal for a quarter-and-a-half, but Jan Stenerud kicked field goals of 48 (left), 32, and 25 yards. Meanwhile, short passes by Dawson to either sideline made the Vikings pass-conscious. The Chiefs then sent wide receiver Frank Pitts on a reverse (right) for 19 yards, setting up Stenerud's third field goal.

At 31, Kapp had come out of the Canadian Football League to become the catalyst of a team that had been reassembled by Grant. Grant had installed 15 new starters since taking over as head coach in 1967. By 1969 it had all meshed. The Vikings limited opponents to 79 yards a game rushing and 116 passing. Carl Eller, Alan Page, Jim Marshall, and Gary Larsen terrorized quarterbacks and runners. Their rush helped force 30 interceptions. Kapp's electric effect on the offense generated an attack that shattered Los Angeles's 11-game streak 23–20. The Vikings easily beat Cleveland 27–7 for the NFL title. Nine years after their inception, they were champions of the National Football League.

Stram and his staff watched film after film. The films were impressive but they also revealed imperfections. There were chinks in that awesome machine, and the Chiefs felt they could be exploited.

"All season long, they hadn't played anybody with an odd alignment," Mays said. "Mick Tingelhoff was a great, great center. He could go out and get a middle linebacker. But he couldn't handle a two hundred eighty-pound tackle on his nose."

Kansas City would use Buck Buchanan, a mobile mountain of a man, squarely in front of Tingelhoff. When defenses dictated that Buchanan be shifted, 265-pound Curley Culp would replace him. Together, Tingelhoff and Culp would shield middle linebacker Willie Lanier, who would become the cutting edge of the defense against Minnesota runners.

The film demonstrated that the Vikings had other shortcomings. "Their cornerbacks were great against a certain type of attack," Mays said, "but they couldn't handle those little curls and turn-ins that we had, and we knew it."

Kansas City's confidence grew as the week went on. The Chiefs' defense worked overtime looking at Minnesota films, running and rerunning them. The more they saw, the more they saw a way to win.

Meanwhile, Grant and his staff were admitting to a problem. "It's hard to plan for a team when you've only seen them in three films," Grant said. "We've got nine years of Bart Starr on film. All we know about the Chiefs is that their style is similar to the Dallas Cowboys'."

The teams were strikingly similar in one basic aspect. Both were highly physical. They had muscle. Kansas City had disguised theirs, however, with the myriad of formations Stram had refined over the decade.

The Chiefs, to be successful, knew they would need exceptional efforts from their offensive tackles (Jim Tyrer on the left and Dave Hill on the right). Hill had to contain Eller. Hill had faced Willie Davis in Super Bowl I and the memory lingered. "I still think about that game today," he said. "I think the biggest difference between our team now and then is experience. I was all shook up before that game. Hell, I was going in against a guy who'd been all-pro for years – I'd seen Willie Davis play when I was a kid."

Stram had seen enough films to convince him there was a method the Chiefs could use to exploit the Minnesota defense. They would throw short, under the deep zone umbrella that had bothered so many NFL teams. They would remain patient and take what the zone offered. But to do that, to open the passing lanes to those quick little "curls and turn-ins" Mays had referred to, Hill and Tyrer would have to chop down Eller and Jim Marshall, with help from the blocking backs. "We can't let them come in with their hands up," Stram cautioned.

The Chiefs were confident they could control Kapp on defense. Obscured in all the attention paid to Kansas City's flamboyant offense was the fact that the Chiefs' defense was just as

devastating in the AFL as Minnesota's was in the NFL. Kansas City had finished the regular season as the leader in 17 of 24 defensive categories. They had permitted only 190 points, and they had choked off seven opponents to no more than a touchdown.

The Vikings opened the week as 13½-point favorites. Oakland quarterback George Blanda recalled that Baltimore had been an 18-point favorite a year earlier before being upset by the Jets. "I think they're doing it again," Blanda said. "They haven't learned a thing. They're underestimating the AFL all over again."

By game day, Dawson's brush with scandal was almost forgotten. He was never called to testify and the entire investigation eventually died. Nevertheless, it had its effect. Dawson, beset by nerves and tension, slept very little that week.

All week the temperatures had hovered near or below freezing, frosting the windows of the Old Absinthe House. The night before the game, red-hatted Chiefs fans and purple-hatted Vikings fans taunted each other across crowded, roped-off Bourbon Street.

Near morning, the weather changed. A warm front moved through, triggering a series of thunderstorms, and the early traffic to Tulane Stadium was a mess.

At the stadium Stram was being wired for sound by NFL Films, which would record his sideline comments during the game. As the teams lined up for the kickoff, Stram said:

"Get it up in the air, Jan . . . Let's go boys. Hey, let's go men. Pop it out of that endzone, Jan. C'mon . . . get it up in the air, get it up in the air."

Stenerud did get it up in the air. The kick sailed deep into the endzone and Minnesota took over on the 20. Kapp trotted out. Four minutes later, he trotted off. Minnesota had failed to score and now it was Kansas City's turn.

With Dawson alternately throwing short to the side and sending Mike Garrett and Robert Holmes on three- and four-yard bursts, the Chiefs moved to the Vikings' 36-yard line. Then Roy Winston threw Dawson for a loss and Page deflected a pass. Stalled, the Chiefs brought on Stenerud, who proceeded to set a Super Bowl record with a 48-yard field goal. The Chiefs led 3–0.

The Chiefs' offense was settling into the game plan nicely. Stram:

"We're catching 'em moving. We're catching 'em moving a little bit . . . they're not ready for that quick count . . . look at 'em running around . . . they didn't know where Mike was . . . they didn't know where he was. . . . They didn't know where to go . . . Kassulke was running around there like it was a Chinese fire drill . . . they look like they're flat as hell . . . "

It was working out just as well on defense. "Our big advantage was that their offense was the kind that our defense was strongest against," said Mays later. "And they would not vary their game plan. They came out and ran into our strength. Every time the defense went in, the coaches would warn us, 'Now wait a minute. We're running that triple stack, but we'll probably have to shift to under. Sooner or later it's going to dawn on them that they can run the same offense to the weakside and make yardage.' So we'd go out for another series, get in our defensive huddle and warn each other, 'Be prepared for a weakside attack.' And it would come strongside, strongside, strongside."

Stubbornly, perhaps not wanting to believe this could be happening to them, the Vikings stuck to their game plan. Dave Osborn and Bill Brown kept slamming into walls of crimson-shirted Chiefs. The Vikings did not gain a single first down rushing in the opening half. Tingelhoff did not reach Lanier.

"For some reason, we were out-hit that day,"

Kapp, the fearless Vikings' commander, found no place to go as Jerry Mays, Curley Culp, and Buck Buchanan hemmed him in (left). Mike Garrett scored Kansas City's first touchdown on a five-yard run (below, left), then hurdled into the arms of well-wishers on the joyous Kansas City sideline.

22
89

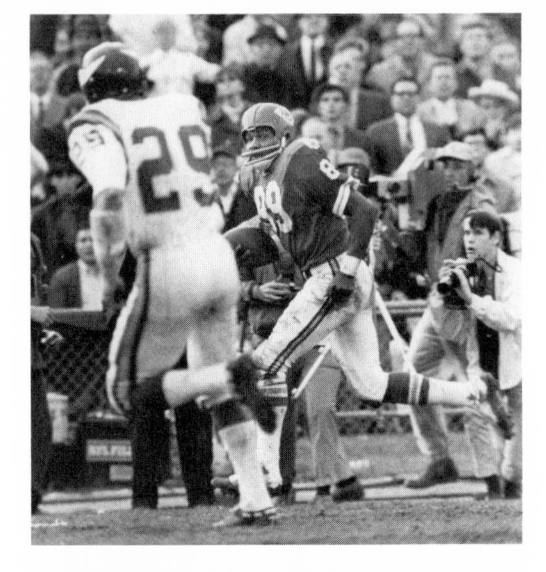
29

22

Wide receiver Otis Taylor made one of the most remarkable runs in Super Bowl history, and assured victory in game IV for Kansas City, when he caught Len Dawson's pass and flowed 46 yards past Vikings defenders Earsell Mackbee (46), Paul Krause (22), and Karl Kassulke (29) for the game's last score. Dave Hill embraced Taylor after the touchdown. Minnesota's final threat was choked off, as Buck Buchanan caught up with Bill Brown (right).

Bill Brown said four years later as he prepared for the Vikings' second Super Bowl game. "After we beat Cleveland, we were ready to play the Super Bowl that very night. We were ready Monday and Tuesday and Wednesday, too. But by Sunday, we'd been up for the game all week. We kind of went flat after the first part of the game. We didn't have the spark we should have."

Osborn and Brown, who had netted more than 1,000 yards between them in 1969, accounted for 22 yards during that first 30 minutes. Kapp added 2 more. On the sideline Stram spoke to Dawson:

"He can't cover that thing, Lenny. Throw it anytime, that hitch on the outside. That's a good time to throw it right there, you see?"

Dawson saw. He had waited a long time for this chance.

Unused by Pittsburgh, ignored at Cleveland, and rusted by five years of disuse, he had finally won his parole from the NFL. He had joined Stram and the Texans in 1962, just in time to lead them to their first championship. He had become what Stram proudly summarized as "the most accurate passer in football."

Now he proved that he was one of the most patient. Working the sidelines, he again moved the Chiefs into field goal range. Stenerud made it 6–0.

"See, that stuff in front is like stealin'. We gotta do it more, do more of it."

Six of Dawson's seven first-half completions were short ones.

"That's it . . . that's the one . . . they can't cover that in a million years . . . no way in the world they can cover that stuff. . . . See that's like stealin' over there, double team those ends . . . keep them down so we can throw over the top . . ."

Minnesota's frustration was beginning to show. "Eller was trying to hurt Lenny," Dave Hill said later. "One time Eller pounced on Lenny after he'd already handed the ball off, knowing Lenny didn't have it. That was a cheap shot. . . . Another time Alan Page punched Lenny when he was down. That's high school stuff. . . ."

"C'mon, Lenny. . . . Pump it in there, baby. . . . Just keep matriculatin' that ball down the field, boys. . . . Keep negotiatin' that ball right down the field. . . ."

If Dawson had been plagued by nerves earlier, they were gone now. Despite four busted plays and an interception by Paul Krause, Dawson guided his team to a 9–0 lead as Stenerud kicked still another field goal. "The first one meant a lot to me," Stenerud said. "It gave us a lead, and it may have settled us down a little bit. The second didn't mean so much but the third one also helped because it made it nine to nothing. That meant that a touchdown wouldn't put Minnesota ahead. The winds weren't bad that day, but there were some soft spots on the field. It had rained all morning. The field had been covered, but there were spots around the seams where the rain leaked through.

"My third field goal [from 25 yards out] was right in the middle of a wet spot," said Stenerud. "I had long mud cleats on. I was scared that I would slip. . . ."

It was on the kickoff after Stenerud's third field goal that the game's first breakthrough occurred.

"We break 'em down with these threes and then we get on the board with some big ones."

Stenerud's kickoff sailed toward Charlie West, who was waiting at the goal line. Either West misjudged the ball or a sudden gust of wind – it hit 14 miles an hour at times out of the south –held the ball up. West was forced to take a lunging step at the 10-yard line. He fumbled, and the ball bounded upfield to the 19, straight at the onrushing wave of Chiefs.

Remi Prudhomme covered it, and the Chiefs

were finally poised for that "big one" Stram wanted. On the first play Marshall poured in to catch Dawson for an 8-yard loss, but Dawson recovered quickly, launching Wendell Hayes on a 13-yard draw play to the Vikings' 14. There, on third and 5, Dawson returned to the proven formula – Taylor and the quick pass. The play took the Chiefs to a first down at the 4-yard line. Then Garrett lost a yard, and on the second down, Dawson had to eat the ball on the fourth broken play of the half. Another third down.

". . . Sixty-five toss power trap. Look for sixty-five power trap . . . they might pop it wide open. . . . IT'S IN THERE . . . YAH HA'! . . . WAS THAT THERE? Yaaah! . . . sixty-five toss power trap, yaaah, ha ha ha ha . . . I told ya that baby would be there. . . .Yessir, boys, yahoo! . . . was that there, boys? The old mentor? The coach pumped that in there, boys."

Garrett, as Tyrer lured Marshall a half turn into a wipeout block by guard Mo Moorman, raced down a wide lane on the left side and into the endzone, scoring the first touchdown of the game. The Chiefs led 16–0.

Garrett said it was the first time the play had worked for a touchdown all season. It was a daring play. If the defensive end ignored Tyrer's fake pull, it was no go. "When we ran it against Oakland, Tom Keating was standing there and just beat on me like a drum," Garrett said.

It was halftime. In the Kansas City dressing room Stram cautioned, "Thirty minutes more and we're world champions. Play control ball."

In the second half, after a holding penalty stopped a Kansas City drive, Kapp finally went to work. He began to demonstrate why he and the Vikings had been accorded so many honors. Kapp had refused the Vikings' most valuable player honors at a banquet earlier. "There is no most valuable Viking," he declared. "There is no Santa Claus, and there isn't any red-nosed reindeer either."

The drive began slowly. After Culp stopped Bill Brown at left tackle, Kapp switched to the air, hitting tight end John Beasley for 15 yards at the Minnesota 46. Brown wedged out 2 yards. Then Kapp, back to pass, ran for 7. At third and one, Minnesota was at the Kansas City 45-yard line and moving at last.

"What in hell's going on out there?"

Osborn, going off left tackle, just made the yard. It was Minnesota's first first down by rushing. The purple hats and pennants in the stands came alive. The Vikings were coming back.

Within four plays Kapp had taken his team to the 4-yard line. From there Osborn rammed over a pile at right tackle, making it 16–7.

There were nearly 20 minutes still left in the game, and on the Kansas City sideline the concern was evident.

"Hey, make sure now. . . . Pick out somebody and block, bring this ball back for us. Let's put out that fire. . . . Lissen, Lenny, again, first down, throw that hitch or square out. . . . They haven't come close to covering it."

Slowly, the Chiefs worked their way upfield, using Frank Pitts on a reverse for the third time in the game. For the third time Pitts netted a first down. Barely. Stram called to the official, pointing to a spot on the sideline chalk.

"Here it is. Move it up a little bit. My God, look where the front of his foot is and where you put the ball."

The official signaled a first down.

"You did good. You did good. You did a helluva job! Nice going! Great job! That's an excellent call. Those officials are doing a helluva job. . . . Was that reverse there, boys? It was there, wasn't it? It was there, wasn't it?"

On the next play Dawson overthrew Pitts, but a personal foul was called on Wally Hilgenberg, moving the ball to the Minnesota 46. Then came the play of the game.

"It was only a six-yard B pass," Taylor would

Hank Stram waved the rolled-up program that was his trademark as the Chiefs carried him off the field after the triumph (left). Len Dawson, exonerated by his play from unnerving pregame charges that he had consorted with gamblers, talked to reporters (right) after he was named the outstanding player.

say later. But that hardly told the story. The play looked simple enough, a pass from Dawson to Taylor into the right flat. It was simple but it wasn't routine. Taylor turned it into a spectacular run, twisting out of Earsell Mackbee's attemped tackle at the 40 and taking off for the goal with long, powerful strides. Only Karl Kassulke stood between Taylor and the endzone. Kassulke had a shot at the 10 but Taylor swept the Viking aside and strode into the endzone. The score was now 23–7.

Only 3 minutes, 10 seconds after Kapp had breathed hope into the Vikings, Dawson and Taylor had snuffed it out. Aaron Brown and the defense would take care of the rest. Two fourth-quarter interceptions, one by Lanier, the other by Robinson, plus a crushing tackle by Brown that sent Kapp to the sideline, erased Minnesota's final hopes.

Three plays from the finish, Mike Livingston was summoned to Stram's side.

"Go in for Lenny."

Dawson trotted off to a thunderous ovation.

"Nice going Len. Good going."

Then the countdown:

Six . . . five . . . four . . . three . . . two . . . one . . .that's it . . . world champions! . . . world champions! . . . we're world champions!"

Kansas City had erased the awful taste of Super Bowl I.

Dawson set a Super Bowl record by throwing only 17 passes. But he also set a record by completing 70.7 percent of them. Garrett, Holmes, Warren McVea, and Hayes had gained 151 yards against the Purple People Eaters. The Vikings finished with only 67.

"The Chiefs' defensive line looked like a redwood forest," said Kapp. "They took the running game away from us. We went into the game wanting to run the ball, and their defense was able to take it away. They didn't do a lot different defensively than we had anticipated. We were well prepared. It was our intention to stay away from Bobby Bell's side of the field as much as we could. But that line – like a redwood forest in California – just seemed to block things out sometimes."

Brown, Buchanan, Culp, and Mays, backed by Bell, Lanier, and Lynch, with Marsalis, Thomas, Kearney, and Robinson deep, had done everything asked.

There remained one final accolade.

"Lenny Dawson," said Minnesota coach Grant, "is very much underrated."

Dawson managed one final, tired smile. "The good thing about this game," he said, "is that we don't have to answer for it for the next three years as we did the last time."

Minnesota	0	0	7	0	– 7
Kansas City	3	13	7	0	– 23

KC – FG Stenerud 48
KC – FG Stenerud 32
KC – FG Stenerud 25
KC – Garrett 5 run (Stenerud kick)
Minn – Osborn 4 run (Cox kick)
KC – Taylor 46 pass from Dawson (Stenerud kick)

December 25, 1971

It was a balmy Christmas afternoon in 1971. For 59 minutes and 25 seconds, the Kansas City Chiefs and the Miami Dolphins had been locked in a game that the Chiefs were never quite able to put out of reach. Each time, the Dolphins had come back. The last time Bob Griese had thrown a tying touchdown to Marv Fleming with less than two minutes left to play.

Momentarily stunned, the Kansas City fans were brought roaring to their feet when Ed Podolak took the ensuing kickoff and burst 78 yards down the sideline. Only a desperate shove by Garo Yepremian kept the one-time Iowa quarterback from scoring and ending it there.

Carefully, Len Dawson used two low-risk plays to position the ball almost directly in front of the goal posts, 25 yards out. The Chiefs called time with 35 seconds left. A familiar figure tugged on his red helmet and began trotting toward his waiting teammates.

Jan Stenerud, the Norwegian ski jumper turned placekicker, was going on the field for the forty-third time in 1971 to try a 32-yard field goal. Stenerud was the holder of pro football's record of 16 straight field goals. He was the AFC scoring leader in 1970. He was the man who had kicked three field goals in Super Bowl IV. Stenerud meant security. The Chiefs were sure that they were home free. It had taken longer than they thought against the pesky Dolphins, but now it was almost finished.

In the bedlam that was Kansas City Municipal Stadium at that moment, there was no doubt the game was finally about to end. The Chiefs would advance to the AFC title game.

Right tackle Dave Hill heard the impact of Stenerud's foot and relaxed his fight. He had kept his Miami adversary from blocking the field goal try. Simultaneously both teams turned to watch the flight of the ball.

As Hill watched the kick, he sucked in his breath in growing disbelief. Instead of taking the little hook most soccer-style kickers produce, the ball hung tantalizingly outside the right upright. It was still outside, wide by inches, when it passed by the upright.

A roar had risen when Stenerud hit the ball. It was now a groan. He had missed! Incredibly, from a range that for him was almost automatic.

Chicago Today columnist Rick Talley happened to be on the sideline at that moment. He described it this way:

"Adrian Burk, the back judge, fidgeted near the goal-line flag. He finally turned to a bystander and blurted, 'Jeez, this is turning into a helluva football game.'

"The Kansas City Chiefs equipment manager Bobby Yarborough knelt on the sideline before the beginning of overtime. He was praying.

"A pale Jan Stenerud stood alone, his head down. Teammate Ed Budde, mud and blood streaked across the number on his red jersey, stormed toward the bench, his face contorted. Stenerud had missed the 32-yard field goal with just 31 seconds to play. All guard Budde could say was, 'Dammit . . . dammit . . . dammit.'"

The 50,374 spectators were now about to witness just the fourth overtime game in pro history. In the first one, in 1958, the New York Giants and Baltimore Colts fought into overtime to settle the National Football League championship. In 1962, the Chiefs (then the Dallas Texans) went 77 minutes and 54 seconds before Tommy Brooker's field goal beat the Houston Oilers for the AFL title. In 1965, Green Bay edged Baltimore on a Don Chandler field goal after 14 minutes and 39 seconds of sudden death for the NFL Western Conference title. Now, it was about to happen again.

History has a bizarre way of creating improbable matchups. The Miami-Kansas City matchup that Christmas Day was one of the most improbable. Just five years earlier, Miami had come into the AFL as the league's first

Dolphins	0	10	7	7	0	3	27
Chiefs	10	0	7	7	0	0	24

expansion team. Its biggest name was Flipper, a dolphin. Flipper, a television celebrity, worked on game days in a tank in the Orange Bowl endzone.

Miami's early history was turbulent, struggling, shoestring – and losing. From a 3–11 record in 1966, the Dolphins "progressed" to 4–10, 5–8, and 3–10–1. During that period, the Dolphins lost six straight times to Kansas City by a cumulative score of 216–47. Four games were shutouts.

Gradually, though, the Dolphins emerged. In 1970 the club brought in Don Shula, the man who had coached the Baltimore Colts to a succession of winning seasons. Shula immediately turned the Dolphins around. Bob Griese, the struggling quarterback, became a cool tactician. Larry Csonka, an oft-injured fullback, became a line-busting terror. Paul Warfield, the incomparable receiver, came aboard from Cleveland to supply the speed. The tools were there – Nick Buoniconti, Larry Little, Jake Scott and the rest – and Shula employed them masterfully, transforming a rag-tag expansion team into a 10–4 playoff team. It lost the playoff to Oakland but its promise was obvious. Now in 1971, after a 10–3–1 season, Miami dreams were all but realized as its defense prepared for the fifth quarter on Christmas Day.

The day had begun with early morning fog, but the sun had broken through by the time the clubs lined up for the kickoff. It was almost balmy at 63 degrees, a temperature more typical of Miami than Kansas City.

Yepremian, who had learned the night before that Stenerud had been voted into the Pro Bowl even though he (Yepremian) had led the league in scoring with 117 points, had spent Christmas eve playing cards in his hotel room. Shortly before kickoff, he walked over and congratulated Stenerud. Yepremian's best wishes were genuine, but he was a powerfully motivated man when the showdown got under way.

Kansas City, moving each time it had the ball, spurted to a 10–0 lead, but the Dolphins came back to tie. Once, in the second quarter, the Chiefs were poised at the Dolphins' 22, and Stenerud lined up for a 29-yard field goal.

"The center [Bobby Bell] was to snap the ball to me, and I was to run around right end," Stenerud recalled. "But somehow he got mixed up on the call. The ball came back like a normal kick, and I kicked it. It was kind of unexpected, both for me and Lenny, and I missed. Miami was really overloaded to one side. Remember, that was when they didn't have the hashmarks so close. This was the perfect situation in which to run. They didn't expect me to run with the ball. This was the right hashmark, and they were overloading on the opposite side.

"Bell told me later that he didn't think that I heard the audible call. The ball came back like a normal kick, and I can remember Lenny yellin' 'Kick it!' I was halfway in motion to run. It looked like a normal kick, I guess. We just missed it by a couple inches to the right."

It was that kind of day.

Tied 10–10 at halftime, the Chiefs moved ahead again at 17–10. Then each team scored another touchdown. The Chiefs were leading 24–17 when Griese marched the Dolphins down the field. With 1:26 left to play, he completed a 76-yard touchdown drive, throwing to Fleming for the final 5 yards.

It was after this that Stenerud missed the field goal that would have won it all. Linebacker Jim Lynch still remembers the kick.

"I was on the wing, and looked downfield toward the goal posts, and those uprights looked about that far apart to me," says Lynch, holding his thumb and forefinger an inch apart. "And it got smaller and smaller.

"I knew it wasn't good. I had a good angle, but I really had to look. Jan allowed for the

The Chiefs and the Miami Dolphins played a marathon game on Christmas day, 1971, that would propel the Dolphins to three consecutive Super Bowls and send the Chiefs reeling into three seasons of relative mediocrity. The score in the divisional playoff game was tied 24-24 after four quarters. Coach Hank Stram watched (left) as a coin toss (below left) started sudden-death overtime. Rival quarterbacks Bob Griese (12) and Len Dawson (16) watched the flip. Running back Ed Podolak was a spectacular performer for the Chiefs; before the game ended, he had totaled 350 yards, including a 78-yard kickoff return (right) in the fourth quarter.

wind, and there was none. People looking from our bench thought it was good."

Stenerud, the carefully concealed Norwegian accent surfacing in a "ve" on occasion, said later, "There was no question in my mind that I was going to make it, and I still don't know to this day how I missed it. I hit the ball perfectly. I hit the ball firm and well.

"There was hardly any wind at all. The turf, especially at that spot, was pretty good. The angle was unusual, though. It wasn't in the middle, and it wasn't on the hashmark. It was kind of in-between. So I still think the only thing I could have done wrong, maybe, was line it up a little wrong. You know soccer-style kickers, we have a little angle. I hit the ball real well. It was straight, high, and nice, and since I was only three or four inches to the outside, it may have been a mental mistake, where I lined up a little bit wrong."

On the sideline, as the teams rested before moving into overtime, there was no place for Stenerud to hide. Coach Hank Stram had patted him on the rump as he came off the field following the miss. What could be said?

The coin toss for the fifth quarter went to Kansas City, just as it had gone to the Texans back in the 1962 overtime against Houston. But this time, the Chiefs wanted the football first.

"Otis – get open!" defensive tackle Buck Buchanan shouted at Taylor as the Chiefs' offensive unit buckled on chin straps and trotted out after the kickoff. But Taylor couldn't find an opening. The Chiefs' game-breaker, one of the heroes of Super Bowl IV, was a marked man. He finished with only three catches for 12 yards.

Miami safety Dick Anderson had an explanation. "When they had Taylor and Elmo Wright on the same side," said Anderson, "I took Otis and hit him. Then I stayed with him. If he broke out, I'd go with him. If he broke in, I'd turn him over to a linebacker. Then I'd try to find out

The two teams punched away at each other until the game became the longest ever—82 minutes, 40 seconds. Jan Stenerud, whom the Chiefs had trusted in dozens of previous pressure situations, failed on a fourth-quarter kick that would have won the game, and had a sixth-quarter attempt blocked (left). His counterpart with the Dolphins, Garo Yepremian, turned the marathon into a Chiefs' nightmare with a decisive 37-yard field goal.

where Elmo was and react to Dawson's eyes."

The Chiefs' offense moved past midfield, again into range for Stenerud. This one was a 42-yarder. The Dolphins didn't give Stenerud a chance to miss this one. Buoniconti blocked it. Later, Yepremian was wide left from 52 yards as the fifth quarter wound down. The quarter closed as Miami's Jake Scott intercepted a pass intended for Wright.

After another short intermission, the sixth quarter began. Obviously the game could not continue much longer. Like punched-out fighters, the two clubs faced each other in the floodlit arena. For 75 minutes, long past dark, the teams had torn and clawed at each other. Something had to end it.

On its first possession in the sixth quarter, Kansas City failed to sustain a drive. Jerrel Wilson punted 50 yards to Scott, who made a fair catch at the Miami 30.

All day, Lanier, Lynch, and Bell had been effective in shutting down Miami's outside running attack. Each time a Miami back started wide, the linebackers fled with him. Now they were to pay a penalty for success.

"We have a lot of plays we like," Griese explained later. "At the time, preparing for the huddle, I was going over them in my mind. There was one play we hadn't called, and I thought it would work. Csonka liked it, and, besides, they had been killing us on end sweeps."

What Griese came up with was the Csonka Special, a misdirection play. It started from the Miami 35. Miami's flow was to the right and Kansas City's linebackers responded. But Csonka cut back, got past Buchanan, and ran 29 yards through a hole off the left side to the Chiefs' 36-yard line.

Three running plays took the Dolphins to the 30. On came Yepremian. On the sideline, Stenerud's agony grew. Eighty-two minutes of play had left the turf rough and torn. Karl Noonan, the Miami holder, smoothed a tiny patch where he would place the ball.

The kick was true. Yepremian, starting to trot off, turned at the last minute to watch his historic accomplishment.

After 82 minutes and 40 seconds, it was Miami 27, Kansas City 24. The Chiefs had lost the last game they would play in their old stadium.

In the Miami dressing room, fatigue was mixed with the joy of winning. Csonka and Jim Kiick sat down for a half hour before they had enough energy to begin undressing.

Griese admitted his fatigue. "When I saw Noonan signal that Garo's field goal was good I broke out laughing," said Griese. "I just laughed. I was so tired."

In the dressing room afterward, Stenerud did not try to hide. "It's unbearable. It's totally unbearable," he said. "I have no idea what I'm going to do now. I feel like hiding. I don't feel like ever playing football again."

Podolak's performance was one of the most memorable in the history of the Chiefs. He accounted for 350 yards, 100 each by rushing and receiving, an additional 150 on returns.

"I suppose," said Stenerud two years later, "that if you look at it from an unselfish point of view, it was a fantastic game. But in my mind, it does not stick out as a great football game. It will stick out as a personal disaster."

Miami	0	10	7	7	0	3 – 27
Kansas City	10	0	7	7	0	0 – 24

KC – FG Stenerud 24
KC – Podolak 7 pass from Dawson (Stenerud kick)
Mia – Csonka 1 run (Yepremian kick)
Mia – FG Yepremian 14
KC – Otis 1 run (Stenerud kick)
Mia – Kiick 1 run (Yepremian kick)
KC – Podolak 3 run (Stenerud kick)
Mia – Fleming 5 pass from Griese (Yepremian kick)
Mia – FG Yepremian 37

The Men

Buck Buchanan

Position: Defensive Tackle
Years: 1963-
Height: 6-7
Weight: 270
College: Grambling

Junious (Buck) Buchanan's father, a 235-pound steel worker in Birmingham, Alabama, once worried that his son would turn out to be the runt of the family.

He needn't have troubled himself. His son grew into such a physical and athletic specimen that he was the first player chosen in the 1963 AFL draft. At 6 feet 7 inches and weighing nearly 280 pounds, blessed with immense physical gifts, Buchanan came to the Dallas Texans just as the signing war between the National and American Football Leagues neared the runaway stage.

Buchanan had been a freshman at Grambling the year Ernie Ladd was a senior. He originally went to Grambling to play basketball. "I didn't care for football in high school," he said. "The only reason I played football during my junior and senior years was because the basketball coach wanted me to stay in shape."

He reported to Grambling at 212 pounds and left weighing 281. "I did some weight lifting, but mainly they just fed me well," he said. "In college I used to eat six eggs and seven or eight pieces of toast for breakfast." That did not break the Grambling eating record. Ladd held that with 56 pancakes at one sitting.

A decade later, Buchanan would be recognized as one of pro football's finest defensive tackles. A member of the College All-Star team that upset Green Bay in 1963, he went on to play in six AFL All-Star games and two Pro Bowl games.

You were the first player taken in the 1963 AFL draft. That must have put a lot of pressure on you.

I suppose, but it didn't bother me. I think the thing that sold me on my ability as a player was playing in the Crusade Bowl in Baltimore. There were players from other areas – the Big Ten, the Big Eight, and the Pacific Eight. We had a couple of practice sessions, and these guys' fundamentals weren't as good as mine. I was as fast or faster than most of them, too. I knew then I could compete. But when I came to camp I had gained so much weight that I had a tough time getting in condition. Coach Stram used to work me every afternoon after practice.

You were huge in your early years as a pro. Was it by choice?

I thought you had to be big. When I signed I weighed two-hundred-seventy-two pounds. When I reported to camp I was up to two-hundred-ninety-six. I was working out constantly, but my wife would cook. I was so tired that I'd just go home, eat, and sleep. I played at anywhere from two-hundred-eighty-six to two-hundred-ninety-two pounds for six or seven years. Then three or four years ago I had my tonsils out. I lost weight and didn't put it back.

Green Bay drafted you a year early, thinking you'd been a redshirt. Were you disappointed when they didn't draft you again?

Not at all. They made it sound as if they'd be doing me a favor by drafting me. Everything was National Football League this and National Football League that. I just wanted to go where I could play right away. So what happens? I went to Dallas and didn't play there. The team moved to Kansas City my rookie year.

Were there any feelings that you were going with a second-class league?

Not really, I just thought that was the place for me to go to develop as a football player. I thought the leagues would merge eventually anyway.

Why weren't you an immediate starter?

Paul Rochester, Jerry Mays, Mel Branch, and Bobby Bell were the starters then. I missed the first four games. Then Bell got hurt against San Diego, and they put me in at defensive end. I've been starting ever since. They had drafted me as a defensive end, but I wanted to play offensive tackle in pro ball. I thought I had been a pretty

99

As a player for the San Diego Chargers, Ernie Ladd (left) gave Buck Buchanan of the Chiefs some lessons in the secrets of defensive line play. Ladd continued his instruction of Buchanan after Ladd was traded to Kansas City. At 6 feet 9 inches and 290 pounds, Ladd was one of the biggest players in football history. Billy Shaw (right) of the Buffalo Bills was, in Buchanan's opinion, one of the great blockers of the American Football League. Ron Mix (far right) of the San Diego Chargers blocked Buchanan consistently during the first game Buck ever played.

good offensive player while I was in college.

When you, Bell, Ed Budde, and the others met that first summer did you sense that this was the group that could win a championship?

As far as Bell was concerned, I just thought about his size. He was a heck of an athlete, but he came to camp weighing only two-hundred-ten pounds. That isn't very big. He wanted to play linebacker, and they were playing him at defensive end. He was very, very small for that position. Budde was big and probably the best-looking lineman we had in the Chicago All-Star camp. I *knew* he was going to play. Once I got to camp and saw Dave Hill, Jerrel Wilson, Charlie Diamond, and Charley Warner, I knew we had a good nucleus.

But it took four years for the Chiefs to become a championship team again. Why?

It just seemed that we couldn't get any momentum going. At the end of the 1963 season we began to realize the kind of team we had. We knew it was just a matter of time.

What difference did Willie Lanier and Jim Lynch make defensively?

A great difference. When they came in, they were both middle linebackers. As I looked at them, the first thing I thought was that Lanier should be the middle linebacker. He was more of a headhunter, a vicious tackler. Lynch was more of a finesse player. We went through camp with both of them at middle linebacker. Then we had a meeting on the field and Stram moved Lynch to the outside. That was all we needed. They're both very smart; they're both students of the game. Linebacking became the key to our game.

With your size and reputation, it was expected that you'd win almost every matchup even as a rookie. What happened?

I found out you really have to have the experience, that somebody forgot to tell the other guy that I was supposed to beat him every time.

Did somebody take you apart that season?

Yes, in San Diego, in the first game I ever played. Ron Mix, a great offensive lineman, was hitting me before I got out of my stance, and I couldn't figure out what was wrong. He wasn't overpowering me, but he was blocking me constantly. Coach Stram finally took me out. Of course Mix did the same to my replacement. He taught me a lot that day. It takes more than brute strength. You have to be a smart player, and from that time on, that's what I tried to be.

Have you learned more from offensive linemen across from you or teammates next to you?

I learned most from Ernie Ladd. He was a big, powerful guy, but he'd tell me things like, "Buck, you can't beat a guy just by overpowering him. You've got to have some tricks." He'd show me different things. When the team started playing the overshift, and I started playing over the center, he showed me a step that prevented the center from blocking me, especially one on one.

You and Ernie weren't even teammates at the time, were you?

No, he was at San Diego. But we'd been great friends for a long time. We were teammates at Grambling in 1960. Whenever we went to San Diego, he'd meet the plane, take me out to his house, and have me in the down stance, coaching me. I didn't resent it at all.

Who are the best linemen you've ever worked against?

When I first came up, I thought the best was Billy Shaw of Buffalo – a great player. Shaw had great quickness and speed. He could come out, pop you, and get back. He could cut you. He could pull. I'll never forget an incident in Buffalo in the 1966 championship game. I'd faked Billy to my right and started my inside move. I really had him out of position. I'd been going outside all day, so I gave him the outside fake and was coming back when he stepped out,

and knocked me dizzy. For about three or four plays, I was out of my head. He hit me that hard. There are others too. The hardest hitting was Bob Talamini of Houston. When he hit you, you felt it all the way to your toes. Gene Upshaw at Oakland was another one.

When you've gone against someone like Upshaw twice a year for seven years, there can't be much he can do that you haven't seen before.

True, but it doesn't matter if you're on your game and moving well. Sometimes you just feel great and everything goes your way.

Is there any one series of plays in all those games that stands out in your mind?

Yes, near the goal line against New York in a playoff game. Every play was such a big one that I'll never forget any of them. They were ready to score, but we weren't going to let them. Willie Lanier was yelling, "C'mon, Red, they're not going to score . . . no way, no way." We were aroused to the point that we *knew* they weren't going to make it, and they didn't. Another satisfying series was in Oakland. We went back every time saying, "They can't score, they can't score, they can't score." It's a funny thing. That championship kind of feeling, a feeling that nobody can beat you. It's hard to explain. I'm sure Miami had those kind of feelings in the Super Bowls. You know you're going out on the field and win.

Did you have that kind of feeling in the first Super Bowl?

No, a lot of our guys didn't think that we could beat Green Bay. Maybe the name Lombardi scared them. Maybe the name Jim Taylor, or Bart Starr. I don't know. I wasn't afraid though and neither was Bobby Bell. We'd played against them in the All-Star game and beaten them. But I think that, as a whole, our guys felt we couldn't win.

Fred Williamson made a lot of statements the week of the game. Later he said that he was trying to distract you from the Green Bay legend. Did what he said bother you?

I was so keyed up for the game that I didn't care what Fred said. I respected him. I never found a guy who worked as hard. I couldn't keep up with him. I've seen him run thirty-five or forty one-hundred-yard dashes back to back. A lot of people can't do that. I mean *work.* I thought Fred had a good game. As you know, he got knocked out, but I can't recall their catching a touchdown pass over him.

What do you remember most about that game?

Willie Mitchell and I, coming down the tunnel. We'd both been crying because of things that had been said about our league. That it was Mickey Mouse. Willie and I were holding hands and consoling each other going down the tunnel.

After the game?

No, *before* the game. I'd never been that emotional before a game. I really felt I could have hurt somebody and been glad I'd done it. I don't normally feel that way. Football's a game. I love to play and to win, but not to the point of hurting somebody. But at that time, I really wanted to hurt someone. On one play Elijah Pitts carried the ball, and when I hit him I said, "You can't run this hole here, man!" He said, "I'll be coming back." I said, "Every time you come back, dammit, I'll be right here waitin' on you." We kept it up throughout the game.

What was different about your emotional approach to that game and your approach to the Super Bowl against Minnesota?

We'd played Minnesota before, we were much more relaxed then. Of course, the two leagues were getting much closer. That week we watched films together constantly, and grew very close as a defensive unit. The things they were doing were so simple that we felt they couldn't overpower us. We were a much bigger and quicker team than they were, too. I thought the Oakland and New York games were bigger ones, because

Buchanan's sack of George Blanda (left) in a 1969 game left the Raiders' quarterback dazed and unconscious (right). Bart Starr of the Green Bay Packers succumbed to the rush of the massive Buchanan during the first Super Bowl in Los Angeles (below).

those teams knew us extremely well. If we could get past those teams, we could get Minnesota.

Even with the controversy about Lenny Dawson running through the week?

We didn't pay any attention to that. We knew Len. When you've been around a guy as long as we'd been around him, you know the kind of person he is.

When did you know you had the game won?

Just before the end of the half, when we got our third field goal. It was nine to nothing and I didn't think that they could come back and catch us. They weren't an explosive team, and we didn't think they could grind it out. Then when Otis Taylor made the big play, there was no way for them to catch up. I was on the sideline and about to go crazy when Otis did that. He's my favorite player. There aren't many players who excite me, but Otis does.

Even after all the years and big plays and championships, one of your favorite memories must still be the way you were signed.

Yes, I met Don Klosterman in Shreveport, and he took me to Dallas in December, 1962. I guess they were hiding me. I stayed in an apartment across the hall from the team officials for four days. There were four players down there. Klosterman called me in and said, "We're going to make you our number one draft choice, and I want you to sign with us." I said, "Well, I don't know." And he answered, "You're going to be the first player in all of football to be drafted." That meant a lot to me, especially coming from a small school.

There's a story that Klosterman's wife had to go next door to borrow food. The players ate so much that she ran out.

She was trying to cook for four big old football players: Jim Kanicki, Don Brumm, me, and somebody else. We must have eaten more than a hundred pancakes every morning. It was ridiculous.

16

Len Dawson

Position: Quarterback
Years: 1962-
Height: 6-0
Weight: 190
College: Purdue

The profile is handsome and unmarked. The gaze is steady, measuring. The eyes are blue. The man seems perfect for his off-the-field role as sports director and on-camera personality for a Kansas City television station.

And the body? "There is no worse body in professional football than Len Dawson's," laughs longtime teammate and friend Jerry Mays. The gentle kidding is exaggerated, since Dawson spreads a well-muscled 190 pounds over a 6-foot frame. But he does seem slight, particularly when he lines up in front of the massive Kansas City linemen in the Chiefs' huddle.

"I don't know how he lasted," Mays says admiringly of the man who was the NFL's 1973 "man of the year." In 1972, Dawson moved ahead of Johnny Unitas to become number one in passing among all-time NFL quarterbacks.

He almost didn't make it. After five wasted years in the NFL, he got his release. He came to the Dallas Texans in the summer of 1962 as a shadow of what his onetime Purdue coach, Hank Stram, remembered from his Boilermaker days, when Dawson led the Big Ten in total offense three times.

"There is no passer in professional football more accurate than Lenny," says Stram. The record book agrees. He led the league in passing four times. Once he threw six touchdowns in a single game. And he survived the threat of scandal to lead the Chiefs to their finest moment, a 23–7 win over Minnesota in Super Bowl IV.

In 1962, Dawson took an uncertain offense and turned it into a devastating force in the old AFL. He led the Chiefs to three championships and finally to their Super Bowl triumph in 1970, earning most valuable player honors for that final game between the AFL and NFL.

You spent five years on the bench at Pittsburgh and Cleveland. That couldn't have done much either for your confidence or for your abilities.

I was hurt all the way around. I had serious doubts whether or not I was still capable. That's the one thing I wanted to find out. The main reason I asked for my release from the Cleveland Browns was so that I could go someplace where I would get an opportunity to play and to find out. I hadn't really played since Purdue. I certainly hadn't done anything of significance.

Had you even started and finished the same game in those five years?

No. In fact I only started in two games. One was my rookie year at Pittsburgh, and I don't think I played the whole half. It was against Philadelphia late in the year, and we were out of it. Buddy Parker told me during the warmup that I was going to start. I had no inkling. I didn't do badly, but on one play I was hit attempting to throw and the ball jarred loose. Then I came out. The other start was against the Steelers when I was with Cleveland. Milt Plum was hurt, and I played the first half. Here again, I didn't do anything significant. Both times I was nervous. That's why I can appreciate a guy coming off the bench. I really wasn't ready. I didn't have the confidence. I doubt I played a total of five quarters over those five years.

How many years did you and Bobby Layne overlap in Pittsburgh?

Two. My rookie year they traded for Earl Morrall, and he played that year. Bobby came in the next year. The only time that I played when he was there was late in the game, after it was all over.

Layne called you the next great pro quarterback, but the two of you were different from each other, sort of an "odd couple." How did it work out with two such diverse personalities?

When Layne called me the next great quarterback, he was referring to physical skills and competitiveness. People display those qualities in different ways. He was an outgoing type, quite verbal. I keep everything inside, but the same

thing is there. We just express it in different ways. I'm not a holler guy, but some of Layne rubbed off on me. When I started with the Texans, I was more vocal than usual. That changed as my confidence built and as I had an opportunity to play, to run a team. I wanted to play and win so badly. Also our team kind of grew together. There are many players who have been with me for years, offensively in particular. It isn't necessary to be vocal. My feeling is that if I can lead by showing rather than by telling, it's better. Sometimes it had to be a combination of both.

Layne would sometimes point at a guy all the way back to the huddle or kick somebody in the fanny. Have you ever done that, or been tempted?

No. Most of the time in the huddle isn't directed at one guy. It's not to single out one guy but several. It depends, too, on whether or not you have a guy like E. J. Holub on your team. With Holub there it wasn't necessary for the quarterback to say anything, because he was constantly on people. You need somebody like that in the middle of the line to spur them on. The quarterback has to concentrate on plays, on the whole picture of what you're trying to accomplish. So if you have somebody else to fire them up, it's better. The logical guy is the center, somebody who's in the pit. Jon Gilliam was that way when he was here. Right now we don't have one.

How did you and Hank Stram get together?

I think I got in touch with him. I'd seen him at a coaching convention in Cleveland in 1960. I had lunch with him and the Purdue coach, Jack Mollenkopf, and Hank asked how things were. I said I wasn't too happy because I wasn't playing. And he said, "Well, if I can ever help you out, if you can get out of the National Football League, let me know." He wasn't trying to entice me. He just said, "Let me know, I'd love to have you." I thought that I would get an opportunity to play with the Browns, but I didn't. After the season I asked for my release, and Paul Brown gave it to me. He'd just made a trade with Detroit for Jim Ninowski, so I wasn't going to play the next year either.

But how could he let you go when he had no proven backup quarterback?

Brown isn't noted for benevolence. He had just drafted a kid out of Texas. I don't think he ever played. But Brown's the type of guy who doesn't bring a lot of people to camp. If he figures this guy's going to be his quarterback and this guy his next quarterback, he won't have others around. At that time he probably went to camp with forty-five or fifty people, fewer than anyone else in the National Football League.

Were you upset when no other NFL team claimed you on waivers?

Let's say it didn't help me any. When I was released, I called Hank. He was going to an all-star game in Buffalo, so he stopped in Pittsburgh on the way. I think he made a hurried trip, because he was afraid I might sign with someone else. But I was ready to sign the contract right there at the airport. I found out much later that many of the NFL coaches were on vacation when I was waived, and they didn't know I was available. A couple of them have told me that. But that's how I got to the Texans.

You were anything but devastating for a while in Dallas.

I was terrible. My footwork, my release, and my quickness were all terrible. Techniques I'd had at Purdue were no longer there. I hadn't worked on them, and they'd rusted. You see, Hank's the only coach I've been with in professional football who really works on the fundamentals of quarterbacking. He's really made a study of it. He breaks it down to every phase: your stance, your ball handling, your footwork in setting up in the pocket, the way you move to

A college star (below) at Purdue, Len Dawson was inactive most of the time at Pittsburgh (left, he holds for a field goal attempt by Bobby Layne). At right, he throws one of his rare passes for Cleveland after he was traded to the Browns in 1960. The Texans secured his services after he was put on NFL waivers in 1962.

get in position to throw with your feet and legs, the release of the ball, your wrist action, everything. Now when I do something wrong, I can stop right there, go back to the fundamentals, break it down, and know what the problem is. Then there's no big problem preying on my mind. It's like a golfer. If a guy really doesn't know his swing, and things go wrong, he doesn't know how to go back to the start, or how to fix it. I didn't know that when I went down there. I was slow, carrying the ball low, winding up, and throwing.

How long did it take before you felt the rust was coming off?

Well, Hank really did me a favor because he'd play me a quarter in one game, a quarter in another, instead of throwing me out there. So instead of looking terrible for four quarters, I'd only look terrible for one. I didn't know anything about reading defenses, and I couldn't pick things up right away. I was indecisive about whom to throw to, and I had all the problems that a young quarterback has. I was worse off than a rookie; I had to break the bad habits I had. Hank worked with me on things like timing in getting back into the pocket. I'd never heard of that. I was taking one point eight or one point nine seconds, but I finally got it down to a consistent one point four, which meant that my feet were getting quicker. I'd never had to worry about that before. I'd just gone back and thrown.

Can you compare the coaching styles of Brown and Stram?

Brown is a great organizer. He does everything by the book – his book. He's a perfectionist with a great football mind. His coaching style and his way of handling people are completely different from Hank's, particularly in my case. Hank knew my personality and worked me along slowly, without yelling and screaming. He had the patience to work with me. With Cleveland and Pittsburgh I was in a different position. I

During the third quarter of Kansas City's Super Bowl I game against the Green Bay Packers, defensive tackle Henry Jordan of the Packers tipped the throwing arm of Dawson (below) and the ball was intercepted by Willie Wood (left). Wood returned the ball to the Kansas City 5-yard line and set up Green Bay's decisive touchdown. A knee injury forced Dawson (right) to miss six games of the 1969 season.

wasn't the number one quarterback, and they weren't looking to me to be the starter. Going to the Texans was a different situation. I went there with a true opportunity to take over as their starting quarterback.

When did you feel that you'd made it?

The last preseason game. I had come along and finally started piecing things together against Houston. I was throwing the ball much better. It was a miserable, miserable night down there, just after a rain. This was before the Astrodome. You know how hot it gets in Houston. It was a tough game, but I was throwing the ball fairly well. Things just seemed to come back. I had confidence in what I was doing. I started the next game, the opener against Boston. Houston really helped, and the Boston game put me there.

Has there ever been a time since then when you've lost your confidence?

Not in myself. There are days when you don't do as well as others, but I'm not afraid like I was before I joined the Texans.

What about the time a few years ago when the crowd booed you through the first half. Stram replaced you with Jacky Lee; Robert Holmes ran wild, and the Chiefs won. Didn't your confidence sag then?

Anytime you're booed, it's hard to take. It irritates the hell out of me, particularly if we're at home . . . and you know it isn't always your fault. The quarterback's performance is the result of what everybody else does, too. I know if it's my fault. When I do something wrong, I don't have to wait for fans to start booing me to get on myself. An athlete's chief competition is himself. He has to get himself ready and perform to his satisfaction. I can truthfully say that there haven't been many times when I didn't put forth my best effort.

Everyone talks about the increasing size, speed, and skill of players. What effect does that have on you?

The depth a quarterback has to drop back is different today. We're going back at least two or three yards deeper, about nine to eleven yards. Teams are playing odd alignments, too, so you may have a guy on your center's nose who's coming somewhere up the middle and impairing your vision. There may be three guys coming instead of two. And players are so much bigger. But these changes have not affected my throwing style. I've never been able to see over people. I don't think there's a quarterback who can. A defensive lineman coming in with his hands up – that's seven-and-a-half feet high! You've got to look between them. That's why you'll see a quarterback move a little to one side or the other at times. At least I do.

What was the worst loss you've had?

The first Super Bowl, because of everything involved and the raps we had to take after the game. Green Bay didn't completely dominate us, particularly the first half when it was still close. At halftime we thought we had something going. Then they came up with the interception.

Was Willie Wood out of position on the interception?

No, the ball was slightly tipped. They had a linebacker coming, and I had the tight end dragging out. All year long they'd shown very few blitzes, and this wasn't a blitzing down. But the guy came, and I really wasn't ready to throw. I was falling back, and he tipped it when I threw. The ball started off. Then it fluttered, giving Wood time to come under it.

Did you ever have your knee repaired after it was hurt in 1969?

No, Hank didn't believe all those doctors when they said it should be operated on. He kept sending me to new ones. It was still five or six to one for operating, but they hadn't really convinced me. I had been hurt before. I'd hurt the same knee in 1962 and it came around without my missing a game. The pain had been just as

Two of the most spectacular receivers who have caught passes from Len Dawson have been Chris Burford (left, being congratulated by Frank Jackson and Johnny Robinson) and Otis Taylor (right).

bad then. I remember getting hurt in Boston and having the doctor check me. He said, "Your knees are loose anyway." He couldn't detect right then whether anything was wrong. I went back in the next time we got the ball. I went a couple of plays, and it still felt loose so I came out. After the game I went back to the doctor and he said, "You'd better wrap it." That night when I got home I couldn't sleep. It was really hurting, and it stiffened up. It didn't swell that much and there wasn't any fluid, but I went to our team doctor in Kansas City and he said it might be torn. It was sort of a twilight area. Nobody said right out, "Your ligament is torn." They took me down to Oklahoma City and put my leg in a cast so that I wouldn't move it. When the cast came off, it felt a hundred percent better. The next day they put weights on both legs. Then they took x-rays so that they could see if there was a difference.

Didn't they call Stram at the time and ask his permission to operate?

My wife Jacqueline was there, and I think that she said go ahead. She was concerned about my safety. But the doctor didn't tell me that I definitely needed an operation. What he told me was, "Now, if you were a thirty-two-year-old housewife I probably wouldn't recommend it. But as a football player, I would recommend it, because seventy-five percent of the people with this damage eventually come back and have to have it done." I didn't want it. I don't think anyone wants an operation. So I saw another doctor. He said, "I could be wrong, but I think with a certain type of therapy – moving therapy rather than a cast – you'll be okay. Stay off it completely. Don't drive, and don't go anywhere without crutches, for two weeks. In the meantime, we'll start with whirlpool therapy and some exercises to keep up muscle tone." I was actually ready to play in Buffalo four weeks later. I was dressed for the Cincinnati game the week before. But I was worried at Buffalo. I was still heavily taped, and it was a sloppy field.

Some of your defensive people have said the tenor of what happened later was set in the ten to six loss in Oakland at the end of the 1969 regular season.

I suppose it could have been. We went out there and threw only a few passes. We knew we were in the playoffs. And we knew when we got there that we still had to win three games.

What about the next time against Oakland in the playoffs? You won despite four fumbles inside your own thirty.

We had things under control. That's what sticks in my mind. All we had to do was hold onto the football, and it would have been no contest. The defense shouldn't have had to work as hard as it did. We just coughed up the football four times. One fumble was on a good hit, but the others were inexcusable.

The week before the Super Bowl game against Minnesota, allegations were made that you'd been involved in gambling activities. That had to put a tremendous amount of extra pressure on you. Do you remember how the news broke?

I believe that I was at lunch when Jim Schaaf told me. The first day was really an ordeal, because we didn't know what was going on. I don't recall Jim's exact words. It was something about a subpoena and a grand jury and that "the reporters want to talk to you." I said, "What about? I don't know anything." Then the team put me into seclusion to find out what was going on. Apparently they talked to the commissioner as well as the league security force. They sent Jack Danahy, the security head, over to the hotel. We talked for a few hours. We were in a different room than my roommate, Johnny Robinson, and he was mad. He said, "What the hell? Here we've been roommates all year. Where have you been? Hell, can't you talk to me?" They were shooting me all around the

Len Dawson is the number one rated passer in the history of professional football, but even the best suffer the occasional ignominy of the postpass position (below). Dawson's face was drawn and tired (right) after his most trying week – Super Bowl IV.

place trying to decide what to say and do. After practice we watched films and then went up to Hank's room. They were calling people. I was just the guy in the background. They were trying to get hold of the league. Then after dinner a couple of reporters came up to the room and asked if I wanted to make a statement. I said, "Not that I know of. Why?" They said, "Well you'd better make a statement because you're going to be hounded until you do. Everybody's going to want to know." I went to Hank's room and told him we couldn't ignore it. So we had a long conference on what to say and how to go about it. We finally went down about eleven-thirty that night. Everyone kept wondering what to say and I kept saying, "Well, why not tell the truth?"

It probably didn't seem so at the time, but is it possible that incident helped distract you from tension over the game itself?

I think it might have had a pretty good effect, looking back. My teammates were definitely on my side, and it might have given me an extra spark. We were playing to show that the first time we were in the Super Bowl we hadn't played the way we were capable of. Now we had another motivating factor. When I started out the game with a pass completion, we moved the ball and were able to keep on moving it and to keep scoring points.

Did it surprise you that when the Vikings got into your territory on their first possession they passed up a field-goal attempt and punted?

Their defense had done the job all year. They were hoping to get us in a hole and break us down there – stop our first drive and maybe come up and get an easy score that would set the tempo. That's why our first drive was so vital. We got three points off it.

How important is the initial series of a game?

It's very important because of the pressure you apply on the other team. If you get out there and they stop you, three downs and out, it helps them. If they weren't fired up before, they're going to be after that. But if you move that ball on *them* and make them start guessing, then they're playing your game. When they go off the field they get together and say: "What the hell did they do?" They're not sure, and it puts more pressure on the offense when the defense is sitting there.

When did you know that you had Super Bowl IV put away?

As soon as Mike Garrett scored. As soon as we had six points. I could have wavered in that thinking when Joe Kapp took them to a touchdown on their first possession of the second half. But we didn't make a big mistake and just give away a touchdown. I knew we had a much better team than we'd had in the first Super Bowl, particularly defensively. Green Bay attacked our corners. Our defense would hold them for the first two downs, then they'd go back and throw those little turn-in patterns to keep their drives going. Our defensive secondary guys were in a sweat because they didn't think they could hold them. And they couldn't. It was entirely different against Minnesota. We had the secondary and the linebackers. Lanier, Lynch, and Bell played a super game. That year our defensive first eleven started every ball game. You've got to be lucky to do that. I don't care how you train, injuries happen. So generally the team that is healthy has a pretty good shot at winning.

Do you fret on the night before a game?

Yes, to a degree. I go over things in my mind. How we're going to do things. What I'm going to do in certain situations. Then I try to forget about it for a while. But I got up about three times the night before the Minnesota game. I eventually took my playbook into the john. I thought I might as well review some things while I was there.

Lamar Hunt

Position: President
Years: 1960-
College: Southern Methodist

Somebody once described Lamar Hunt as a man whose idea of a big time was a Dr. Pepper and a hamburger at a standup lunch counter. That's a peculiar biography for a man whom *Fortune* magazine once estimated is worth several million dollars, whose father is one of the wealthiest men in the world, and who facelifted the profile of professional football in the United States. His father, H. L. Hunt, wears white socks and brings his lunch to work in a brown paper bag. Some say he rivals J. Paul Getty in net worth. He once told Lamar, "The money will run out long before the deals do."

Lamar Hunt: owner of the Kansas City Chiefs; founder of the American Football League; co-owner of a professional soccer team; minority owner of a professional basketball team; onetime owner of a professional minor league baseball team; developer of Worlds of Fun, a multimillion dollar amusement center north of Kansas City; guiding spirit of the World Championship of Tennis; owner of oil stocks.

In 1960, the sports world scoffed at Hunt's vision of an American Football League. More than a decade and a half later, nobody is laughing anymore. Now over 40, Hunt is a bespectacled, respected, admired administrator, a builder who has turned dream into reality and desire into fact.

The man who once spent evening hours watering the lawn in front of the Dallas Texans' headquarters now resides on an 11-acre, $2 million estate. But the old Lamar isn't gone. One biographer recorded that Hunt, redesigning a flower bed at the new home "told his wife to buy plants that were smaller to save $18 or $20. He said that the plants would grow."

"I'm the last person to claim personal justification," he said in July, 1972, when he became the first member of the AFL to be enshrined in the Professional Football Hall of Fame in Canton, Ohio.

"My selection is symbolic of all the general managers, coaches, and players who worked for the growth of the American Football League."

At the age of 26, Hunt had started the league that shook the establishment and eventually forced its reworking into an expanded 26-team league. He moved his own team from Dallas to Kansas City because he thought it would be good for the AFL. He watched his team become one of the bellwether teams of all of pro football.

He helped force and forge the changes that are now taken for granted in the geography of the sport – two 13-team conferences and six divisions, spread from coast to coast.

"He is now making a lot of money on his own," says a friend. "He's emerging from the shadow of his father, and he likes it." A non-drinker, he once startled onlookers in a post-championship dressing room celebration when he actually stuck out his tongue and allowed some champagne to trickle on it after somebody poured a bottle over his head. "Damn" is about the strongest "off-color" word he uses.

But, as the friend continued, "You learn not to get Lamar mad. In the end you wind up playing the game by his rules which are money rules, and hell, there is no way you're going to beat him that way."

There were many shaky moments in the early years of the American Football League. Was there ever a time when you thought it might die?

Yes, twice. Once in Denver in 1960, the seventh week of our first year. Before the game, Bob Howsam, Denver's owner, asked if I could come to see him at the stadium. He told me he wasn't sure they were going to be able to finish the season. They were going to do their best to play their remaining games, but they wouldn't be back the next year. But the grimmest moment of all was midway through the 1962 season. The New York Titans had to be supported by the league. We paid their bills, yet we weren't allowed to take them over. Harry Wismer was fighting to keep them, and he obstructed everything, as he generally did. We had to have a New York franchise with a good public image. Unfortunately, at that point, the Titans were our weakest club. It was the most miserable operation imaginable. We were worried that they might just drag the whole league down with them.

If that was the league's worst time, what was its best?

The turning point for the league was the next spring, when Sonny Werblin and his group took over the New York club.

You mean that was even more meaningful than the thirty-six million dollar television contract which came a little later?

I really think so, because Sonny gave us immediate believability with the press, even though the Jets didn't have immediate success on the field – or even at the box office. But they soon had a big-league operation, and it was easy enough to see that success would follow. And, of course, they would be opening Shea Stadium in 1964.

The television contract kept several clubs afloat, though, didn't it?

Yes, it was the single most dramatic thing of that nature, and it drew the attention. The Werblin thing was not so immediately apparent. The television contract gave the league the stability and financial ability to compete for players for five years. Before that, we just had year-to-year television contracts.

Wismer was one of the league's most controversial figures. It's said that when Minneapolis was being wooed by the NFL while the AFL was holding its first draft in November, 1959, he stalked into a meeting and called Max Winter a "Judas." Did he?

I don't remember the "Judas" part, but I do remember "the Last Supper." Harry had a flair for the dramatic. It was a Sunday night. We were there in Minneapolis for a Chicago Cardinals game. They were playing their last two "home" games on the road that year before moving to St. Louis. We were sitting in the room as various people filtered in from the Sunday afternoon game. Wismer came in and he already had the Monday morning papers under his arm. He'd bought about ten copies on the street. They all had big headlines that said, "Minneapolis to Get NFL Franchise." The source of the story said that the group that was going to get the NFL franchise was the same one that had agreed to an AFL franchise. Winter was in the group. Wismer threw the papers on the table and said, "Boys, it looks like it's the Last Supper." He and Winter got into a heated exchange.

Minneapolis defected to the NFL only a few months later, leaving you with only seven teams.

Well, that certainly hurt, but we went ahead. We'd gotten our eighth team, Boston, three days before that first draft meeting in Minneapolis. No one had actually met Bill Sullivan of Boston until that meeting. It was sort of a telephone franchise. They had no stadium. God, thinking of all the problems, I can't believe we made it. It gives me cold chills to recall them. Frank Leahy, who was general manager of the Chargers, vouched for Bill. We went ahead and had the draft, but although the Minneapolis people said they didn't plan to go into the NFL and wanted to continue with us, they were very evasive.

The draft was an unusual one, by any standards, wasn't it?

It was sort of an out-of-the-hat-deal. We put what we thought were the top eight quarterbacks in a hat and each team picked one without knowing his name. Then we'd put the eight centers in and do the same. We continued through each position.

The members of the "Foolish Club" of American Football League owners are shown at right in 1961. They are, seated left to right: Bud Adams, Houston Oilers, and AFL commissioner Joe Foss; and standing, left to right, Bill Sullivan, Boston Patriots; Cal Kunz, Denver Broncos; Ralph Wilson, Buffalo Bills; Hunt, Dallas Texans; Harry Wismer, New York Titans; Wayne Valley, Oakland Raiders; and Barron Hilton, San Diego Chargers.

Lamar Hunt commands a diversified empire of sports and entertainment that not only includes the Chiefs, but the Dallas Tornado of the North American Soccer League (left, their brilliant young star, Kyle Rote); the World Championship of Tennis professional tennis tour (right, 1974 champion John Newcombe); and a new amusement park near Arrowhead Stadium in Kansas City called Worlds of Fun (below).

How did you determine the top eight?
Through a committee of employees from the various teams. We'd hired Will Walls early to analyze talent for us in the fall, and he worked along with Leahy, Don Rossi of the Texans' staff, and Dean Griffing of Denver. They met in one room while the owners met about other things in another room.

In view of all the uncertainty, did you ever consider taking some of the NFL offers made to you and Bud Adams to withdraw from the AFL?

Not really. We'd conditioned everything in the AFL on the fact that everyone was a partner. I'd gone out and solicited these people to become part of the new league. Anything we did would have to take them all into consideration. That wasn't in the NFL's thinking.

It's been said that the NFL wanted just you, Bud Adams, and Barron Hilton of the Chargers.

They didn't want individuals, necessarily; they wanted cities. There was some talk that Bud could have Houston, I could have Dallas, and Barron could possibly be brought into the Rams' ownership.

Another report said that when both your team and the Cowboys were in the formative stages, Clint Murchison called and told you he'd either buy you out or you could buy him out.

That was in October, 1959, but it didn't happen exactly like that. Clint actually said he'd step completely out of the picture. We had a meeting initiated by my cousin, Stewart Hunt, who also was a distant relative of Murchison's. Clint said, "Look, I'll get out completely. My main goal is to see that Dallas gets an NFL team. Lamar, you take it. But you've got to take the NFL franchise." I said I couldn't. We were committed to the AFL people, and they were committed to us. We just couldn't pull out. He called back that evening and amended what he'd said. He said that since he'd worked on it,

he would like to stay in the picture – for a percentage. He was well-intentioned in his thinking.

Did you have an amicable relationship with him after that, even though you became competitors in Dallas?

I never knew Clint very well. The competition was there, but we kept things on a jocular basis. One time, in 1960, some of his friends wrapped me up in a box and presented me as a Christmas present at a party at Clint's house. A mutual friend of ours had asked me to do it.

It's been reported that you lost two-hundred-thousand dollars in 1962, the year you won the league championship. How heavy were your Dallas losses?

We've never announced figures, either in Dallas or Kansas City. We broke even our first year in Kansas City, fell behind the next two years, and have shown a profit since 1966.

Despite intense promotions in Dallas – milking contests, ticket campaigns – you never drew as you'd hoped you would, and you started looking around. Why did you pick Kansas City?

In the late fifties a number of us used to go up to Kansas City from Dallas a couple of times each year for a baseball weekend, usually to watch a Yankee series. It was always sold out, and that made an impression on me. I felt that Kansas City was a good sports town. I also wanted a city relatively close to Dallas, because of the expenses involved in a move. So that narrowed it even more. I really considered only two cities: Kansas City and New Orleans. H. Roe Bartle, who was then mayor of Kansas City, had as much to do with the decision as anyone. He was very persuasive. He has since embellished some of the things surrounding our trips to investigate the city, but he seriously introduced me as Mr. Lamar and Jack Steadman as Jack X in an effort to protect our identity on those visits.

In your first preseason game in Kansas City, against Buffalo, you had five-thousand fans and thirty-five-thousand empty seats. Did that make you want to move back to Dallas?

We announced sixty-two-hundred fans, but we exaggerated a lot in those days. It was sobering, to say the least. We really thought we'd do better. We had sold more than fifteen-thousand season tickets, and although we hadn't tied our preseason games to season tickets, we thought there would be more of a carryover. The next year the season sale dropped to ten thousand and then, in 1965, it dropped even more. I remember vividly when at the first game my brother, Bunker, said to someone, "Your crowd is far too gentlemanly." He was saying that you need the man in the street to support a program, and it took us a while to build that kind of support. We made a mistake in not starting our ticket campaign soon enough. We waited until March or so.

You were very active in all the team's operations in those first years. You even traded Cotton Davidson.

That was with Hank Stram's knowledge, but without his consent. I felt we were not progressing as a franchise. There was complete dissatisfaction and a feeling that we weren't going anywhere as long as Cotton was our quarterback. From what I'd seen I felt Dawson was going to be fabulous, and we also had an outstanding rookie, Eddie Wilson. With the thirty-three-man rosters of those days, you couldn't afford the luxury of three quarterbacks. There also was the opportunity. Oakland was the dredge of the league then. I felt trading Davidson to them would give us the opportunity to get the number one player in the country the next year, which we did in Buck Buchanan. It's the only time I ever did anything like that, and I think I escaped lightning. It was just a feeling. I was lucky. Since then, trading has been Hank's domain, although he always checks with me on any deal. I might make comments and try to talk him out of one aspect or another, but basically it's his duty.

Do you keep as close a hand on team operations in other ways as you used to?

No, the distance makes some difference, but basically it's the fact that we have a mature organization and a super staff. I was very active in the recruiting end of it at first when timing was so important. We had to sell the organization to the draft choice before he signed with some other team. That's not nearly as important now. I even used to water the lawn out in front of the old Texans' office. I've always got to be doing something. One time I was talking to Dave Dixon, who was in from New Orleans trying to get a franchise. I watered the grass while we talked.

Does one exceptional, even historic, game stand out in your mind?

You know, it's funny, but the most memorable one for me was that sixty-six to twenty-four preseason win over the Chicago Bears. It came the summer after our Super Bowl loss, and there was much more at stake than just the game. It was our first return game against an NFL team. It's interesting that Fred Arbanas said the same thing when he retired. Here was Fred, the all-time AFL tight end on that team picked to represent the league for its first ten years, and the Chicago game was also his fondest remembrance.

What was the Chiefs' worst moment?

Well, I've seen a number of games that I wish I'd missed, but around the Chiefs' office we talk about the loss to Oakland in 1963 as the worst. Any loss is a bad one but Oakland had never beaten us at home. They were just emerging from being the downtrodden members of the league. They beat us twenty-two to seven, and we did some strange things, including Jerrel Wilson's punt into the backside of our own goal posts, giving them a safety. Another bad moment was when we left Dallas. But we couldn't afford the luxury of an unsuccessful franchise. That move also was tempered by the optimism with which we went to Kansas City.

It's been said the Chiefs were not on a par with the Packers – or any upper-echelon NFL team – at the time of the first Super Bowl.

The game was very disappointing, primarily because we didn't play good football. We played three poor games that year, losing thirty-four to thirteen to Oakland, then twenty-nine to fourteen to Buffalo, and then thirty-five to ten to Green Bay. But we beat Oakland once that year after losing to them and Buffalo twice. We did have a letdown in the second half against Green Bay, and I certainly think the Packers were the superior team.

How did you coin the term "Super Bowl?"

It was an accidental thing. I didn't really coin it. I was a member of a merger committee along with Ralph Wilson and Bill Sullivan from the AFL, and Tex Schramm, Art Modell, and Dan Reeves from the NFL. We had meetings every three or four weeks and in talking about details of the game, we kept referring to it as the "final game" or the "championship game," or whatever. It was kind of awkward. One day "Super Bowl" just came out. "When we get to the Super Bowl . . ." I happened to say, and everybody immediately knew what I was talking about. I don't know where the term came from except that my daughter Sharon had a "super ball," a little, rubber ball, with phenomenal bouncing ability. It would literally bounce over a house. I've never seen anything like it. So it must have come from that. There was never a formal announcement using the words "Super Bowl." People just began using it. The press used it and probably they are responsible for its becoming the official title. After about three years the title "AFL-NFL World Championship Game" was done away with. It was too much of a mouthful.

Lamar Hunt and Hank Stram, two men who have guided a team from its infancy to its present status as one of football's best, watch their charges at work.

Jerry Mays

Position: Defensive End
Years: 1961-69
Height: 6-4
Weight: 252
College: Southern Methodist

Gold cufflinks form the numerals "75." Along with the size of the man and his permanently displaced knuckles ("your hands begin to go after a while, and you have trouble gripping your opponents"), the cufflinks he wears are one of the few reminders of his former occupation. A calculator rests on the desk. A worn briefcase leans against it. Piped music drifts through the office. It's an office in Johnson County, just over the state line from Kansas City on the Kansas side. Jerry Mays, contractor, talks wistfully about Jerry Mays, football player.

Mays captained the Kansas City Chiefs through their days of greatest glory. He ruled by desire, example, and emotion. He made all-league as a tackle, and when he moved to end, he made all-league there as well. "He's the only man I've known," coach Hank Stram once said, "who could play every offensive and defensive position in the line."

Mays was named to the 10-year all-AFL team in the Hall of Fame. He was co-captain and all-Southwest Conference at SMU before the old Texans drafted him fifth in 1961. He toyed with the idea of playing with Minnesota in the NFL, but he wanted to move into the contracting business his father conducted in Dallas. A civil engineer, he is now vice-president in charge of the Kansas City branch of Avery-Mays Construction Company. He also has done the commentary for Chiefs radio broadcasts.

He retired from football in the spring of 1971 – before he had to – and sometimes he wishes he hadn't.

Do you miss playing?

I've missed it since the minute I quit. It gets a little better at times, and I suppose it will finally get bearable; but I loved it – every part of it. I enjoyed being exhausted and feeling as if I had paid the price; and I loved the glory of winning. I even enjoyed practices. I dreaded them, but once they were accomplished, I got great satisfaction out of them. There was great joy for me, right after a practice or a tough game, just sitting in the dressing room and contemplating. I miss that as much as anything. Then there's the camaraderie and the discipline. I thoroughly believed in Hank's discipline and enjoyed having it administered to me, even though it was a pain in the rear sometimes.

Discipline isn't a very popular word anymore.

I know, but I'm kind of old-fashioned. I was really one of Hank's boys. I believed in everything he did. He got a little corny at times, but it's fun to play for Hank Stram. I talked to an ex-football player not long ago and he said, "Man, I don't miss it a bit." He asked me why I did, and I said I didn't really know, that I'd just loved it.

Is professional football *really* fun?

I had fun every minute and so do most pros. Take Bobby Hunt, one of my best friends. I had lunch with him a while ago, and we were talking and joking. He was starting off on a new career, and we were talking about how it wasn't the same anymore. Then he looked at me and said, "I wouldn't trade one minute of it." Tears started running down his cheeks – two years after he retired.

Was that a normal reaction?

I don't think that too many people have the privilege of making a living from something they'd almost do for nothing. Football can be the most miserable thing to a guy who doesn't love it, but it's the most joyous to a guy who does.

What is there in Stram and the Chiefs' system – they seem almost synonymous? What makes it enjoyable?

First, Hank is unpredictable. You can never tell what the "Little Caesar" is going to do. He's enthusiastic, and it rubs off on other people. He has fun, so he makes it fun for others. There have been few occasions when I've seen Hank

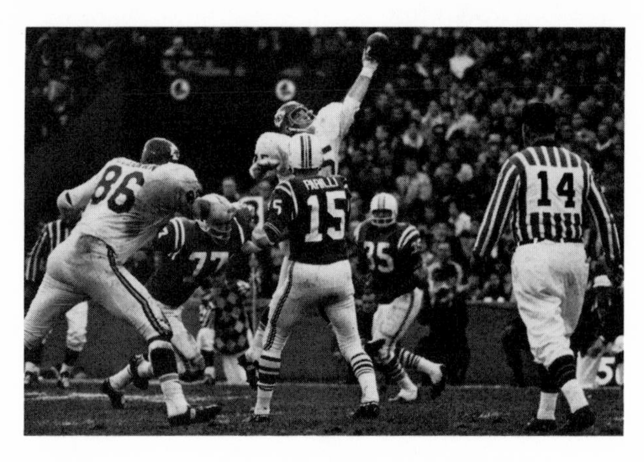

really get down and lose that Stram enthusiasm.

What makes him that way?

The worst thing that can happen to Hank is to come to a point of the season where he realizes he's out of the race, that there isn't even a remote set of circumstances that can make him a champion. When that happens, it's sad. Hank can believe, with three games remaining, seven teams will do exactly what needs to be done to let us win. I think the Chiefs have won many games on his optimism, on what he stimulates and nurtures. He and the Chiefs are very fair too. They probably give a player more of a chance than some clubs. Sometimes they carry it too far, but few players leave the Chiefs without feeling they've been given a fair shake.

What was it like walking into Arrowhead knowing you'd never play in it?

Really that made it easier for me. The first year after I retired, I'd go into the old stadium with all those memories. It was agony.

And how is it sitting at home, watching on television?

I can't be a quiet rooter. As much as I love the team it's sometimes better if I don't watch them. I still have strong feelings about teams I like or dislike.

Such as Oakland?

Yes, I can't think of any circumstance where I'd ever pull for Oakland. And the only time I'd pull for Dallas would be against Oakland.

As much as anyone, you seem to be associated with the American Football League.

Yes, and I loved it. It was part of me, and the merger made it easier for me to retire. I realize that it was an intelligent business decision to combine the AFL and NFL. But it sure took a lot of the fun out of it. I was AFL from start to finish, proud of the league, tickled to death I'd played in it, and jealous of the NFL for years. It was a cause bigger than football. It was the little guy against the big guy.

You were drafted by Minnesota. How did you wind up with the Dallas Texans?

The AFL had its draft very early; the NFL didn't have its draft until after Christmas. The rumor got around that I'd signed with the Texans before the NFL draft. I got maybe fifteen calls the night the NFL was drafting. All night long, first one club, then the other . . . things like, "We've heard you've already signed." And "Don't do a thing until you've talked with us." Minnesota finally drafted me, and I talked to them. But they said they'd trade my draft rights to the Cowboys because my father was in business in Dallas and I'd grown up there. I finally signed with Jack Steadman, the Texans' general manager, at my home.

You came to the Texans during the AFL's second season. Weren't you one of the league's few really professional teams in terms of organization, structure, and budget?

That's true, and we used to worry about it. That's what made the AFL so enjoyable. We not only wanted to beat the other clubs, we worried about them. When the New York Titans' paychecks started bouncing, our players started asking, "What can *we* do?"— as if we had anything to do with it. But we did feel like a part of it. When Denver burned its vertical brown and yellow striped socks, we were happy because we were part of it. That was something that made us look bush.

Did you sense, then, that you were in a second-class league?

I knew it, but I never did admit it. If you'd said that to me then, I'd have argued with you violently. I'd have told you, "Just bring 'em on; we'll play any of them." Of course, the thing we wanted more than anything else was to play the Cowboys — and to beat them.

Could you have done that?

We had the talent in the early years. I think that any time in the first three years we would

Jerry Mays, blocking a pass by Babe Parilli of the Boston Patriots at left, was one of the greatest defensive players in the 10-year history of the American Football League. John Unitas of the Baltimore Colts was, according to Mays, one of the most vocal NFL critics of the Chiefs after Kansas City's loss in Super Bowl I. The Chiefs got even in 1970 after the merged leagues began interconference play. Bobby Bell racked up Unitas (right), Johnny Robinson made three interceptions, and Kansas City won 44-24.

have given the Cowboys a heck of a good battle.

Maybe you could have done it on emotion. That was one of your main assets, wasn't it?

Yes, and I enjoyed it. Sometimes I knew that my emotions were getting away, getting control of me. I think I probably argued with myself and gave in pretty easily.

Did you have them in check against the Packers in the fourth quarter of the first Super Bowl game?

I don't even remember that quarter. It was such a horrible disappointment, such a crushing thing, that I've wiped it out of my mind. I remember it only to the point we *had* to remember it, to learn the lesson we had to learn to make us Super Bowl champions later.

Tell us about that lesson.

We were behind only fourteen to ten, and we were driving. Then they intercepted. When they went ahead twenty-one to ten, we changed our game plan and lost our poise. Green Bay used to do that to everybody. Afterward, the only writers who treated us favorably said that everything was fine until Lenny Dawson threw the interception. It would have been easy for us to say, "If only Lenny hadn't done this or that." One of the great things Hank did was to tell every player on the team: "Look, it wasn't Lenny. It was the Chiefs – the coaches and everything – that lost the game." The interception became a turning point not because Lenny threw it, but because the defense collapsed and everyone lost his poise. In other words, it was a turning point in the history of the Chiefs because we didn't make excuses. We realized our weaknesses and where we'd gone wrong. We could look at Green Bay and get mad at Vince Lombardi because he had made a statement saying, "True, they're not in our class." But he was just as right as he could be. Emotionally we weren't mature – yet.

How did you begin putting things back together again?

I had to go to an All-Star game the next day, and I dreaded it more than anything because I had to see my AFL teammates – guys like Lance Alworth, who had come up to us before the Super Bowl, grabbed our arms, and said, "No matter what, you can do it." I remember how I wanted to get out of that All-Star game. I wanted to hide. I didn't want to see anybody, any public or press. The week after the Super Bowl – that whole spring – was agony.

There was an incident that spring when John Unitas said some things. It simmered for several years, didn't it?

The most vocal of all the NFL critics after the Super Bowl was John Unitas. He said we were inferior and that our quarterback was inferior. The Chiefs have been involved in two games where they were emotionally charged to the absolute peak. Both of them had to do with our Super Bowl loss. One was with Chicago the summer after the loss to Green Bay. The other was the first time we played Baltimore. We stomped them on that Monday night. Killed them. Everybody on our team had Johnny Unitas's quotations in his back pocket and billfold. Hank didn't have to put them on the bulletin board. We went out there and had them thirty-five to six at halftime. We ran Unitas out of the ball park – and that was four *years* after he'd rapped us.

Your 1962 AFL title team had a formidable defense.

We were small in the line but very mobile. I was two-hundred-forty pounds, Paul Rochester was about two-hundred-fifty-five pounds, and Bill Hull and Mel Branch were about two-hundred-thirty. Hull was six feet, seven inches. He looked like a basketball player. We called him "Giraffe" for a while, but one day Mel Branch got confused on his animals and called him "Zebra." That name stuck.

You eventually got tremendous help out of

75

Joe Kapp of the Vikings was forever finding Mays or some other member of the Chiefs in his path, and went through four quarters of frustration in Super Bowl IV. The Chiefs won the game 23-7.

An exhausted but satisfied Mays watched the last seconds tick off the Shea Stadium clock after Kansas City defeated the New York Jets in the 1969 playoff.

the 1963 draft. Were you aware of how good your draft was at the time?

No, it took a while. We got Wilson, Buchanan, Budde, Bell, and Hill. With the common draft now, I don't know if there ever will be another draft like that. We had a good draft in 1961, too. Arbanas, Tyrer, Holub, and myself. But 1963 was the best of them all.

How impressive was Buchanan as a rookie?

Everybody knew he was a super athlete. The guy we weren't really sure about was Bobby Bell. He started out as a defensive tackle. He was awfully small and a bit uncoachable. That's very natural now that I know Bobby. He's one of my favorite people. He's such a superb athlete that he can do something wrong and still be successful. He can run around a block and get away with it, he's so quick. What success I had was greatly attributable to the fact that I understood Bobby Bell and let him play his kind of game. The styles we played were on opposite ends of the pole. He was a shoot-the-gap type. I was a fundamentalist. Step with the right foot, be in the right position. He steps on the wrong foot, lines up wrong, goes wrong, and still makes it.

Isn't it important that an end and a linebacker have a rapport?

Sure. I resented Bell at first. I was a little jealous. No one could play football the way Bobby Bell did and be successful. But he did. He had a little trouble as a lineman, but once he became a linebacker, there was no stopping him.

Why did the team drop off so badly from 1962 to 1963?

Part of it was the disruption due to the move from Dallas to Kansas City. Then, after winning as the youngest team in football, we became immature and egotistical. We felt that all we had to do was throw our jocks on the field and we'd be champions again. The truth is, we could have been–if only we had worked hard for it.

You beat Minnesota in Super Bowl IV. Was that particularly satisfying?

Heavens, yes. We really liked Minnesota. I had the utmost respect for their players. But it was beating the NFL that gave us the satisfaction. The only thing we hated about Minnesota was that they were in the NFL.

Were you conscious of the weather in New Orleans that Sunday in January, 1970?

No. We were concerned about the field because of how much rain had fallen, about it becoming a quagmire where the canvas had leaked. I don't think football can be played after a two-inch rain on a dirt field late in the season. The game doesn't resemble football under those circumstances. We played a game at Municipal Stadium against San Diego after about three inches of rain. People could have drowned, there was so much water. Fumbles became the big thing. On the big play, John Hadl, the San Diego quarterback, reached back to pass. As he squeezed the football, it squirted straight out of his hands and flew up. He reached over, caught it, and threw a pass to Alworth for a touchdown. That touchdown beat us. If the ball had squirted the other way, we'd have caught it.

75
42

WILSON

Hank Stram

Position: Head Coach
Years: 1960-
College: Purdue

The big red and yellow "cherry picker," as the telephone repair people call it, was wheeled to the center of Arrowhead Stadium. Hank Stram, attired in high top, highly polished red football shoes, and a red warmup suit with yellow piping, stepped into the basket and was whirred aloft to look critically at the team on the Tartan surface below.

"Watch for that pattern to come open out there on the left," he called to quarterback Mike Livingston. "Yeah, that's the one, that's the one," he said, falling into a habit of repeating key words and phrases as his Chiefs ran through a practice during one of the off-season's monthly camps.

Later, after he had been lowered to the ground, Stram was throwing deep passes to defensive linemen, chiding them when they missed; and being chided himself when they had to slow down to wait for the ball. Both sides were enjoying it hugely. At the midpoint in his life, Stram was a man in love with his work. "I've never wanted to be anything else," said the only head coach the Kansas City organization has ever had.

Inside the Chiefs' new stadium, Stram works in the luxury of two offices. One is a working office with one wall made up of immense pictures of his players. Another wall is dominated by a blackboard (Stram is a compulsive "x" and "o" man.) The third wall gives him the depth chart of every team in the league at a glance, while the fourth lists the Chiefs' player status. Upstairs, the second office is bedecked in regal splendor – hidden cabinets, indirect lighting, soft music, paneling, deep carpets, a glass wall opening onto banks of seats for his special guests at a game.

Stram, the only coach in the old AFL to take his team to two Super Bowls, is also the only one to survive all 14 years since the league was founded. Surrounded by the trappings of success and content with his work, he is a long way from the 35-year-old assistant who seriously considered giving up coaching altogether. Only a phone call from Lamar Hunt rescued him from a career as a sporting goods salesman. No one doubts he would have been a good salesman. But the AFL, and football in general, would have wound up a lot poorer.

In 14 years, Stram's team have won 119, lost 67, and tied 10. His teams also have won five of eight playoff or championship games. He is one of only nine pro coaches with 100 or more victories. His triple stack defense, the moving pocket, and tight end I have become familiar because of the success with which he used them.

"My father wanted me to be a baseball player," he says. "He used to bring home baseballs, bats, and gloves for me." Stram traded them for football equipment.

An all-state halfback at Gary, Indiana, Stram wanted to go to Notre Dame. But the new Irish coach, Frank Leahy, wasn't excited by 5-foot 7-inch, 160-pound backs, so Stram went to Purdue. There he earned seven letters, four in baseball and three in football, and remained as an assistant after graduation.

Quickly earning a reputation as a good offensive coach, he went on to SMU and then Notre Dame. The Notre Dame stop was memorable mostly for its ending. In 1958, Stram and his wife, Phyllis, decided on a Notre Dame theme for their Christmas cards. "So we ordered these cards with a picture of our kids wearing Notre Dame sweaters in front of the Christmas tree," he said. "The greeting said 'Cheer, Cheer From Old Notre Dame.'"

The day the cards arrived from the printer, Notre Dame head coach Terry Brennan and his staff, Stram included, were fired.

Stram went on to Miami, where he remained until Hunt offered him the Texans' coaching job.

The merger between you and Lamar Hunt has been as important in the Chiefs' history as

the merger between the NFL and the AFL. How did you first get together?

I was working at the University of Miami, and Lamar was coming to Miami on business. He called me and said he was in the process of formulating a new league. He said that he had met me at SMU, but I didn't remember. Then he said he'd like to visit with me about the possibilities of the new league. We went out to dinner after practice and talked at great length about a lot of things – about the people we knew in Dallas, about the possibilities of the AFL. We looked at some films, and he wanted to know about philosophies. Basically, that's where it all started, but not once during the whole discussion did he ever mention coaching. It was obvious to me that he just wanted to get a feel for me; what I felt about football, my family, that kind of thing. He said he'd be in touch later, but he didn't make a job offer. I told Andy Gustafson, the Miami coach, about it, and he said that Hunt wouldn't have come that far to visit me unless he had something in mind. He said I'd hear from him eventually. At the end of the season I attended a banquet in Gary, Indiana, at my old high school. It was then that I got a long-distance call from Lamar. He asked me to come to Dallas the next day to visit with him about the team.

Did you have any reservations?

Not really. I had a couple of other tempting opportunities to take head coaching jobs in colleges. But I was excited about the challenge of a new professional league – and pro football. The excitement dominated my feeling about whether or not to take the job.

You felt you were ready?

I did, and I was in a very restless stage. I had set a goal for myself when I first started coaching. If I hadn't become a head coach at a certain age, I'd consider something else. I had an offer from a sporting goods company, more money than I was making in college coaching. I thought it would be better than fighting it out as an assistant coach. If you haven't made it as head coach by a certain time, people have a tendency to look at you and say, "Well, there must be something wrong with him. If he were that great a prospect, somebody would have given him the chance before now." I had served a twelve-year apprenticeship, and I'd been a candidate for several head jobs. I felt I was coming into a very critical stage of my career.

Kansas City has been a consistent winner for almost fifteen years. Why?

Initially you start with philosophy and responsibility. A lot of credit has to be given Lamar Hunt for having the foresight, patience, and understanding to establish and maintain a consistency, a continuity of people who are responsible for running the program. Then once a coach is given the opportunity, it's equally important that he be given supreme authority. Someone has to have that in any organization. Unless someone does, a lot of problems arise because of divided responsibilities. There's just no way in the world you can survive that. The problems that are created are self-inflicted, because of the nature of the organization. I think young people are looking for leadership. They want to know who's in charge.

Would you call it a benevolent dictatorship?

Yes, I think it almost has to be. It depends on the personality of the individual. Dictatorship is a strong word but we're in a strong business.

What about a coach having a dual job as general manager?

I think we have an ideal situation in Kansas City. I'm responsible only to Lamar, so there isn't any divided responsibility. We had one situation – the Cotton Davidson trade in 1962 – where he overrode me. But that's the only time we had a misunderstanding, if you want to call it that. I didn't want to trade Cotton. I feel very

The 1955 Purdue University football team. Seated at the end of the second row, next to All-America end Lamar Lundy, is backfield coach Hank Stram. Seated on the fourth row, extreme left of the photo, is junior quarterback Len Dawson.

At left, the Hank Stram family of Kansas City in 1964 (left to right): Stu, coach Stram, Gary, Hank, Jr., Mrs. Stram, one-year-old Mary Nell, Dale, and Julie. At right, the Stram family 10 years later in 1974 (left to right): Mrs. Stram, Hank, Jr., Mary Nell, Dale, Gary, Stu, Julie, and in the rear, coach Stram.

strongly that you can't let other people run your business. You can't survive without fans – they're very important – but you can't let fans decide who's going to play quarterback. Regardless of criticism, you have to do what *you* feel is best for the team. I thought Cotton was a victim of circumstances because he had played at Baylor. There was a strong denominational factor at the schools that were represented in the Dallas area. And there was strong sentiment in other ways, too.

What happened early in the 1962 season?

I decided to start Lenny Dawson against Boston, and he had a big night. I felt Cotton would be a super backup quarterback. We had Eddie Wilson, a rookie from Arizona, and he had good potential; but I thought it was important for us to have two experienced quarterbacks. But Lamar made the trade with Oakland, and it turned out to be a good one in that we got Buck Buchanan as a result. I still think, though, we'd have been a better team with Lenny and Cotton.

You hadn't coached Dawson for five or six years. What triggered the thought to go with him in 1962?

Having coached him in college, I always felt he had the ability to be a great pro. He isn't the easiest person in the world to know and understand. He's quiet, reserved. As a result, if you don't know him, you'd think he's aloof and uninterested in you. Nothing could be further from the truth. He is intense and involved. So I thought a lot of the things I heard about him as a pro at Pittsburgh and Cleveland were caused by lack of understanding and lack of opportunity. I'd heard that he couldn't throw long, that he really wasn't a student of the game, and that he wasn't as involved and dedicated as they thought he should be. He was at Pittsburgh with Bobby Layne and at Cleveland with Milt Plum, the wrong places at the wrong times.

If you hadn't known him well, would you have kept him after the way he looked that summer of 1962?

I definitely wouldn't have. He played poorly. I had a lot of friends in Dallas who said they just couldn't understand why I was being stubborn and overly loyal to a man who played for me at Purdue. They said there was no way he could succeed. He was over the hill. Why would a great coach like Paul Brown give up on him if he still had any skill? Why would Buddy Parker? The next question was why everybody in the National Football League let him get through if he still had the ability to play. That was the common argument. They also said Lenny would get me fired.

When you saw him, did you think maybe they were right?

I've used the expression that he was like sterling silver that had been tarnished and just needed a lot of polish. Mechanically he wasn't throwing the ball well; he wasn't using his body. He dropped the ball before he got it into trigger position. His footwork was bad and so was his timing going back into the pocket. It was obvious that he hadn't drilled in many areas while he'd been in professional ball. His spiral wasn't as tight as I remembered it in college, and he didn't have an overabundance of confidence. Anytime you stand around as long as he did, you've got to be unsure, and wonder if what they're saying is true. Lenny concealed his feelings well though, and as we practiced, you could see that he was getting better and better. The spin was a little tighter, and the footwork and techniques were better. It was starting to come back. Lenny threw the ball very well from our moving pocket. It was what we had put in at Purdue in 1949.

So the moving pocket is a legacy from Purdue?

Well, it's a little different. It was a rollout at Purdue, rolling right or left with the option to run or throw. The tight end released in the pat-

tern; so did the flanker and the near back. So you had a flood action on the strong side. In the Chiefs' moving pocket our tight end didn't release. He blocked. He destroyed the containment responsibility of the defensive end. We did it that way because Fred Arbanas was such a great blocker, and because those huge San Diego players, Ernie Ladd and Earl Faison, would invariably knock down six or seven balls every game if you tried to throw from the normal pocket. So the moving pocket is movement by design to an area behind the tight end. The first time we used it was against San Diego. We completed our first eleven passes and won by a big score. Things kind of turned around for us in the San Diego series then, about 1964.

Do you see yourself as primarily an offensive or defensive coach?

My interests have always been offensive; I'm slanted more that way. But if you're not careful, you're so involved on offense that you lose sight of the fact you can't win consistently unless you have great balance.

How did you start using the I formation?

Abner Haynes was a very skillful runner. He had a great capacity to find seams, running room, and daylight. And the great thing about the I is that it's one formation from which you can take advantage of pursuit. The I provides you with the opportunity to counteract pursuit, because you're in a balanced position when the ball is snapped. We put our tight end into the I in 1966, experimenting a lot. In 1967, we came out with it full scale, because everybody was going to a strong and weak safety. It was always geared to where the tight end was. The strong safety was always going to where the tight end was. So we thought if he didn't know where the tight end was going to go, then there would be confusion as to where he'd line up – movement with our movement. So we put him in the backfield and shifted him. That made one of two things happen. Either the strong safety had to shift with him, or the weak safety had to become the strong safety. That's something you don't want to do defensively. It creates a mismatch. We felt we had an advantage – dominating the defense by making it do what we wanted it to do, rather than the other way around. I remember very vividly that when we started using the I, a lot of people around the league pointed the finger and said that there was no way in the world to use a college offense in pro football.

There was a lot more than the I formation being talked about in those early "war" years between the AFL and the NFL. Do you miss any of the intrigue?

Yes, it was a very exciting time. I think those of us who were involved in it from the beginning liked and enjoyed it. We took great pride in the league, in the way it grew and developed. The intrigue really was a fascinating aspect. It still is. This is the real excitement of professional football. The game plan, the camouflage, and other things that go on trying to win a game hold great appeal.

Why did pro football's two great camouflage teams – the Cowboys and the Texans – come out of the same city?

Camouflage and variety are what we've sold since the beginning of our football team, both offensively and defensively. The Cowboys have a varied offensive personality and a simplistic defensive personality, which is unique. Tom Landry has always felt strongly about his basic four to three coverage, and that kind of thing. He helped create it when he was with the Giants, and he has done a fantastic job with it. But it's a split personality. I know we're not known for a variety defense, but we have one. People talking about our triple stack don't realize that it's part of our variety. We've always used the zone defense, even in the early 1960s, and we started

Hank Stram (left) has been closely identified with some of the most dramatic technical innovations in professional football over the last decade. Three of them are shown below. They are (top to bottom) the tight I formation (also seen at right), the triple stack defense, and the moving pocket.

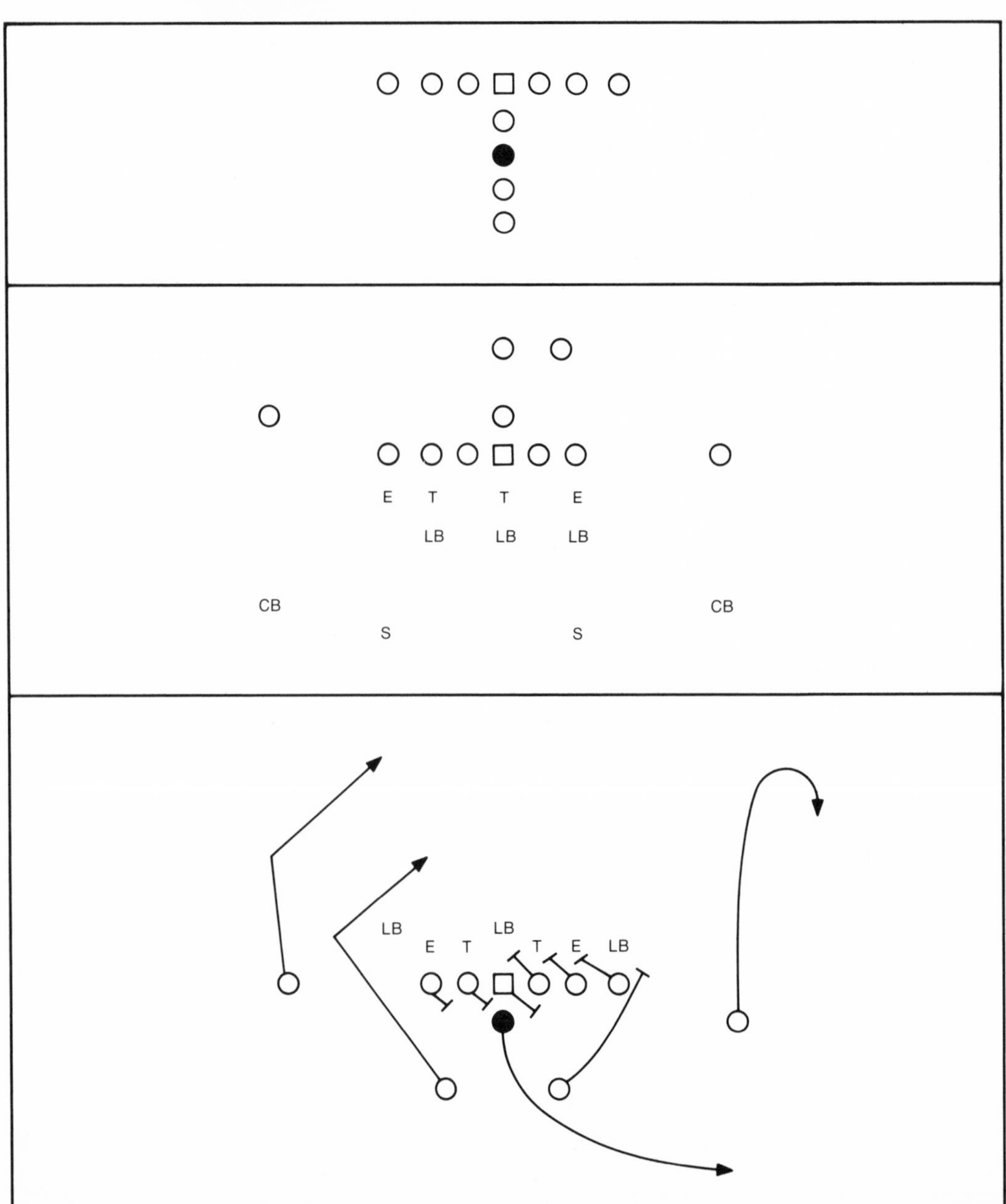

16
59

There was a moment for Hank Stram after Super Bowl IV, a moment when all the ebullience washed from his face and he reflected on his career as he clutched the most coveted trophy of all.

the triple stack in 1962. We used it in the championship game that year. Buck Buchanan helped us a lot in that defense because of his bulk and size. But we used the zone and the Oklahoma, which is kind of a triple, because at that time we didn't have many outstanding linemen. We did have outstanding linebackers: Walt Corey, Smokey Stover, Sherrill Headrick, and Ted Greene. We used some four-linebacker, three-down-linemen defenses. Then E. J. Holub came in at linebacker. We've always used odd and even spacing on defense, which is the variety I'm talking about. And here again, if you believe in variety, then you would think it would carry over into both segments of your thinking, offensively and defensively. We're consistent from that standpoint.

You won in 1962 and lost in 1963. You won in 1966 and lost in 1967. The year after you won the Super Bowl wasn't as good as you'd hoped. What is it with some championship teams that creates a dropoff the following season?

That's very difficult to understand. A lot of factors are involved. Number one, if you are goal-oriented, I think it's the nature of the beast that you don't have the same zest and determination after you've achieved the goal. You don't have the same willingness to make sacrifices you did before you won the Super Bowl or the world's heavyweight championship, or whatever. If you're not careful, you subconsciously take winning for granted. You don't admit this to yourself or even realize it's happening, but it happens. Then too, once you become a champion, every team you play has a different approach toward you. Maybe last year you were just another team, and they played you that way. They weren't quite as mentally involved as they are against a champion. The measuring stick becomes, "Well, we're going to find out what kind of team we are this week because we're going to play the world champions. If we can beat them, we can beat anybody."

What are the most intense games the Chiefs have played?

Our games with Oakland are always intense. There are two kinds of rivalry – the kind that's *just* a rivalry and a really bitter rivalry. Our rivalry with Oakland is bitter. With a bitter feeling, if you're not careful, you won't play to your capacity. The first Super Bowl was a very intense game for us, too. There were a lot of intangibles – the pageantry of the game, the rivalry between the two leagues, and playing one of the great glamour teams in professional football [the Green Bay Packers]. The New York Jets playoff game the year we played in Super Bowl IV is another one you'd have to classify in this category. And there was always great intensity in the early years against Houston and San Diego.

What was it like that day after the loss in Super Bowl I?

It was a professional blow. We had a chance to become the ultimate, the champions of professional football. It was a loss to all of us with the Chiefs, but it was also a loss to the whole American Football League. It's a little different now. When you lose it now, you and your organization lose it. At that time the whole league lost. It was a very intimate feeling. You'd hear from the owners, and they were pulling for you. We had made great strides and felt we were as good as the National Football League. Yet the way we played in the second half hurt our image. People said, "Well, they really aren't as good." I thought it was important not to dwell on that loss, but instead to turn around and make it a positive thing. We won eighteen and lost only three that season, so it was really a fantastic year. We were proud of what we'd achieved. We would use the setback as a stepping stone.

KC
CHIEFS

TYRER
77
77

Jim Tyrer

Position: Tackle
Years: 1961-
Height: 6-6
Weight: 270
College: Ohio State

Sunlight embellished the red hair, worn much fuller than when he came out of Ohio State coveted by both the Cleveland Browns and the Dallas Texans. That was in 1961.

With a 6-foot 6-inch, 280-pound body, good speed and quickness, and a quality of toughness, Jim Tyrer was the rarest of men. He was an offensive tackle who could be placed into a starting job as a rookie and take command like a veteran. Since the Texans already had a right tackle, Tyrer was sent to the left side. He remained there until injured midway through 1973, establishing a Chiefs' record for consistency and longevity by playing 13 years and 180 consecutive games.

Through the 1960s Tyrer was an almost automatic selection as the left tackle on the AFL all-star teams. He played prominent parts in all five of the Chiefs' championship and Super Bowl games.

As a rookie playing in the East-West Shrine game, he was matched against another rookie, E. J. Holub, who soon would be a teammate. "The Beast" from Texas Tech was voted the day's outstanding defensive player, but he shrugged off the honor: "That Tyrer should've got something. He just cut me down like a blade."

Despite his size, Tyrer displayed amazing quickness. As a rookie he was the lead blocker as Abner Haynes scored five times in one game on sweeps, still a Kansas City record.

Like others on the old Texans, Tyrer was reluctant to come north when the franchise moved in 1963. Now he makes his home in Kansas City, where he conducts a successful business in which he represents athletes in commercial ventures.

There was an obvious stigma attached to the American Football League in its early years. What influenced you to sign with Dallas?

I was drafted number one by Cleveland and talked to Paul Brown. He couldn't see why an Ohio boy would want to play for anyone but the Browns. But they had Mike McCormack, the offensive captain, as their right tackle and Dick Schafrath as their left tackle. I'd beaten Schafrath out at Ohio State, but he had played one season already and pretty well established himself. In talking to Lamar Hunt and the Dallas people, I saw a great opportunity. The AFL was only one year old. Besides, the AFL offered me more money.

You got off to a rocky start in Dallas.

It was unique anyway. Jerry Mays, Fred Arbanas, E. J. Holub, and I had all played in the College All-Star game on a Friday night. Then we got on a plane and flew to Dallas, where we all started against the New York Titans. My wife met us at the airport in our old Ford station wagon. It was a northern station wagon; that is, it had no air conditioning. We all drove to the clubhouse and I encouraged my wife, who was pregnant, to wait inside the team offices, where it was cooler. While we were drawing equipment for the game, somebody stole all the luggage from the back of our car.

What was it like in the early AFL years?

Well, we played in places like Midland, Texas, and Wichita, Kansas, and P. C. Cobb Stadium in Dallas before ten or twelve thousand fans . . . and it wasn't an honest crowd count. In New York my locker consisted of a nail driven into a two-by-four, and a folding chair underneath. It was right before the Polo Grounds closed and they certainly weren't putting any money into it.

Didn't you play the Titans the week their checks bounced?

Right. The league stepped in and guaranteed the checks. The league made laundry payments, too, because the team couldn't get its uniforms out of the laundry before the game either.

The stadiums themselves weren't too fancy either, were they?

I remember one time we were playing Boston

The career of mighty tackle Jim Tyrer has spanned 13 years of Chiefs history. He helped running back Abner Haynes to AFL rushing records in the team's early years (right), and he was there at Super Bowl IV pass blocking for quarterback Len Dawson (below).

up in Boston. Cotton Davidson was our quarterback, and we were behind by six late in the fourth quarter. We got down to their ten-yard line and had time left for one pass. Cotton threw it, but it was knocked down and we lost. When we saw films of that pass, which was meant for Chris Burford, we saw some guy run out of the stands and knock it down. Then he ran back in the stands. That's how we lost. The officials didn't see it, and neither did our coaching staff. But the fans were in that close. There were a lot of other places like that, Buffalo and Denver, for example. Young guys coming in today can't really appreciate what the American Football League achieved. They can relate to tradition that is given to them by older players, but most of the oldtimers are gone now. I'm the senior member of our team.

What was the state of your own team that first summer?

I think we've always been further advanced from a management standpoint than most teams. This depends heavily on the capabilities of Lamar and Jack Steadman. From a football standpoint, it goes back to Hank. Organization is one of his true fortes. I always felt we were very well organized.

Hank's reputation outside the club is one of an innovator.

More than that, he's a stickler for fundamentals. Everything proceeds from the proper fundamentals. He'll say, "Do it again," or "Let's go over that again, fellas." Even now, after all these years, he'll have me going back over the fundamentals. And he'll work with quarterbacks, giving them the individual attention they need. He's many-faceted, but his feeling is that everything begins with fundamentals, and a proper attitude. He expects a consistent attitude, eliminating peaks and valleys, on both good Sundays and bad Sundays. He hasn't had a substantial amount of turnover in his staff. He's built peo-

ple around him who think as he does. He's very demanding of himself, his coaching staff, and his players. Hank puts everything in a word: "Win." I hear a lot of talk about old teams and young teams. In 1962, we averaged only twenty-three years of age. But if you win, all of a sudden you can forget about the old, the young, and the mistakes. If you win on Sunday, you're a great guy on Monday.

What about the transformation from 1961 to 1962?

In 1961, we were going through a pretty desperate period. Jack Spikes was hurt, and everything fell down on our heads. Cotton was reaching a plateau in his career and didn't have a whole lot of confidence. It was affecting our concentration. Hank was trying to find that right quarterback. Even at that time our offense was pretty technical. When Dawson joined us, most of us thought he was an NFL reject, a guy who never had the opportunity to make it. He had no credentials, per se. Of course, the AFL at that time was made up of marginal ball players, former NFL players, and guys who had been out of school a couple of years and come back to try out. It was a catch-as-catch-can group of people. The nucleus of our ball club was old NFL players – Ray Collins, Paul Miller, and guys like that. They only lasted a couple of years and were phased out.

Has the style of the Texans/Chiefs changed over the years?

They say it has, just as they say the entire style of the AFL did when it merged with the NFL. We were wide-open, razzle-dazzle types once – Abner Haynes types who start one way, stop, change direction, and come back the opposite way, the Paul Lowe type, and the Keith Lincoln type. Now with the dominating defenses in the NFL, it has to have changed some. But not that much.

You and Ed Budde have played beside each other for a decade. Can you communicate now in a game without talking?

You wage your own wars in the line, but you grow to know the man next to you. This is what pro football's all about. We know our strong points. Ed and I are both good on running plays. Because of our size, we like it when the team runs. That gives our quarterbacks confidence.

In Super Bowl IV against Minnesota, when Mike Garrett scored the touchdown that put the game almost out of reach, you had a key "influence" block.

That goes back to tendencies. We had one. We don't have it as much as we did with Abner Haynes. In those days it was a toss thing with the tackles and guards pulling. Well, I don't care who you are or how well you're schooled, in the heat of battle you'll invariably react momentarily to the movement of an offensive lineman. Jim Marshall of the Vikings did. He turned his body just slightly. That gave Ed a chance to make a quick trap. It just takes that second, that slight eye or head movement, and it's all over. The play was designed to come over the left side with my making a false pull to my left, and if I could, influence the defensive end to turn to react to me enough to enable my guard to make the trap. Then the back was to hit the right hole, a straight dive.

Do you recall how you felt when Garrett scored to make it sixteen to nothing?

With the amount of strain during that game, it took me nearly a week to sit down and analyze what we'd accomplished. There was so much leading to that game. I think the big plus was that we'd been there before. There was such great pressure the first time – playing for our league against the great NFL. There was so much emphasis placed on what the game represented. There probably was also some doubt in some players' minds that we could win. In the first game we had confidence, but it really didn't

16
HILL

This offensive line was an important reason for Kansas City's success in the late sixties. Its members were, clockwise: guard Ed Budde, tight end Fred Arbanas, tackle Jim Tyrer, tackle Dave Hill, and guard Mo Moorman. Moorman joined the group in 1968; the other men were together from 1963 to 1970.

Away from the football field, he is Jim Tyrer the tycoon, operator of a Kansas City promotion company and typical business-minded Chiefs player.

show. It was individualistic, not team. And that two-week training thing in Long Beach was too much for us. We didn't need two weeks for mental preparation. And we didn't change our offense for Green Bay that much. We changed it a lot less than we would have against somebody from the AFL, where we were so used to odd defenses, triple stacks, that kind of junk. Green Bay just gave us a plain old ordinary defense, a four-three-four. Our second Super Bowl was different. It's like having had an operation. You've been there. You know what to expect.

How much of a factor was pressure from the press the first time?

A very small part. What harassed me more than anything else was people calling for tickets. I went into the ticket business, it seemed. I got twenty to thirty calls a day, voices out of the past. These are the things the average fan doesn't realize. The game itself is no problem. It's the environmental aspects.

Does anything stand out in your mind as much as the Super Bowls?

Two things. The 1962 championship game, because everything was involved in it, and that game against the Bears in the summer of 1967 when we came back from the Super Bowl. We weren't really playing the Bears; we were playing the NFL. It was the pride aspect. Here was a team that was one of the basic foundations of the NFL, and we kicked the hell out of them. Hank didn't work us up for the game. He's big for clippings, but I don't remember any clippings or special films that time. It was preseason, and it was hot. But we were well-conditioned. The score was sixty-six to twenty-four, and they didn't get the twenty-four until late in the game. The win was fun, and it also meant a lot to us.

What championship ring do you wear?

Usually the one from 1962. All it has on it is a picture of the Cotton Bowl with a red "D" in it. But I use it as an example, past and present.

Was that 1968 game against Oakland, where you just ran and ran and ran, the most physical game you've ever been in?

Only to the extent that it was so constant – bang, bang, bang. We're like Oakland. We don't like a team that just goes at us and at us. Pro football's evolved to the point where the defensive linemen don't want any contact at all. The contact they have with me just slows them down in getting to the quarterback. In the case of a run, if they're messing with me, they can't get off to make the tackle.

The Packers used to talk of love. Kansas City has always talked of a strong sense of team. What ingredient is it that best distinguishes a winner?

Confidence. It grows with victories and success. You can say it's love in the case of the Packers. Again it goes back to philosophy. Any successful person has critics. Hank has his in Kansas City. But whatever he's done, he's done something right because we've won. I look around at the number of ball players who started with me in the AFL or NFL. For example, if I'd played with the Cleveland Browns, I'd never have been in a Super Bowl game. And the likelihood of playing in even one all-star game would probably be nil. Much of that is individual ability, but a lot of it is team ability and popularity. When you get right down to it, you play for many reasons – love of the game, the contact, the ego trips it gives you to be an athlete, the fan appeal, the charisma of the NFL, and the hero worship. But everything you do is preparation for that big one in January. We've been there twice, so Stram is doing something right. Even though I don't agree with his philosophy at times, I'll go along with it.

The Other Years

The rain that had threatened Super Bowl IV returned after the game and continued through the night. It was still coming down as people rushed from taxis to the airport in New Orleans that Monday morning.

Inside the jetliner bound for Dallas, almost every seat was filled. There were red souvenirs. Those belonged to Kansas City fans. There were purple pennants. Those belonged to Minnesota fans. All the eyes seemed a little bloodshot. The people with the red souvenirs definitely looked happier.

Less than 24 hours earlier, Kansas City had defeated Minnesota 23–7.

Near the rear of the tourist section, a young businessman found a seat, tucked his raincoat into the overhead rack, and settled down. He fastened his seat belt and let his knees straddle the shopping bag he rested on the floor in front of him. The man was Lamar Hunt, owner of the Kansas City Chiefs and founder of the American Football League. The shopping bag was jammed with Chiefs souvenirs and the accumulated sports pages of a week that had climaxed a 10-year struggle. His Chiefs – his league, in fact – had been vindicated. After a decade of work, Hunt celebrated the triumph in tourist class, where he always rides. His team was at its peak. They were world champions. The press clippings between his knees said so.

This was Lamar Hunt's finest moment. He and his league had climbed to the top of the mountain. For every peak, of course, there's a valley, and if this was the summit, what was the lowest point in those 10 years? Was it the day Hunt finally decided to abandon Dallas and move to Kansas City, even as his 1962 Texans team was winning its first title? Was it the disappointment of some losing seasons, or was it a game such as the Green Bay Packers' victory in Super Bowl I? Or was it going onto the floor of Kansas City's Municipal Stadium for the first time, only to find just 5,000 spectators for the game? Which would rank as the bleakest memory? Curiously, it's none of these.

"Around the office, we sort of refer to that loss to Oakland that gave them a sweep over us in 1963 as our worst moment," says Hunt from the vantage point of the mid-1970s. "They were just beginning to emerge in the West, and that was the first time they swept a series."

Just as Kansas City cannot be removed from the fabric of the AFL, the Raiders can never be taken out of any story on Kansas City. Together, the two bitter rivals won their way into three of the four Super Bowls before the leagues completed their merger. As regularly as Christmas or Thanksgiving, and at about the same time, it was Kansas City and Oakland, head to head for the title. While some teams could win division championships with eight victories, the Chiefs and Raiders were so good they sometimes went into double figures and still finished second to the other.

But this came after the two teams had become the class of the ambitious young league. In the earlier years, those other years while the AFL struggled against the NFL, the rivalries were different. In those days, Houston and San Diego were powerful. Then Buffalo grew as a threat and dominated for a couple of years just before the merger.

All the while, Hunt's young team was often held up as the shining example, the ideal. "The best money can buy," was one quip making the rounds in those days, and one that used to goad the young owner at times.

Once, after a disappointing season, he told an interviewer that the image was distorted. The Chiefs had players such as Jim Tyrer, Jerry Mays, Buck Buchanan, and Bobby Bell, but Hunt said, "there are other teams in this league with excellent people, too." The image of excellence, of a superabundance of talent, has clung

Quarterback Len Dawson and his running backs, Curtis McClinton (32) and Abner Haynes, led the Texans, champions of the American Football League.

to the franchise throughout its history. It has been both an asset and a liability.

It began almost as soon as the team opened for business in Dallas. It faced an immediate challenge from the NFL's Cowboys. The two Texas teams sought the same players, the same fans, and sometimes even the same coaches. While searching for a head coach, Hunt had considered a young New York Giants' assistant, Tom Landry, but he has never regretted the decision he made to pick Hank Stram. Landry went to the Cowboys; Stram went to the Texans. Each forged a power.

That pioneer period in Dallas was an exciting one, both on the field and in the box office. Knothole gangs were set up to lure kids – and hopefully their parents – into the Cotton Bowl. At halftime, balloons were released, some with season tickets in them. Promotions abounded. Lovely girls sold tickets in downtown Dallas. There was even a milking contest featuring players from the Texans and Cowboys. The Texans won. It was the only face-to-face meeting during the teams' three-year crosstown rivalry. But it typified the zany things that happened in the intensely competitive atmosphere.

For all the Texans' success in the promotional duels, they never dominated the Dallas market. They probably featured a better team, but the Cowboys could boast of better, more famous opponents. Who was going to pay to watch Boston if they could wait to see the Packers?

In putting together the Texans, Stram and Hunt had wanted it to be a team that was essentially theirs, rather than a collection of castoffs from other clubs, although they knew they would have to fill key positions with such men for a period. This would require tryout camps.

"They'd bring in almost anybody and give them a look that first year or so," says Bobby Yarborough, the equipment manager. Yarborough has been with the club since it began and is the unofficial historian and collector of anecdotes. "That first summer, before we went to training camp at Roswell, New Mexico, they had a camp in a park in Dallas. The coaches would look at each other and say, 'Well, what are we gonna do with these guys? Let's have some calisthenics.' So they'd do that a while. Then they decided it was time for agility drills. Leapfrog was one of them. This was summer, remember, and it was hot. Dallas hot. And I remember Al Reynolds, who became a real good guard for us, leaping over one poor guy and heaving right down his neck." From that camp came Reynolds, Smokey Stover, and defensive back Dave Webster.

The actual training camp opened in July at a military school in Roswell. Those who attended that first camp recall it principally for the brutal work schedule. Then there was the heat, and the mosquitoes. An irrigation canal ran along one side of the practice field, and weary players used to flop into the shallow trench, equipment and all, at the end of a drill.

Hunt would fly up to watch regularly as Stram began piecing together the team he would take into the AFL's first year. Camp opened with seven quarterbacks, but ex-Baylor star Cotton Davidson quickly moved ahead. Rookies Jack Spikes, Johnny Robinson, and Abner Haynes were obviously going to provide a sound group of runners.

The Texans moved through a good summer that finished with four straight preseason wins. They wound up 8–6 in their first regular season. The Los Angeles Chargers won the division with a 10–4 record. The Texans drew 171,500 fans, a figure that, from all accounts, was probably inflated by a number of free passes.

It took a late-season tongue-lashing by Stram to snap his team out of a two-game losing streak that did as much as anything to cost the Texans the title that year. Although frequently ham-

Often the target of photographers, owner Lamar Hunt tried his own hand at shooting the action from the Texans' bench (left). Dawson (number 16 at right), Fred Arbanas (84) and the Texans were in the national spotlight after their nationally televised six-quarter championship struggle against the Houston Oilers.

pered by injuries, the team was still in contention until losing 42–14 to the Patriots and 41–35 to the Titans. The Tuesday after the loss in New York, Stram had a message for his team. "You have played the two worst games anyone has ever played for me," he said. "Perhaps you are immature. Perhaps you are not very smart. Each man has to get himself ready for each game with what is inside him, but I am going to help you along a little. Any man who scores less than seventy percent in our ratings in any of our three remaining games will be fined five hundred dollars." Nearly a third of the squad had missed the 70 percent mark in the two previous games.

The incentive program worked wonders as the Texans won their final three games by a cumulative score of 82–7. But it was too late. They could only take consolation later with one of their finest drafts, selecting E. J. Holub, Bob Lilly, Jim Tyrer, Claude Moorman, Jerry Mays, Fred Arbanas, and Curtis McClinton. They signed everyone except Lilly and Moorman.

Ironically, the fact that the Texans drafted Lilly probably made it easier for the Cowboys to eventually get the big defensive star from Texas Christian. "If it hadn't been for Hunt drafting Lilly and Holub," said Cowboy general manager Tex Schramm later, "we wouldn't have had a chance at them. As it turned out nobody wanted to get in a bidding war with Hunt."

The Cowboys had traded away their number one draft choice a year earlier, sending it to Washington to obtain quarterback Eddie LeBaron. They had gone through 1960 without a victory, managing one tie. Cleveland, thirteenth in the draft order, had just selected Jim Tyrer when the Browns received word that an aide had contacted the Ohio State tackle and learned he already had signed with the Texans. Paul Brown quickly withdrew the name, and the Browns' staff was huddling to find a replacement when Schramm went to their table. He proposed to trade the following year's number one and Paul Dickson, a tackle from Baylor, for the Browns' choice. Cleveland agreed, and Dallas took Lilly. Holub was the second-round choice of the Cowboys.

The Cowboys then signed Lilly, making it imperative that the Texans get Holub. Holub finally signed on the final day of December, after Hunt had spent most of the week in Palo Alto, California, where Holub was practicing for the East-West Shrine game.

Armed with some impressive new talent, plus a new general manager in Jack Steadman, a former employee of a Hunt Oil Company subsidiary, the Texans moved into their second season. At the owners' meetings in Houston in January, it was announced that Hunt's league had lost an estimated $3.5 million in its first year. But it was still in operation, even though Los Angeles soon would move to San Diego. Even this news did not dampen the team's optimism.

Unhappy with the Roswell arrangement, the Texans leased a couple of air-conditioned fraternity houses on the SMU campus the next summer and shifted their training camp to Dallas. Says Yarborough: "We had our offices and training rooms off the North Central Expressway, with the practice fields just behind the building. In June we'd have some of our guys working out there, as well as guys from other clubs who were living in Dallas. We even had a couple of Cowboys. We'd have some hellacious touch football games there off the expressway. Fifteen hundred people or so would stop off on their way from work in the evenings to watch.

"We had a big billboard in front of the office, and we'd have to change the signs every once in a while when Lamar sent out a new saying, or a new team was due in town.

"Lamar used to come out in the evenings. We

had beautiful Bermuda grass in front of the office, and he used to sit out there for hours in the evening. He'd water the grass as we talked. He and Hank would sit out there sometimes. Lamar would roll up his sleeves, loosen his tie and just water the grass. Once, when Dave Dixon [a New Orleans businessman who wanted the Texans to move to New Orleans] was in town, he and Lamar stood outside talking business while Lamar watered the lawn."

Even the players seemed drawn back to the site. Says Yarborough: "They'd get a couple cases of beer and sit out on the curb there after preseason games. No girls or anything else; just the players. They'd sit and drink beer and hack the game over."

It was, in many ways, a comfortable, homey, friendly, typically Texas kind of life for those first three years. Stram and Hunt were gradually putting together the talent they needed, and the players had settled nicely into the city. Indeed, few adjustments had to be made; the first year, 15 of the 35 active players were from Texas. The ratio remained about the same for several seasons. The Texans had been well-named.

But Stram still could not find the consistent pattern he was after. He had made a reputation developing quarterbacks – Len Dawson at Purdue, Charlie Arnold at SMU, George Izo at Notre Dame, and Fran Curci at Miami – but Davidson was proving too erratic for any serious championship thrust. At one point in 1961, Davidson was completing less than 40 percent of his passes. The Texans were being hit by crippling injuries, and they lost six straight games to fall out of the title picture quickly. The losses carried to the attendance as well. Only 123,000 showed up for the seven Cotton Bowl dates as the Texans slumped to 6–8 for the season. San Diego was first with a 12–2 record.

By this point in the team's development, it was becoming clearer and clearer the Texans needed a proven quarterback. For several reasons they had not drafted a quarterback the previous year. They knew that they already had ex-Iowa star Randy Duncan coming down from Canada, and they thought they might also get Sam Etcheverry, another Canadian who eventually went instead to St. Louis. Duncan did not prove to be the product Stram remembered. So by late 1961 the Texans were back in the market. They talked to another Canadian star, Joe Kapp, but they did not get him. They also attempted to get Oakland's rights to Roman Gabriel.

If the Texans were uncertain at quarterback, Hunt left no doubt who his coach would be as the Texans opened their third year. "Hank Stram will definitely be our coach next year. Don't make that sound like a vote of confidence," Hunt said. Then he launched into a discourse on quarterbacks.

"You hear so many good and bad things about players. You'll have to ask Hank why [Duncan] isn't playing. That's his department. I'll give you an example. San Diego is real high on John Hadl. I can't believe it. If he makes it, anybody can," said Hunt of the quarterback who would one day lead all 26 teams in passing.

It was not an auspicious draft in 1962 as four of the Texans' top six choices, including number one, Baylor fullback Ronnie Bull, went to the NFL. Still, Arizona's Eddie Wilson was signed, as was Miami end Bill Miller, and some later round choices, including Bobby Ply, Bobby Hunt, and Tommy Brooker.

Two of the hardest years were behind the Texans as Tyrer, Mays, and others began to move into positions they would occupy with all-league ability for years. Arbanas had been a 1961 casualty, however, missing the entire season with a back ailment that had troubled him since college. Called the "finest blocking tight end I've ever seen" by his coach at Michigan State, Duffy Daugherty, Arbanas had under-

Cartoonist John Chase delighted Chiefs fans with the covers he drew for game programs. His offering for the team's inaugural game in Kansas City (left) depicted a Chief about to carve a Buffalo Bill. Sherrill Headrick (right) was a far-ranging linebacker.

gone surgery as a rookie. "Then I got an infection in my lower back," he said. "The doctors didn't think that I was going to make it. Jeff Chandler, the movie star, had died the month before with the same thing. I was lucky."

In the 1961 season, the Texans' long losing streak finally ended against Oakland. Leading 43–0, Stram sent in both Davidson and Duncan. Even for Stram, this obviously heralded something different and the Cotton Bowl crowd murmured. Duncan took the snap, whirled, threw to Davidson, who threw it as far as he could. Chris Burford made a sensational catch. But the Texans were penalized five yards for being offside.

Later in the game, the Texans had a fourth down on the Oakland 36. On came Davidson and Duncan again. Duncan knelt to take the snap for a field-goal try. Davidson kicked the ball squarely into a startled lineman's rump, and the ball bounced back to the quarterbacks. Turning soccer stylist, Davidson whacked at it again, this time with the ball moving toward him. It bounced toward the sideline with Davidson in pursuit. He kicked it out of bounds, cursing.

In an earlier game in Boston, Davidson had taken the Texans deep into Patriots territory in a last desperate attempt to pull out a victory. On the final play, as he tried to throw to Burford in the endzone, a fan jumped from the stands and ran into the endzone nearly to the goal before veering off. None of the Texans even knew it until they spotted the intruder on films the next Tuesday, since the lighting in that end was poor and fans already were ringing the back of the endzone.

Incidents such as this caused one Dallas reporter to comment, "The AFL games I've seen had a feeling of wild freedom, as if at any moment somebody would run ninety-eight yards, turn a somersault, and throw the ball into the air; then somebody else would grab it, run ninety-nine yards, step on a turtle, and break his leg; and a big flag would pop out of the scoreboard and go *BANG!*"

Stram hoped to change that image with his 1962 club. Arbanas was healthy; Davidson had looked good in the first AFL All-Star game; Haynes continued to get better and better, now ranking among the top runners in the game; Mel Branch and Mays anchored a good defensive line, with Holub, Corey, Headrick (whom San Diego's Sid Gillman called "the best middle linebacker in football"), and Ted Greene at linebacker. Robinson was to shift to defense, since it appeared Curtis McClinton was as good as everyone thought. Frank Jackson, the "Preacher" from SMU, was an excellent backup for Haynes and could also play as a receiver.

As usual in those years, the winter months were filled with reports of double signings, athletes who had signed contracts in both leagues. The Texans and Cowboys even got into the act. The Cowboys lost defensive tackle Ray Jacobs to Houston. The Texans lost offensive lineman Irv Goode to St. Louis and tackle Charles Hinton to Cleveland.

The Texans did get Auburn quarterback Hunt, although there were some worrisome moments. The 6-foot 1-inch, 185-pounder was sought as a defensive back both by the Texans and Cowboys. No NFL team had drafted him, and the Texans had waited until the eleventh round.

Jim Beavers, an employee of Hunt Oil Company who was skilled in negotiations, had been sent to start talking to Bobby right after the AFL draft. But Hunt said, "No, I promised the NFL I wouldn't sign until after their draft." When he wasn't chosen, he called Steadman. "I'm ready," he announced. Beavers flew to Atlanta and was in the terminal making arrangements to get to Auburn when he saw Bobby walking to a reservation desk with Jim Myers, the ex-Texas A&M coach who was working as a scout for

69

11 53
CHIEFS 35 VISITOR 7
1 DOWN 10 TO GO 3 QTR
86
87
BEATHARD
10
33

Eight-year-old Dale Stram cleaned the Municipal Stadium mud from the cleats of towering Buck Buchanan (left) during a 1964 game. Safetyman Bobby Hunt (right) had been the object of a signing war between the Texans and the Cowboys.

the Cowboys, and who now had the prize in tow.

They were going to Dallas. "Not without me," Beavers said. Bobby Hunt then flew to Dallas sandwiched between the two, Myers whispering Cowboys in one ear and Beavers murmuring Texans in the other.

This continued in Dallas, as Hunt was shuttled back and forth. Finally Hunt called Steadman. The Texans rushed over and signed him.

By summer, bolstered by rookies like Hunt and McClinton, the Texans were back near the North Central Expressway. A newcomer named Len Dawson began to look better as the summer moved quickly toward the opening game against Boston.

Hopes were high as usual. So were spirits, and the final night of training camp in Dallas was a memorable one for Yarborough and others.

"Wayne [Rudy, the trainer] and I were sleeping in the recreation room of an SMU fraternity house while the players shared the regular rooms upstairs," says Yarborough. "Everything was air conditioned, but the air conditioner that fed the players' rooms went out about two-thirty or three in the morning. Pretty soon the rec room doors started opening, and the players started coming in, dragging their mattresses with them.

"About five, Headrick came in," Yarborough remembers. "He couldn't sleep any more. He couldn't sleep half the time anyway. I happened to wake up and see him. There were about thirty-five people in that room by then, spread out wall to wall. Headrick got hold of the rope to ring the biggest bell you ever saw and was about to ring it when I whispered, 'No, no, don't ring it.' Sherrill kind of looked at it longingly, and then he went off down the hall.

"But by six-thirty he couldn't stand it any longer. He rushed back in, grabbed the rope, and started ringing the bell. You never saw such mayhem in your life. They started throwing mattresses and everything all over that room."

So, with a bell-ringing, mattress-heaving fight, the Texans wound up their last summer camp in Dallas.

The Texans sped through the season with Haynes and Dawson leading the charge. They finished with an 11–3 record, then beat Houston 20–17 in overtime for their first title. It came just two days before Christmas, 1962.

Within six weeks the team was staring at the morning headlines and listening to the radio with disbelief – the Texans, champions of the AFL, were moving to Kansas City. Hunt had abandoned the costly competition with the Cowboys in a city that could support only one professional football franchise.

Haynes's reaction was probably typical. "Believe it or not, I was in my bed that morning about five o'clock, wide awake, and I heard on the radio that I'd been moved to Kansas City," he said. "It was the first I had heard of it, and it was a shock. I had a good job, and I was at home in my own community. Now I was being uprooted, taken to Kansas City. We were being put into a situation where we had to do another selling job all over again. It took us out of a good situation into a new area, one that was basically college-oriented. It was the same for the other guys. They had developed tremendous roots in Dallas. We were definitely accepted there. We were drawing better than the Cowboys. I had signed with the Texans partly because I wanted to play in Dallas.

"I just lost all the way around, including a job. I had a hell of a time getting work in Kansas City. If it hadn't been for Hank Stram, I don't know what would have happened. On his own, he called Pepsi Cola and got me a job driving a truck."

Tyrer said it was a big adjustment for his family. "We didn't know where to shop, where to find a doctor, or how to get to different

Chris Burford (left) and Frank Jackson were Kansas City's star pass receivers during the mid-1960s. Defensive end Mel Branch was a sturdy member of the defense during the same period. On pages 170-171, he grabs the jersey of Buffalo quarterback Jack Kemp.

places," he said. "It was all new. When you are worrying about those things, you don't concentrate as well on football."

It was a different lifestyle in Missouri, one to which the Texans would have to adjust. It took its toll on the Texans, who were renamed the Chiefs.

In their three years in Texas, the Texans had won 26 and lost 17. They had begun to feel at home. Now all that was changed. There was one comforting factor: They would take an excellent football team north, one bolstered by one of the finest drafts any team in the AFL enjoyed. Buck Buchanan, Ed Budde, Bobby Bell, Jerrel Wilson, and Dave Hill were now Texans – or rather Chiefs.

Stram was back at the drawing board with more ideas. On defense he was sometimes using three linemen and four linebackers, as he had done on occasion in 1962. All through that first summer in Missouri, he also used part of his daily practice time to introduce a formation new to the pros, the I. "It gives us a quicker way to get to certain areas from a running standpoint," he said.

The lure of a new team, a championship one at that, seemed lost on Kansas Citians. The Chiefs defeated Buffalo 17–13 in their first game in Municipal Stadium that summer, and only about 5,000 fans watched.

"We moved north for this?" one veteran asked as they lined up for the National Anthem. It was the final touch on a day in which they had come into their dressing room to get ready, only to discover that Charles Finley, owner of the baseball team that also occupied the room, had refused to allow the Chiefs to use the same dressing stalls. Finley had ordered plywood sheets nailed over them to seal them off. The Chiefs used nails driven into these boards to hang their clothes.

It would not be a memorable year. Nor would it be a happy year, perhaps explaining Haynes's decline after he had established himself as one of the game's top runners. He had scored 19 touchdowns in 1962, but for much of 1963, he averaged only a little over two yards per carry.

The season had taken a tragic turn on a hot August night in Wichita, Kansas, in a preseason meeting between the Chiefs and Oilers. It was their first game since the Texans had won the championship battle in overtime the previous December.

The hitting, as expected, was ferocious. Late in the first quarter, Haynes and his boyhood friend, Stone Johnson, were standing in the endzone awaiting a Houston kick. Haynes had talked Johnson into going with the Texans the previous fall. Johnson, who had once recovered from back surgery to run for the United States in the Rome Olympics, was a good prospect that summer of 1963, and an eager one. He had arrived in the hotel lobby a half hour before the bus departed for the stadium, then waited there fidgeting anxiously. When the Oilers kicked, the ball drifted toward Haynes. Ten years later he described what ensued: "Stone jumped in front of me and got the ball. He was on the kickoff return team. In that situation, Kansas City uses the goal posts to determine which deep man takes the ball. If the ball comes across a certain position, right or left, one or the other back takes it."

Haynes's voice broke at the memory. "Stone was so excited about showing well that he just took the ball. He was moving on a guy and got ready to make a turn, sort of a fadeaway turn, when his feet slipped. While he was in the slide, the guy hit him head on.

"I have never seen a man's pants knocked down below his knees before. He was hit that hard. The position of his body . . . I couldn't explain it to you. There were certain things he was saying to me while he was lying on the

field; I heard them for two years afterward in my sleep."

Eight days later, totally paralyzed in the interim, Johnson died. Haynes, Dawson, McClinton, Burford, Mays, and Stram served as pallbearers at the funeral.

In 1962, the Chiefs had gone to camp needing a quarterback, secondary people, a tight end, a fast flanker to complement Burford, another running back, and more defensive linemen. They filled every need, and in 1963 Stram had a new list: a punter, a defensive end, and a flanker. Curt Merz, a second year man from Iowa, was counted on to replace Bill Hull, who had gone into the service. Jackson was shifted to flanker, solving that problem; and Jerrel Wilson immediately convinced everyone he was the punter they were looking for.

"Wilson," said personnel chief Don Klosterman, "is a man without a governor. He can't kick short. He doesn't just kick the ball, he ruins it." That was welcome news on a team that had been sorely troubled by lack of a punter all through 1962. Wilson played golf the same way he punted. "We were playing at this country club in Kansas City, and we came up to this par-three, two-hundred-thirty-yard hole," said Klosterman. "Wilson took out an eight-iron. We all go 'ha, ha' and he hits the thing over the green." Wilson finished his rookie season with a 43.5-yard average.

From the way the Chiefs launched their 1963 season, it looked as if they would never need a punter. Stunning Denver with the "I," they defeated the Broncos 59–7 in a game Stram described as "the greatest performance ever by the Chiefs."

But the fast start was misleading. The Chiefs' injury list lengthened and they lost frequently. Some of the carefree confidence of the earlier Haynes was missing, left perhaps on the field in Wichita in August. His 4.8 average fell to 2.6, and the Chiefs' running game, a major element in the success of 1962, was like a car with missing cylinders.

Kansas City lost 7 of 10 games after the Denver win, and it didn't regain anything approaching form until the end of the season. The Chiefs won their last three games by lopsided margins, and finished with a 5–7–2 record, their worst ever.

The front office reported one bright note. "We achieved breakeven status in our first season," said Steadman. An audit before Christmas disclosed an average of 22,509 fans per game, and season tickets sales of 15,185.

More good news followed. Late in January, 1964, it was announced that the league had concluded a five-year contract with the National Broadcasting Company. It would net $36 million, beginning in 1965. That amounted to $900,000 per team, compared to $261,000 from ABC in the final year of its contract.

"It gives them substance," one NFL owner admitted when informed of the television package during NFL meetings in Miami Beach. There were estimates that it took about $800,000 to break even for most AFL teams. So the new contract virtually assured the AFL of success. The long-range effect was a major one, particularly in NFL circles, which had been confidently waiting for the AFL to die of malnutrition. The AFL wouldn't die now.

Armed with a new five-year extension of his coaching contract, Stram set out to repair the damage of 1963, only to run into more problems. Of Kansas City's top 12 draft choices that year, only the first, USC quarterback Pete Beathard, and the fourth, tackle Ed Lothamer of Michigan State, signed with the Chiefs. All the others went to the NFL.

And, for a while in the spring, Stram was uncertain about second-year guard Budde, who had been hit over the head with a pipe by a man

33
78

BRANCH
87
15

81

Tommy Brooker (left) set an American Football League record by kicking 149 consecutive extra points. Guard Ed Budde (right) returned to football despite a skull fractured in an off-the-field incident.

in a bar. It fractured the big lineman's skull, and a metal plate had to be inserted. It wasn't until the following summer that either Budde or Stram could be certain whether or not the 6-foot 5-inch, 265-pounder would ever play again.

Budde adopted a unique testing method. In camp, he lined up opposite the "ding-ding bag," a 500-pound monster suspended from a heavy crossbar. Admitting that he was a little apprehensive about the whole process, Budde then proceeded to smash into the bag repeatedly, using his helmeted head. "It wasn't easy going out there the first time," he said. "If it was going to give me trouble, I'd sure pull out, but I had to find out right away."

Budde had no ill effects, but even a 4–1 preseason record in 1964 couldn't disguise the growing number of Kansas City injuries that threatened the season before it began. Dawson missed three games of a crucial stretch. Other starters had to be replaced, but the Chiefs were still within reach (only two games behind the Chargers) when they played their first "must" game in two years.

After a recession in 1962, the Chargers, led by Tobin Rote and Lance Alworth, had moved solidly back into their former place on top. They arrived in Kansas City for the November 15 game with a 6–2–1 record; the Chiefs were 4–4. But there was still another game between the two later in the season, so the Chiefs could help themselves considerably by beating the Chargers.

It seemed even the weather was against Stram's squad that afternoon. It rained except for a stretch through the second quarter when the Chargers scored all the points of their 28–14 victory. Hadl completed 11 of 19, including a 38-yard touchdown to Dave Kocourek and a 47-yarder to Alworth, who also dashed 19 yards on a reverse. Paul Lowe ran 50 more for another touchdown. Both of Alworth's scores came within a minute of each other, as the Chargers won to take a three-game lead.

The Chiefs were never able to make up that margin. They wound up 7–7 to the Chargers' 8–5–1. Still, it had not been a total washout. The Chiefs had unearthed a powerful rookie fullback in Mack Lee Hill, the first free agent ever to make the team as a runner. At 238 pounds, Hill was recommended by Buchanan, who had seen him play at Southern University. Talent scout Lloyd Wells had signed Hill for a $300 bonus just before Christmas after nobody drafted him in either league. Even though he had developed a magnificent physique stacking 190-pound boxes of tobacco in the summer in Florida, Hill somehow had escaped notice until Buchanan told the Chiefs about him.

Haynes also had rebounded in 1964, winning the AFL's comeback player of the year award as he averaged 5.2 yards per carry, just two-tenths behind Hill's league-leading rookie average.

In the draft, the Chiefs lost their number one choice, Gale Sayers, to the Chicago Bears. It wasn't until a Prairie View pass catcher named Otis Taylor came up in the fourth round that the Chiefs landed another of the big-play people whom they would use in the years ahead.

Taylor's signing is a well-chronicled example of the intrigue and counter-intrigue common during the war years. Wells had been close to Taylor's family in Houston, so close that he figured he would not have to worry about the big pass receiver. So Wells went off on other scouting duties only to learn that Taylor had disappeared.

Wells flew home and began checking, patiently tracing Taylor from Prairie View to Houston to Dallas through a series of motels. At one, the NFL sitters and several collegiate players, including Taylor, had merely walked through the front door, through the lobby, out a

The high drama and intrigue of the signing war between the rival leagues was at its most intense stage when scout Lloyd Wells (left, with coach Hank Stram) and the Chiefs spirited brilliant receiver Otis Taylor away from the NFL and signed him for Kansas City. At right, Taylor fights for the football with Jim Hudson and Johnny Sample of the New York Jets. Once the most celebrated player in the American Football League, Abner Haynes (pages 176-177) was traded to the Denver Broncos in 1965.

side door, and into waiting autos for a trip to yet another motel.

With the help of one of Taylor's girl friends, Wells finally learned that the players were in a motel north of Dallas, although none of them was registered under his own name.

Here is how Wells described the rest of the story to Milton Gross of the *New York Post:*

"I got some of the bellboys and some of the cooks and kitchen help I knew and learned they were in suites 101-105. I went to one of the rooms and a big, burly guy came out and asked me what I wanted. I had an unloaded camera around my neck, so I told him I was a newspaper man. He said, 'Okay, come on in.'

"I went into Taylor's room, and the boy acted all excited and intimidated. Obviously, he didn't want to stay. He had been cooped up for the last two or three days, ever since he'd been spirited off the Prairie View campus in a cab."

Wells wanted Taylor to leave with him right then, but Taylor said no, not until his teammate, Seth Cartwright, who was out at the moment, also could go. Wells told Taylor he'd return at midnight.

Wells left, called the Chiefs, and went into the dining room for a snack. The man who had admitted him to the suite also was there, studying Wells and pointing him out to a companion. When Wells returned to his own hotel in Dallas, one of the pair followed him.

Wells returned to the motel at midnight, just as a patrol car arrived. "I was trying to get up to Taylor's room," said Wells, "when this policeman asked me what I was doing around there. I said I was looking for a friend. He asked me if I was registered in the motel, and when I said I wasn't, he said. "You're prowling then. Get off this property, and if I catch you on it again I'll put you in jail.'"

The scout returned to Dallas, where he got a 3:30 a.m. call from Taylor. Wells again drove north and knocked on Taylor's window. Taylor, Cartwright, and another player had their bags packed. They got into Wells's car and drove straight to Love Field in Dallas.

"It was about four forty-five," Wells said, "but I saw some suspicious people hanging around the Braniff counter when I drove up. I figured they were waiting to intercept Taylor and Cartwright there. I decided to avoid trouble and drove to the Fort Worth airport, where we got a seven-forty plane to Kansas City."

The breakeven season was achieved only by winning the last three games. One of them, a 49–7 rout of San Diego, is notable because it was the first time Stram used the moving pocket. It was a tactical device designed specifically to help Dawson find passing lanes through the Chargers' huge linemen. The tactic worked so well that Dawson hit his first 11 passes and finished with 17 of 28 for 220 yards and 4 touchdowns. Rolling left or right, with line blocking varied slightly, Dawson was able to offset the reaching hands of Faison and Ladd, and Stram made the pocket another permanent part of Kansas City's weaponry.

On the following day, it was disclosed that another tragic event had struck the Chiefs. This time, Arbanas had undergone eye surgery after being assaulted on the street the previous Thursday. Police later theorized his unknown assailant must have used brass knuckles. Arbanas lost the use of one eye.

The new year opened on another discordant note. The AFL All-Star game was shifted from New Orleans to Houston at the last minute after Haynes helped to lead a revolt of black players who found the discrimination in New Orleans intolerable.

On January 21, 1965, the Chiefs traded Haynes to Denver for punter-linebacker Jim Fraser and cash. It was an ignominious finish for the dancing, dazzling runner who had

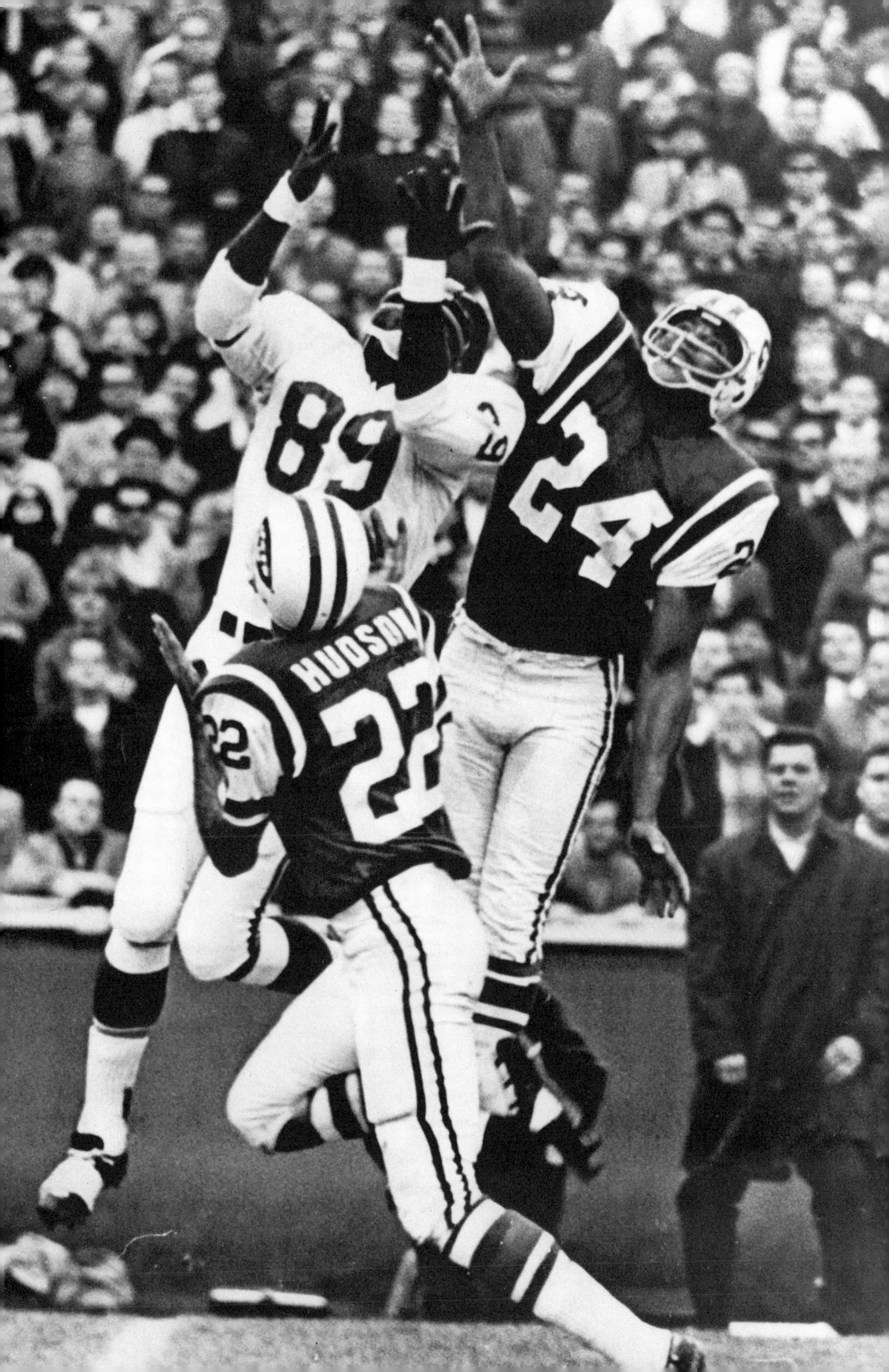
89
24
HUDSON
22

33

28
64
CLONE
64

The trade of Dave Grayson (left) brought Fred (the Hammer) Williamson to the Chiefs. Owner Lamar Hunt was one of the "babysitters" who stayed with defensive end Aaron Brown (right) to ensure his signing with the AFL rather than Minnesota of the NFL. An unknown from Southern University, Mack Lee Hill (pages 180-181) made the Chiefs' roster in 1964 and became the team's starting fullback.

brought so many people to their feet over the past five years.

"I'm glad to be moving," he said, "although I thought they might have gotten more for me in the trade. There are seven or eight others up there who would like to be traded, too. But some of them haven't got the nerve to say so. But I went to Hank Stram at the end of the season and told him I would like to be traded. It's obvious by the kind of deal they made for me that they felt they had to get rid of me. And not just because I wanted to leave Kansas City. There are other reasons."

Haynes had enjoyed his best year since 1962; he finished fifth in the league in rushing. "I guess they felt there wasn't much chance of some of the other players being satisfied as long as I was there," he said. "I hadn't been happy since we'd moved from Dallas, and I influenced the others. You want to play in a city where you can relax, but there was a lot of tension among the players in Kansas City, particularly after Fred Arbanas got hurt walking along the street. And before that Ed Budde had been injured in a fight with a couple of guys. You sort of wonder about your popularity in a town like that. But I believe what really forced the trade was my stand about the treatment of Negro players in New Orleans. I still think we were right in pulling out of there."

Haynes, one of the league's first great stars, was gone, but the questions and postmortems continued. In a question and answer series with Tom Marshall of the *Kansas City Star,* Hunt was asked about Stram's status, and about the fact that the Chiefs seemed to have great personnel, yet they failed to win as they should.

"There is a misconception regarding the material," said Hunt. "We have excellent material, but there are three teams that have equal or better material. There are six teams that could win the title.

"It seems to be our image that we should crush everybody, that we should go undefeated every year. We're still fighting this, trying to overcome this impression that there is no other material in the league."

In Lubbock, Texas, where Holub was recuperating from his sixth knee operation and tenth operation overall, the big linebacker was up every morning doing a six o'clock sports show. Holub also was trying to analyze what had happened since the team left Dallas. Where had it gone, that championship touch?

"I wouldn't be honest," said Holub, "if I didn't say that a lot of the guys still have their minds in Texas. Maybe I'm just being a big old baby about it, but it's just easier to breathe down here. But that should not have caused us to lose as much as we have. It's really irritating. We have the best personnel in the league – more talent, more speed, more everything – but each of the last two years, we've hit a slump in midseason and dropped out of the race."

Another major trade materialized in April, when the Chiefs sent Dave Grayson to Oakland for Fred Williamson, thus dispatching a man who would become a fixture on all-league teams for one who would become a focal point of controversy in the first Super Bowl. At the time, however, the Chiefs felt they had much the best of the deal. Williamson, who liked to tape his shoes so they seemed to be white, was 6 feet 3 inches tall and weighed 215 pounds. He was 5 inches and 29 pounds bigger than Grayson. Williamson thrived on public print and loved to advertise his "hammer," a forearm he delivered across a receiver's head, often with devastating effect.

In camp that summer, Bert Coan, acquired two years earlier in a trade, assumed greater importance now that Haynes was gone. Bell was moved exclusively to left linebacker after working at defensive end, but for the fourth time in

six years the season began with a loss. Dawson, who completed only 3 of 16 and even pitched out into an interception by Grayson, said he could not recall a worse personal game "even in high school" as the Raiders won 37–10.

It was one of the rare lopsided scores in a year in which the Chiefs finally moved back over .500 and had 10 games decided in the final minutes. "The Chiefs were about four plays away from a 10–2–2 season, which would have won the Western Division championship," wrote Bill Richardson in the *Star*.

Taylor, waiting until nearly midseason for his first starting job, had proven worth every bit of Wells's maneuverings to get him. Coan, at 230 pounds, and McClinton, at 232 pounds, had teamed in a power backfield much different from the one that had featured Haynes's sweeps.

Although the Chiefs finished third behind San Diego and Oakland, the promise for better things in 1966 was obvious. The Chiefs won three of their final six games.

Even the draft again seemed to be going their way, as they quickly signed Aaron Brown, the All-America from Minnesota. The 6-foot 5-inch, 240-pound Brown played the 1965 Big 10 season with a broken jaw, but he arrived on the Chiefs' scene just in time – Branch was due to retire following the 1965 season.

Borrowing NFL tactics, the AFL babysat Brown until the draft, with Hunt serving as one of the guardians. "We took an approach like the NFL's," said Hunt. "If you can't get him for your team, then get him for the league."

Hunt, Klosterman, and Wells met in Brown's hometown of Port Arthur, Texas, on Friday, the day before each league was to draft in late November. They went to Brown's home, where they met his parents. An NFL agent was already there. "It was a wild evening," said Hunt.

It was not a pleasant draft for Brooker, the hero of the 1962 championship game. Plagued by leg problems the previous two years, he watched as the Chiefs selected two kickers. They took Charlie Gogolak of Princeton in the seventh round, and then named Montana State's Jan Stenerud third on their future list.

In a game against Buffalo in 1962, Mack Lee Hill was injured on a blind-side tackle. Two days later he died on an operating table. At first, it was thought he had suffered a blood clot blockage. A more detailed autopsy seemed to rule that out. He may, it was suggested, have been the victim of his own superb muscular development. It may have placed him in a special risk group prone to sudden high fever during anesthesia. The autopsy revealed definite signs of heat stroke, while seeming to eliminate the earlier theories of a blockage.

Years afterward, Dawson said the second-year fullback seemed to have an inordinate fear of surgery. "He was deathly afraid of hospitals," said Dawson. "On the bus from the Buffalo stadium to the airport, he was trying to convince himself, as well as us, that it wasn't as bad as everyone knew it was. I saw the play on which he was hit. I think it was Mike Stratton who got him on the side and it was a good, clean tackle. The cleats stayed in and the knee went.

"On the bus ride, Mack was standing up. Somebody said 'Hey, sit down, don't be crazy.' He said, 'No, I'm fine. I'm all right. I want to stand here.' We almost had to force him to sit. I think he was afraid to admit then how bad it was.

"I talked to him the day before he went into the hospital. I knew he was apprehensive, but he knew it had to be done. He was talking about afterward, about going back to Florida."

The surgery had gone routinely for repair of a torn ligament in Hill's right knee. He was in the process of being prepared for return to the hospital bed when it was discovered at 2:35 p.m. that the canister in the breathing machine where

16
36

65

36

Mack Lee Hill and Hank Stram leave Shea Stadium after a 1965 Chiefs' victory (left). Hill died after he was injured during a game in 1966.

soporifics, oxygen, and the patient's respirations mix, had become abnormally warm.

A check showed that Hill's body temperature had soared to 108 degrees. After a desperate battle that included ice water enemas and alcohol baths, Hill was pronounced dead almost exactly two hours later.

Two words ran through all the reports on this additional Chiefs' tragedy: unpredictable, unpreventable. Dawson spoke at the services. McClinton sang the Lord's Prayer.

A solemn team assembled on Tuesday to hear the team physician explain the death to relieve anxiety for those who might some day face surgery. Then they prepared for their final game against Denver.

Playing with an abandon they seldom had shown, the Chiefs led 21–0 by the time the Broncos managed only three plays. They took the opening kickoff to a score. They held Denver and then scored again. They then got the ball on an onside kick and scored again. There are some veterans who still feel that Hill's death somehow galvanized the Kansas City Chiefs as a team.

The three trouble-plagued years in Missouri were finished, about to be replaced by a steady succession of triumphs that would carry the franchise powerfully into the 1970s.

The power seemed to ebb in 1973, but even after the Chiefs had finished their season with a 7–5–2 record and watched Oakland gain the playoffs ahead of them, there was no hand wringing at Arrowhead.

Stram had come to similar crossroads too often in the past, and he had emerged with an I formation, a zone, a moving pocket, and a "crisis in recognition," to help his team regain its old status. There were hints that the Chiefs might become the first team to take a long and serious look at the option series the colleges were running so successfully.

An interviewer asked Stram about his post-1970 Super Bowl comments that had been widely, if somewhat incorrectly, quoted. "I said simply that I felt the 1960s had been a decade of simplicity, and that the 1970s would be a decade of variety," he said. "I did not mean it would be the decade of the Kansas City offense, as some quoted.

"I felt the seventies would see quarterbacks as bigger, stronger, and better athletes. In the sixties, they were anchored. They went back into the pocket, planted, and threw. They had no running responsibility."

Stram is a man who loves his work. "I thrive on this job," he said. "I've had the opportunity to express my skill or talent – or whatever you'd call it – in something I enjoy. I'm a lucky man.

"We're now at a stage with the Chiefs where we have to recapture a championship and then successfully defend it. I've always had the ambition to be a consistent winning coach, and defending a championship is the only challenge we have not met yet. It has been a very bitter disappointment to me. But we don't have any problems we can't solve."

Stram moved to the blackboard in his office. He drew some diagrams. The movements were quick, decisive. Attack here, deceive, execute.

But the option? A college attack? Stram smiled. Years ago, a pro coach told him the zone would not work. Stram used it anyway, intercepting George Blanda five times in one afternoon. Years ago a coach told him that the I formation would not work. Stram made it the heart of one of the game's most diversified offenses.

"I think that the added dimension of a quarterback running will really help our game," he said. "That's the next step. We have to incorporate the option; we have to carry the ball out there to the fringe areas of the defense and pressure them."

The Names and Numbers

Kansas City Chiefs Victories 1960-1973

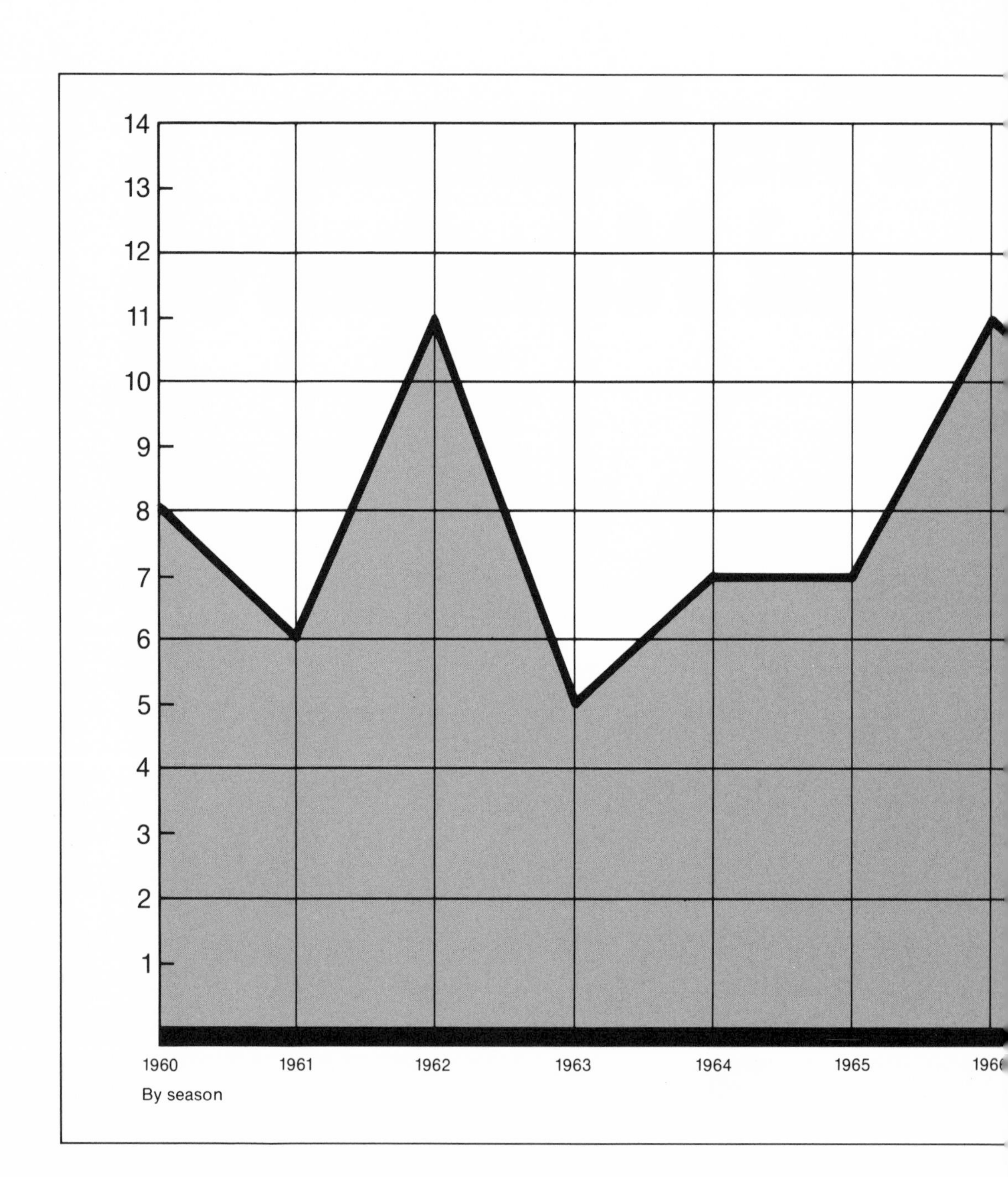

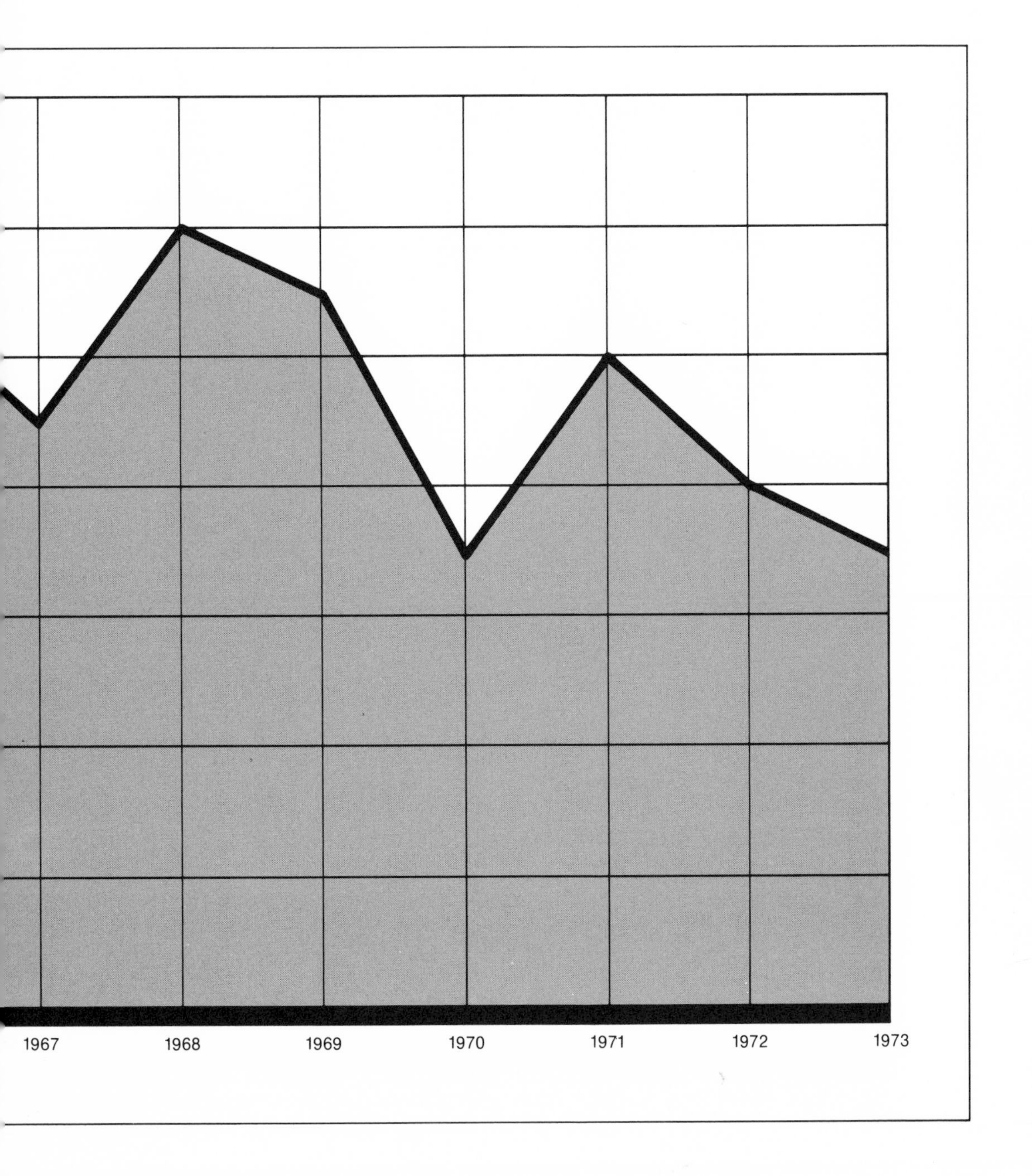
1967
1968
1969
1970
1971
1972
1973

Chiefs All-Time Scores

Dallas Texans

1960

8–6–0, second place, Western Division

Coach: Hank Stram		Texans	Opp.
Los Angeles	(A)	20	21
Oakland	(A)	34	16
Los Angeles	(H)	17	0
N. Y. Titans	(H)	35	37
Oakland	(H)	19	20
Houston	(A)	10	20
Denver	(A)	17	14
Buffalo	(A)	45	28
Denver	(H)	34	7
Boston	(A)	14	42
N. Y. Titans	(A)	35	41
Houston	(H)	24	0
Boston	(H)	34	0
Buffalo	(H)	24	7
		362	253

1961

6–8–0, second place, Western Division

Coach: Hank Stram		Texans	Opp.
San Diego	(H)	10	26
Oakland	(A)	42	35
Houston	(H)	26	21
Denver	(A)	19	12
Buffalo	(A)	24	27
Houston	(A)	7	38
Boston	(H)	17	18
Boston	(A)	21	28
Buffalo	(H)	20	30
San Diego	(A)	14	24
Oakland	(H)	43	11
N. Y. Titans	(A)	7	28
Denver	(H)	49	21
N. Y. Titans	(H)	35	24
		334	343

1962

11–3–0, first place,
American Football League

Coach: Hank Stram		Texans	Opp.
Boston	(H)	42	28
Oakland	(A)	26	16
Buffalo	(H)	41	21
San Diego	(A)	28	32
Boston	(A)	27	7
N. Y. Titans	(H)	20	17
Houston	(A)	31	7
Houston	(H)	6	14
N. Y. Titans	(A)	52	31
Denver	(A)	24	3
Oakland	(H)	35	7
Buffalo	(A)	14	23
Denver	(H)	17	10
San Diego	(H)	26	17
		389	233
AFL Championship			
Houston	(A)	20	17

Kansas City Chiefs

1963

5–7–2, third place, Western Division

Coach: Hank Stram		Chiefs	Opp.
Denver	(A)	59	7
Buffalo	(A)	27	27
San Diego	(A)	10	24
Houston	(H)	28	7
Buffalo	(H)	26	35
San Diego	(H)	17	38
Houston	(A)	7	28
Oakland	(A)	7	10
Oakland	(H)	7	22
Boston	(A)	24	24
N. Y. Jets	(A)	0	17
Denver	(H)	52	21
Boston	(H)	35	3
N. Y. Jets	(H)	48	0
		347	263

1964

7–7–0, second place, Western Division

Coach: Hank Stram		Chiefs	Opp.
Buffalo	(A)	17	34
Oakland	(A)	21	9
Houston	(H)	28	7
Denver	(A)	27	33
Buffalo	(H)	22	35
Boston	(A)	7	24
Denver	(H)	49	39
Oakland	(H)	42	7
San Diego	(H)	14	28
Houston	(A)	28	19
N. Y. Jets	(A)	14	27
Boston	(A)	24	31
San Diego	(A)	49	6
N. Y. Jets	(H)	24	7
		366	306

1965

7–5–2, third place, Western Division

Coach: Hank Stram		Chiefs	Opp.
Oakland	(A)	10	37
N. Y. Jets	(A)	14	10
San Diego	(A)	10	10
Boston	(H)	27	17
Denver	(A)	31	23
Buffalo	(H)	7	23
Houston	(A)	36	38
Oakland	(H)	14	7
N. Y. Jets	(H)	10	13
San Diego	(H)	31	7
Boston	(A)	10	10
Houston	(H)	52	21
Buffalo	(A)	25	34
Denver	(H)	45	35
		322	285

1966

11–2–1, first place,
American Football League

Coach: Hank Stram		Chiefs	Opp.
Buffalo	(A)	42	20
Oakland	(A)	32	10
Boston	(A)	43	24
Buffalo	(H)	14	29
Denver	(H)	37	10
Oakland	(H)	13	34
Denver	(A)	56	10
Houston	(H)	48	23
San Diego	(H)	24	14
Miami	(H)	34	16
Boston	(H)	27	27
N. Y. Jets	(A)	32	24
Miami	(A)	19	18
San Diego	(A)	27	17
		448	276
AFL Championship			
Buffalo	(A)	31	7
Super Bowl I at Los Angeles			
Green Bay	(A)	10	35

1967

9–5–0, second place, Western Division

Coach: Hank Stram		Chiefs	Opp.
Houston	(A)	25	20
Miami	(A)	24	0
Oakland	(A)	21	23
Miami	(H)	41	0
San Diego	(A)	31	45
Houston	(H)	19	24
Denver	(H)	52	9
N. Y. Jets	(H)	42	18
Boston	(A)	33	10
San Diego	(H)	16	17
Oakland	(H)	22	44
Buffalo	(H)	23	13
N. Y. Jets	(A)	21	7
Denver	(A)	38	24
		408	254

1968

12–2–0, second place, Western Division

Coach: Hank Stram		Chiefs	Opp.
Houston	(A)	26	21
N. Y. Jets	(H)	19	20
Denver	(H)	34	2
Miami	(A)	48	3
Buffalo	(A)	18	7
Cincinnati	(H)	13	3
Oakland	(H)	24	10
San Diego	(H)	27	20
Oakland	(A)	21	38
Cincinnati	(A)	16	9
Boston	(H)	31	7
Houston	(H)	24	10
San Diego	(A)	40	3
Denver	(A)	30	7
		371	160
Western Division Championship			
Oakland	(A)	6	41

1969

11–3–1, Super Bowl Champions

Coach: Hank Stram		Chiefs	Opp.
San Diego	(A)	27	9
Boston	(A)	31	0
Cincinnati	(A)	19	24
Denver	(A)	26	13
Houston	(H)	24	0
Miami	(H)	17	10
Cincinnati	(H)	42	22
Buffalo	(A)	29	7
San Diego	(H)	27	3
N. Y. Jets	(A)	34	16
Oakland	(H)	24	27
Denver	(H)	31	17
Buffalo	(H)	22	19
Oakland	(A)	6	10
		359	177
Inter-Divisional Playoff			
N. Y. Jets	(A)	13	6
AFL Championship			
Oakland	(A)	17	7
Super Bowl IV at New Orleans			
Minnesota		23	7

1970

7–5–2, second place, AFC Western Division

Coach: Hank Stram		Chiefs	Opp.
Minnesota	(A)	10	27
Baltimore	(A)	44	24
Denver	(A)	13	26
Boston	(H)	23	10
Cincinnati	(A)	27	19
Dallas	(H)	16	17
Oakland	(H)	17	17
Houston	(H)	24	9
Pittsburgh	(A)	31	14
St. Louis	(A)	6	6
San Diego	(H)	26	14
Denver	(H)	16	0
Oakland	(A)	6	20
San Diego	A)	13	31
		272	234

1971

10–3–1, first place, AFC Western Division

Coach: Hank Stram	Chiefs	Opp.
San Diego ....(H)	14	21
Houston ....(H)	20	16
Denver ....(H)	16	3
San Diego ....(A)	31	10
Pittsburgh ....(A)	38	16
Washington ....(A)	27	20
Oakland ....(H)	20	20
N. Y. Jets ....(H)	10	13
Cleveland ....(A)	13	7
Denver ....(A)	28	10
Detroit ....(H)	21	32
San Francisco ......(H)	26	17
Oakland ....(A)	16	14
Buffalo ....(H)	22	9
	302	208
AFC First Round Playoff		
Miami ....(H)	24	27

1972

8–6–0, second place, AFC Western Division

Coach: Hank Stram	Chiefs	Opp.
Miami ....(H)	10	20
New Orleans ....(A)	20	17
Denver ....(A)	45	24
Cleveland ....(A)	31	7
Cincinnati ....(H)	16	23
Philadelphia ....(H)	20	21
San Diego ....(A)	26	14
Oakland ....(H)	27	14
Pittsburgh ....(A)	7	16
San Diego ....(H)	17	27
Oakland ....(A)	3	26
Denver ....(H)	24	21
Baltimore ....(H)	24	10
Atlanta ....(A)	17	14
	287	254

1973

7–5–2, second place tie,
AFC Western Division

Coach: Hank Stram	Chiefs	Opp.
Los Angeles ....(H)	13	23
New England ....(A)	10	7
Oakland ....(H)	16	3
Denver ....(H)	16	14
Green Bay ....(A)	10	10
Cincinnati ....(A)	6	14
Buffalo ....(A)	14	23
San Diego ....(A)	19	0
Chicago ....(H)	19	7
Houston ....(H)	38	14
Denver ....(A)	10	14
Cleveland ....(H)	20	20
Oakland ....(A)	7	37
San Diego ....(H)	33	6
	231	192

Chiefs Records

SCORING
Most Points
Lifetime — 770, Jan Stenerud
Season — 129, Jan Stenerud, 1968
Game — 30, Abner Haynes vs. Oakland, Nov. 26, 1961
Most Touchdowns
Lifetime — 58, Abner Haynes
Season — 19, Abner Haynes, 1962
Game — 5, Abner Haynes vs. Oakland, Nov. 26, 1961
Most Points After Touchdown Made
Lifetime — 233, Jan Stenerud
Season — 46, Tom Brooker, 1964
Game — 8, Tom Brooker vs. Denver, Sept. 7, 1963
Mike Mercer vs. Denver, Oct. 23, 1966
Most Field Goals Made
Lifetime — 179, Jan Stenerud
Season — 30, Jan Stenerud, 1968
Game — 5, Jan Stenerud vs. Buffalo, Nov. 2, 1969
Jan Stenerud vs. Buffalo, Dec. 7, 1969
Longest Field Goal
55, Jan Stenerud vs. Denver, Oct. 4, 1970

RUSHING
Most Attempts
Lifetime — 780, Abner Haynes
Season — 236, Mike Garrett, 1967
Game — 28, Ed Podolak vs. Chicago, Nov. 12, 1973
Most Yards Gained
Lifetime — 3,837, Abner Haynes
Season — 1,087, Mike Garrett, 1967
Game — 192, Mike Garrett vs. New York, Nov. 5, 1967
Most Games, 100 or More Yards
Lifetime — 7, Mike Garrett
Season — 4, Mike Garrett, 1967
Longest Run From Scrimmage
80, Abner Haynes vs. New York, touchdown, Nov. 29, 1964

PASSING
Most Passes Attempted
Lifetime — 3,321 Len Dawson
Season — 379, Cotton Davidson, 1961
Game — 46, Len Dawson vs. Buffalo, Oct. 13, 1963
Most Passes Completed
Lifetime — 1,884, Len Dawson
Season — 206, Len Dawson, 1967
Game — 25, Len Dawson vs. Buffalo, Sept. 22, 1963
Most Yards Gained
Lifetime — 25,996, Len Dawson
Season — 2,879, Len Dawson, 1964
Game — 435, Len Dawson vs. Denver, Nov. 1, 1964
Longest Pass Completion
93, Mike Livingston to Otis Taylor vs. Miami for 79, lateral to Robert Holmes for 14, touchdown, Oct. 19, 1969
Most Touchdown Passes
Lifetime — 225, Len Dawson
Season — 30, Len Dawson, 1964
Game — 6, Len Dawson vs. Denver, Nov. 1, 1964
Most Passes Had Intercepted
Lifetime — 166, Len Dawson
Season — 23, Cotton Davidson, 1961
Game — 5, Cotton Davidson vs. Houston, Oct. 16, 1960
Len Dawson vs. Oakland, Nov. 23, 1969

PASS RECEPTIONS
Most Pass Receptions
Lifetime — 391, Chris Burford
Season — 68, Chris Burford, 1962
Game — 12, Ed Podolak vs. Denver, Oct. 7, 1973
Most Yards Gained
Lifetime — 5,505, Chris Burford
Season — 1,297, Otis Taylor, 1966
Game — 213, Curtis McClinton vs. Denver, Dec. 19, 1965
Most Touchdown Passes
Lifetime — 55, Chris Burford
Season — 12, Chris Burford, 1962
Game — 4, Frank Jackson vs. San Diego, Dec. 13, 1964

INTERCEPTIONS
Most Interceptions By
Lifetime — 57, Johnny Robinson
Season — 10, Johnny Robinson, 1966 and 1970
Bobby Hunt, 1966
Game — 4, Bobby Ply vs. San Diego, Dec. 16, 1962
Bobby Hunt vs. Houston, Oct. 4, 1964
Most Yards Returned
Lifetime — 741, Johnny Robinson, 57 interceptions
Season — 228, Bobby Hunt, 1963, 6 interceptions
Game — 108, Bobby Ply vs. San Diego, Dec. 16, 1962, 4 interceptions
Longest Return
99, Dave Grayson vs. New York, touchdown, Dec. 17, 1961

PUNTING
Most Punts
Lifetime — 727, Jerrel Wilson
Season — 80, Jerrel Wilson, 45.5 average, 1973
Game — 10, Jerrel Wilson vs. N. Y. Jets, 39.9 average, Sept. 18, 1965
Highest Average
Lifetime — 44.4, Jerrel Wilson
Season — 46.1, Jerrel Wilson, 1965
Game — 56.4, Jerrel Wilson vs. Boston, 5 punts, Oct. 11, 1970
Longest Punt
72, Jerrel Wilson vs. San Diego, Sept. 29, 1963

PUNT RETURNS
Most Punt Returns
Lifetime — 56, Willie Mitchell
Season — 29, Larry Marshall, 1973
Game — 5, Abner Haynes vs. Buffalo, Nov. 12, 1961
Noland Smith vs. Houston, Oct. 22, 1967
Larry Marshall vs. San Diego, Nov. 4, 1973
Larry Marshall vs. Houston, Nov. 18, 1973
Most Yards Returned
Lifetime — 689, Noland Smith
Season — 311, Ed Podolak, 1970
Game — 111, Mike Garrett vs. Buffalo, Nov. 12, 1967
Longest Punt Return
80, Noland Smith vs. N. Y. Jets, touchdown, Sept. 15, 1968

KICKOFF RETURNS
Most Kickoff Returns
Lifetime — 84, Dave Grayson
Season — 41, Noland Smith, 1967
Game — 9, Noland Smith vs. Oakland, Nov. 23, 1967
Most Yards Returned
Lifetime — 2,231, Dave Grayson
Season — 1,148, Noland Smith, 1968
Game — 244, Noland Smith vs. San Diego, Oct. 15, 1967
Longest Kickoff Return
106, Noland Smith vs. Denver, touchdown, Dec. 17, 1967

Team Records

SCORING
Most Points
Season — 488, 1966
Game — 59 vs. Denver (7) Sept. 7, 1963
Most Touchdowns
Season — 55, 1966
Game — 8 vs. Denver, Sept. 7, 1963
vs. Denver, Oct. 23, 1966

NET YARDS GAINED
Most Yards Gained
Season — 5,114, 1966
Game — 615 vs. Denver, Oct. 26, 1966

RUSHING
Most Rushing Attempts
Season — 537, 1968
Game — 60 vs. Oakland, Oct. 20, 1968
Most Yards Gained
Season — 2,407, 1962
Game — 398 vs. Houston, Oct. 1, 1961

PASSING
Most Attempts
Season — 439, 1963
Game — 46 vs. Buffalo, Oct. 13, 1963
Most Completions
Season — 231, 1963
Game — 25 vs. Buffalo, Sept. 22, 1963
vs. Boston, Nov. 20, 1966
Most Yards Gained
Season — 2,871, 1964
Game — 435 vs. Denver, Nov. 1, 1964